damselfishes
of
the
south
seas

by dr. gerald r. allen

ISBN 0-87666-034-0

Distributed in the U.S.A. by T.F.H. Publications, Inc., 211 West Sylvania Avenue, P.O. Box 27, Neptune City, N.J. 07753; in England by T.F.H. (Gt. Britain) Ltd., 13 Nutley Lane, Reigate, Surrey; in Canada to the book store and library trade by Clarke, Irwin & Company, Clarwin House, 791 St. Clair Avenue West, Toronto 10, Ontario; in Canada to the pet trade by Rolf C. Hagen Ltd., 3225 Sartelon Street, Montreal 382, Quebec; in Southeast Asia by Y.W. Ong, 9 Lorong 36 Geylang, Singapore 14; in Australia and the south Pacific by Pet Imports Pty. Ltd., P.O. Box 149, Brookvale 2100, N.S.W., Australia. Published by T.F.H. Publications Inc., Ltd., The British Crown Colony of Hong Kong.

Dedicated to John E. Randall and Walter A. Starck II, whose assistance has been instrumental in making this book possible.

Photos by the author unless otherwise credited.

PREFACE

This book is an outgrowth of my earlier work on anemonefishes which was published by T.F.H. Publications. A short time after the *Amphiprion* study was completed, I had the good fortune to meet Dr. Walter A. Starck II, who was voyaging around the South Pacific aboard his research ship, *El Torito*. I had originally intended to write only a brief research paper on the damselfishes of Micronesia, but Dr. Starck encouraged me to abandon these plans and instead write a book on the pomacentrids of the entire tropical West Pacific. At the Palau Islands Walter and I dived together on a daily basis and I soon became interested in the elaborate equipment which he used for photographing small fishes. Walter suggested that I should purchase similar gear and attempt to compliment my anticipated study with a close-up underwater photograph of every damselfish inhabiting the "South Seas." The magnitude of this task at first seemed unrealistic, but nevertheless I followed his advice and began a relentless pursuit of photos and specimens which lasted for more than two years. The work was tremendously satisfying, but several serious set-backs were encountered along the way. The worst of these included the flooding of three expensive Nikon cameras and the loss of 40 rolls of exposed film of New Guinea pomacentrids by the Australian postal system. The collecting and photography phase of the study was completed in November, 1973 after having traveled over 42,000 miles and after shooting nearly 4,000 pictures. Dr. John E. Randall completed my coverage with photos of crucial species from Southeast Oceania which I was not able to observe personally. The end result is *Damselfishes of the South Seas*.

Hopefully the book will strike a happy medium as far as the requirements of scientists and marine aquarists are concerned. Much of the text is specifically designed for use by systematic ichthyologists, but even this portion can be used by the layman after mastering a few ichthyological terms. The common denominator, which will prove of equal value to scientists and hobbyists, is the many color photos providing quick and easy species identification. Ecological and distributional notes which are included for each species will also be of interest to aquarists and diver-naturalists.

At this writing I have made a tentative agreement with T.F.H. to provide a more or less definitive work entitled *Damselfishes of the World* to be published approximately five years from now. This book will include comprehensive treatment of all the damselfishes, including those from the Indian and Atlantic Oceans and the eastern Pacific. The five-year time period has been set to allow for the completion of several pomacentrid studies now in progress by various colleagues, which will allow an up to date coverage of the family. Also, any species subsequently discovered in the "South Seas" or any nomenclatural alterations pertaining to this region will be incorporated.

GERALD R. ALLEN
SYDNEY, AUSTRALIA.
March 12, 1974.

ACKNOWLEDGMENTS

I thank the following people who offered logistic support during the field portion of the study: Mr. P. Bevridge, Mr. B. Carlson, Mr. K. Cassiday, Mr. T. Chivers, Mr. and Mrs. S. Domm, Dr. G. Filewood, Dr. P. Fourmanoir, Dr. and Mrs. B. Goldman, Mrs. P. Kailola, Mr. R. Kuiter, Mr. and Mrs. M. McCoy, Mr. B. Marr, Mr. B. Parkinson, Mr. D. Popper, Mr. A. Power, Mr. P. Ruaoul, Mr. B. Russell, Dr. W. Starck, Mr. R. Steene, Dr. F. Talbot, and Mr. P. Wilson.

Thanks are also due Dr. M. L. Bauchot, Dr. M. Boeseman, Dr. W. Eschmeyer, Mr. M. Gomon, Mr. D. Hensley, Dr. G. Palmer, Dr. J. Randall, Dr. R. Taylor, Dr. V. Springer, Dr. S. Weitzman, and Mr. P. Whitehead for specimen loans and information regarding type specimens. Mr. W. Deas, Mr. W. Doak, Mr. R. Kuiter, and Dr. R. Robertson provided several of the color photographs. Mrs. G. Leigh prepared the maps in Chapter III.

I am particularly thankful to Dr. J. Randall, who has provided many excellent photographs and copies of several hard-to-obtain species descriptions. Dr. Randall has also given freely of his time in the field to procure comprehensive pomacentrid collections on my behalf. Mr. Bruce Carlson of Suva, Fiji has also performed beyond the call of duty in providing specimens of both undescribed species and new locality records.

Special thanks are due Dr. F. Talbot, Director, and the Board of Trustees of the Australian Museum for providing financial assistance and laboratory facilities. I also thank Dr. J. Paxton, Dr. D. Hoese, Mr. G. Whitley, Mrs. C. Allen, and Miss H. Dlugaj, of the Australian Museum, Department of Ichthyology, for their help and co-operation. I am especially grateful to the National Geographic Society, Washington, D.C., which provided funds for travel to Easter Island, Lord Howe Island, and the Solomon Islands.

Finally I would like to thank my wife Connie for typing the manuscript.

CONTENTS

Chapter I

INTRODUCTION

There are few groups of coral reef fishes which are more numerous than the damselfish family Pomacentridae with regards to both number of individuals and species. Indeed, it is estimated that there are at least 200 forms inhabiting the world's tropical oceans. A few are also encountered in temperate seas. The present volume includes a comprehensive treatment of the classification of the species inhabiting the vast region which comprises Oceania, Melanesia, and the Great Barrier Reef. It is the result of nearly four years of research, including 27 months of field work. A significant portion of the work was accomplished aboard *El Torito*, an ultramodern research vessel of miniature proportions. Owned and operated by marine biologist Dr. Walter A. Starck II, the ship is fully equipped for biological field studies. In addition to a well stocked library-laboratory, the ship's equipment includes a complete range of underwater photography gear, mixed gas breathing apparatus for deep diving and conventional SCUBA, two decompression chambers, air compressors, closed-circuit underwater television, a 22-foot dive boat, and a two-man submarine. Although only 64 feet in length, the steel-hulled *El Torito* has a mammoth 28 foot beam and cruising range of 4,000 miles. I spent $8\frac{1}{2}$ months aboard the vessel while studying the damselfishes of New Guinea, the Great Barrier Reef, Lord Howe Island, New Caledonia, Loyalty Islands, New Hebrides, and the Solomon Islands. In addition to these travels, I spent 10 months at Eniwetok Atoll, six months at Palau, one month each at Hawaii and Truk, and one week each at Fiji and Ponape. I also participated in a National Geographic expedition to Easter Island and the Society Islands in 1969 with Dr. John E. Randall. In addition, Dr. Randall has kindly supplemented my own observations with photographs and specimens taken during his extensive collecting trips to the Society and Marquesas Islands, Tuamotu Archipelago, Pitcairn Group, and Rapa.

This book represents a unique ecological approach to the classification of a complex group of reef fishes, encompassing over 1,000 hours of undersea study. Traditionally, taxonomic studies of tropical reef fishes are based almost entirely on preserved museum specimens. These are often procured by museum or university sponsored expeditions. Ichthyologists participating in these ventures are usually unable to focus their entire attention on a given genus or family. This could only be accomplished at the risk of failing to gather a large comprehensive collection, which is usually the purpose of such missions. Consequently, there remain huge gaps in our knowledge of the more complex reef families, such as the Pomacentridae, Gobiidae, Apogonidae, Labridae, and Scaridae. Unfortunately the worker who must rely on museum collections alone is frequently confronted with the task of sorting out nomenclatural problems on the basis of inadequate material. Furthermore, the nature of museum collections results in serious distributional gaps, thus hindering a thorough understanding of zoogeographic relationships. To be sure, museum study is an indispensable part of taxonomic research, but with certain coral reef groups, such as the pomacentrids, it needs to be supplemented with the study of freshly procured material and observations of live fishes in the sea. My previous work with anemonefishes underscored the value of observing living animals in their natural habitat. Many of the species exhibit very different adult and juvenile color patterns, which are difficult to link without observing living intermediates.

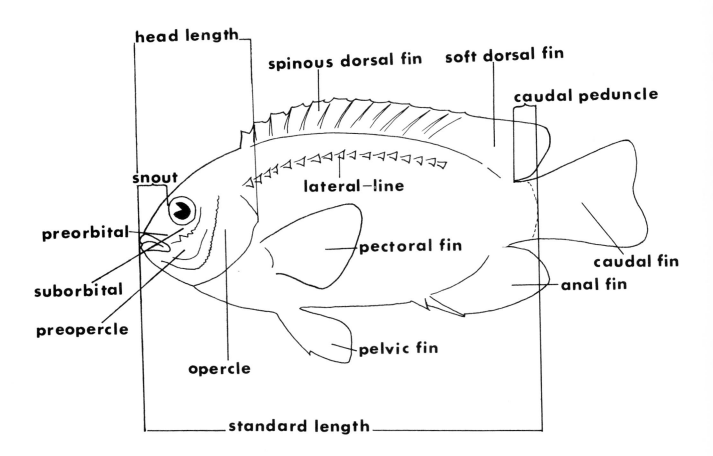

External features of a typical pomacentrid.

The present research was initiated at Palau, the westernmost district of the Caroline Islands. It required nearly six months of intensive study to familiarize myself with the 77 species which occur there. This initial work formed a solid foundation for future investigations in the Melanesian-Great Barrier Reef region. I soon discovered that in certain cases it was considerably easier to differentiate closely related species by studying their behavior, ecology, and live colors, rather than relying on preserved museum specimens and sketchy descriptions in the literature. I am convinced that many of the problems resolved in this fashion could not have been cleared up otherwise.

Comprehensive collections, species check-lists, and notes on ecology and behavior were made at each locality visited during the study. In addition, a close-up color photograph was taken of nearly every species in its natural habitat. While aboard *El Torito*, species identifications were facilitated by the excellent shipboard library. Taxonomic problems not solved in the field were put aside until I had access to the library and inter-museum specimen loan facilities at the Australian Museum. Most of the damselfishes were collected with specially constructed multi-prong spears and quinaldine (an anaesthetic) which allowed a greater degree of selectivity than is offered with standard poisoning methods.

The results of this study were extremely gratifying. Aboard *El Torito* I collected 130 species (including 14 which were undescribed) at Palau, Melanesia, and the Great Barrier Reef. The highest number of damselfishes formerly known from the entire Indo-Australian Archipelago was 85 (De Beaufort, 1940). At nearly every locality we visited, the previously recorded pomacentrid fauna was increased more than twofold. Many of the species included in the present volume have never been illustrated and are known only from brief descriptions in the literature.

METHODS OF PRESENTATION

Keys to the subfamilies and genera of damselfishes occurring in the "South Seas" are included in Chapter IV. In these keys the generic name is followed by the number of the chapter which deals with that group. The individual species accounts appearing in Chapters V-XXV are arranged alphabetically and include a brief diagnosis plus notes on ecology and distribution. In addition, at the beginning of each account there is a short synonymy, which in most cases incorporates only the original description. However, additional synonyms may be listed, particularly if the name has been commonly misused or if the synonymy was previously undetected. In these abbreviated citations the author name(s) is followed by the year of publication, page number, and type locality. For more complete information the reader is referred to the bibliography which appears at the end of the book.

The ichthyological terms which appear in the keys and diagnosis sections are explained in Allen's *Anemonefishes* (1972) and Randall's *Caribbean Reef Fishes* (1968). Many of these terms refer to features which are illustrated in the figure given. The term "biserial teeth" as used for damselfishes refers to the condition in which there is an outer row of larger teeth and a secondary row of slender buttress teeth behind, usually in the spaces between the outer row teeth. Frequently the dentition is biserial only at the front of the jaws. The tubed lateral-line counts pertain to the continuous upper series only, excluding the detached series of pored scales which are sometimes present on the caudal peduncle.

Appendix Tables I and II give a complete listing of the species which appear in this book according to locality. Only species which were either collected (observed only in a few cases) by me, or examined in museum collections are included. The records in Appendix Table I are based on the following localities:

Marshall Islands
Eniwetok Atoll

New Guinea
Madang
Cape Nelson
D'Entrecasteaux Islands
Samarai Island
Egum Atoll
Port Moresby

Great Barrier Reef
Off Cairns to Port Douglas
Capricorn Group

Solomon Islands
N. Guadalcanal
Savo Island
Florida Island
Alite Reef

New Hebrides
Vila, Efate
Luganville, Espiritu Santo
Pulu Iwa Reef

New Caledonia-Loyalty Islands
Noumea
Puetege Reef
Uvea Atoll

Fiji Islands
Suva

Chapter II
ECOLOGY

Damselfishes are extremely successful from an evolutionary standpoint, having invaded nearly every inshore habitat in tropical seas. A few species penetrate freshwater streams and brackish estuaries, others are found to depths of at least 200 meters, but the majority of species inhabit the relatively narrow zone where reef building corals flourish. Tropical damselfishes usually demonstrate a definite preference with regard to substratum and depth. Thus each species is more or less restricted to a particular portion or zone of the reef where conditions are suitable. There are several species which are relatively ubiquitous, occurring both shallow and deep and over a variety of substrata. At subtropical localities ubiquity is frequently the rule rather than the exception. Because of reduced competition, each species is free to penetrate habitats from which they are generally excluded. For example, the three damselfishes which occur at Easter Island (*Chromis randalli*, *Eupomacentrus fasciolatus*, and *Glyphidodontops rapanui*) frequent a variety of habitats ranging from knee-deep tidal pools to depths of at least 40 meters. One of these, *E. fasciolatus*, is a wide ranging form known from the tropical western Pacific and Indo-Australian Archipelago. At most tropical localities it is restricted to a very narrow zone usually situated on the outer reef in areas of moderate to slight surge at depths less than about three meters. However, at Easter and Lord Howe Islands, which are subtropical, this species is found in a variety of habitats to at least 40 meters depth. This lack of vertical zonation is exhibited by other families as well at these localities.

In the tropics the number of species encountered on a given section of reef is extremely variable and directly reflects habitat diversity and availability of food. The average number of damselfishes recorded for 30 lagoon and outer reef areas at Palau and various Melanesian localities was 33 species. In each case the area sampled was approximately 100×50–100 meters. Only six species were noted over a stretch of sandy lagoon bottom off Muli Island, Loyalty Islands, while 61 species were counted on a seaward reef at tiny Naura Islet, off Ferguson Island in the D'Entrecasteaux Group.

The various habitats where pomacentrids occur are discussed in the following paragraphs under separate headings for each major environment. In addition, ecological notes are included for each species in the generic chapters. Marine habitats are sometimes difficult to categorize due to local physiographic influences. For instance, the gradually sloping outer reefs near Vila Harbor, New Hebrides, are partially lagoon-like with regards to the fish fauna because of the protective influence of nearby mountains. Another unusual habitat situation was found at the mouth of Sandfly Passage, Florida Island in the Solomon Group. The shoreline there consisted of steep cliffs which plunged vertically into the sea. The precipice continued its descent for at least 100 meters below the surface. In the shallow portion of the dropoff there were relatively few corals and associated fishes. Instead, species normally confined to deep outer reef slopes such as *Chromis analis* and *C. elerae* were found in only two meters. Perhaps similar situations at other localities account for the occasional presence of deep dwelling reef species in the collections of early naturalists. The inner maze of coralline shoals which constitute the bulk of the Great Barrier Reef are also slightly aberrant compared with the reefs of Oceania. The shallow reef top areas and lagoons are essentially the same, but the outer edge is not truly characteristic of oceanic slopes, plunging only to a depth of about 40 meters. They are perhaps most similar to the reef passages of Oceania which connect outer slope and lagoon. However, the true oceanic outer reef is encountered on the outermost edge of the Great Barrier Reef system.

DAMSELFISH HABITATS

Harbors; silty coastal reefs; brackish inlets and freshwater streams:
These are relatively homogeneous environments offering shelter to a very limited number of species. They are characterized by reduced visibility, little or no coral growth, occasional fluctuations in salinity, and soft silty bottom conditions with relatively little shelter except that which is man-made. Most of the damselfishes in these areas are benthic dwellers which feed chiefly on algae. However, members of *Neopomacentrus* are plankton feeders which form aggregations around wharf pilings, wreckage, rocky outcrops, etc. At least one species, *N. taeniurus*, appears to be restricted to brackish estuaries and the lower reaches of freshwater streams. The following species are typical residents of murky harbors and silty coastal reefs (species marked with an asterisk in the following lists are largely restricted to the specified habitat):

Abudefduf sp.	*N. cyanomos*
A. coelestinus	*N. violascens*★
A. saxatilis	*N.* sp.
Amblypomacentrus breviceps	*Pomacentrus albimaculus*
Amphiprion polymnus	*P. amboinensis*
Dischistodus chrysopoecilus	*P.* sp.
D. perspicillatus	*P. pavo*
D. prosopotaenia	*P. smithi*
Glyphidodontops biocellatus	*P. taeniometopon*
Neopomacentrus anabatoides★	*P. tripunctatus*★

Lagoons:
Generally two types of lagoons are encountered in the tropical western Pacific: atoll lagoons, and coastal lagoons, which lie inside a fringing reef and are more or less adjacent to a high island. Due to greater habitat diversity, lagoons support a much richer pomacentrid fauna than harbors and coastal reefs. Water circulation in most lagoons is relatively good because of daily influxes of oceanic water during tidal fluctuations. Underwater visibility is generally moderate. Substrate conditions are variable and include rich coralline areas, vast sandy stretches, rubble, and isolated dead and live coral patches of various size. Lagoons are frequently surge-free and offer a relatively high degree of shelter. Conditions vary from ultra-protected waters such as those found among the rock islands of the Palau Archipelago to more exposed habitats like those on the windward side of Egum Island, situated in the center of Egum Atoll (lagoon diameter 24 kilometers) in the Solomon Sea. Shallow lagoon margins are typically composed of sand, rubble, or wave-scrubbed beach rock and support a relatively small number of pomacentrids, most of which are algal grazers. The following species are typical inhabitants of the lagoon fringe:

Abudefduf sp.★	*Glyphidodontops biocellatus*★
A. bengalensis	*G. cyaneus*
Dascyllus aruanus	*G. niger*★
D. melanurus	*G. unimaculatus*
Dischistodus chrysopoecilus★	*Pomacentrus flavicauda*★
D. notopthalmus	*P. bankanensis*
D. perspicillatus	*P. pavo*
D. prosopotaenia	*P. wardi*
D. pseudochrysopoecilus	

Deeper parts of lagoons (from about two to 20 meters) and sheltered shallow localities, such as those at Palau and in the lee of atoll and fringing reef islets, frequently support rich coral growth and a corresponding greater number of damselfishes. Although benthic algal feeders predominate, certain species, including members of *Amphiprion, Chromis, Dascyllus,* and *Lepidozygus,* are dependent mainly on zooplankton. Species typically found in this habitat include:

Abudefduf coelestinus
A. saxatilis
Acanthochromis polyacanthus
Amblyglyphidodon curacao
A. leucogaster
*A. ternatensis**
Amphiprion akindynos
A. clarkii
A. mccullochi
A. melanopus
*A. percula**
*A. rubrocinctus**
A. perideraion
A. polymnus
A. sandaracinos
*Cheiloprion labiatus**
Chromis amboinensis
C. atripectoralis
*C. caerulea**
C. lepidolepis
C. margaritifer
C. retrofasciata
C. ternatensis
*Dascyllus aruanus**
*D. melanurus**
D. reticulatus
D. trimaculatus
Dischistodus notopthalmus
D. perspicillatus
D. prosopotaenia
Eupomacentrus apicalis
*E. lividus**

*E. nigricans**
*Glyphidodontops azurepunctatus**
*G. cyaneus**
G. flavipinnis
*G. hemicyaneus**
G. rollandi
*Hemiglyphidodon plagiometopon**
Lepidozygus tapeinosoma
Neopomacentrus anabatoides
N. sp.
Paraglyphidodon behni
P. carlsoni
*P. melanopus**
P. melas
P. polyacanthus
Plectroglyphidodon dickii
P. lacrymatus
Pomacentrus albimaculus
*P. burroughi**
*P. grammorhynchus**
P. lepidogenys
P. sp.
P. alexanderae
*P. opisthostigma**
P. pavo
P. popei
P. taeniometopon
P. vaiuli
P. wardi
P. amboinensis
Premnas biaculeatus

Lagoons vary widely with regard to depth; coastal lagoons may average only three to five meters, while those of oceanic atolls are frequently between 40 and 60 meters. The lagoon bottom, particularly at depths below 15 meters is usually composed of extensive sandy areas. The few species found there congregate around available shelter. Typical damselfish inhabitants, particularly at depths greater than 20 meters, include *Amblypomacentrus breviceps, Amphiprion polymnus, Glyphidodontops tricinctus, Pomacentrus amboinensis, P. species,* and *Pristotis jerdoni.*

Inter-islet channels and passages which connect the lagoon and outer reef are intermediate between these two areas with respect to the fish fauna. Generally there are more species of *Chromis* and other plankton feeders. In this regard the passages are more similar to the outer reef.

Outer reefs:

The outer reef is generally composed of shallow reef flat, coralline ridge, surge channels and the outer slope. However, in some localities the first three may be lacking, and a rich coral plateau extending from the lagoon at depths of about three to 10 meters abruptly falls away to deeper water.

The shallow reef flat and coralline ridge represent the least diversified outer reef environments and only a limited number of species occur there. The substratum of these areas consists largely of coral-free, consolidated beach rock. Surge conditions vary from extremely heavy to mild depending on exposure to prevailing winds. The species which are largely restricted to this zone are predominantly algal grazers and include:

Abudefduf septemfasciatus	*G. unimaculatus*
A. sordidus	*Plectroglyphidodon imparipennis*
Eupomacentrus albifasciatus	*P. leucozona*
E. jenkinsi	*P. phoenixensis*
Glyphidodontops glaucus	*Pomacentrus bankanensis*
G. leucopomus	

These same species may be encountered in shallow lagoon areas which are relatively exposed and subject to surge.

Surge channels represent a transitional area between the reef flat and upper portion of the outer reef slope. The fishes which occur there also represent a compromise between these two zones. The following species are particularly representative:

Abudefduf coelestinus	*Glyphidodontops rex*
A. saxatilis	*Neopomacentrus azysron*
A. whitleyi	*Parma polylepis*
Chromis acares	*Pomacentrus bankanensis*
C. lineata	*P. coelestis*
C. vanderbilti	*P. philippinus*
Eupomacentrus gascoynei	*P. wardi*
E. fasciolatus	

The upper edge of the outer reef slope is consistently the richest habitat with regards to both number of species and individuals. The oceanic waters which bathe the outer slope abound with plankton organisms which support a large assemblage of damselfishes. Visibility on the outer slope frequently exceeds 30 meters. Substrate conditions on the upper edge range from extensive beds of live coral to areas which are largely composed of sand, rubble, and boulders. This environment is the stronghold of the genus *Chromis*. Indeed, all the species except *C. caerulea* have their largest concentrations there, frequently occurring in large midwater feeding aggregations. Most *Chromis* are poorly represented in museum collections because of the inaccessability of the outer slope to early collectors. Indeed, 30% of the new locality records presented in Appendix Tables 1 and 2 belong to this genus. Throughout most of Oceania the outer reefs fall away rather steeply to deep water, although the uppermost portion of the slope may be gradual or form a nearly level bench to depths of 10 to 15 meters before giving way to a steep precipice. The following species, in addition to *Chromis* and the surge channel dwellers already mentioned, are typical inhabitants of the outer slope at depths ranging from about four to 25 meters:

Topside equipment on *El Torito* includes a 15,000 lb. capacity crane, submarine, and decompression chambers.

Abudefduf abdominalis
A. notatus
Acanthochromis polyacanthus
Amblyglyphidodon aureus*
A. curacao
A. leucogaster
Amphiprion akindynos
A. chrysopterus*
A. clarkii
A. latezonatus*
A. melanopus
A. leucokranos*
A. perideraion
A. sandaracinos
Dascyllus reticulatus
D. strasburgi
D. trimaculatus
Eupomacentrus apicalis
E. aureus
E. emeryi
Glyphidodontops flavipinnis
G. galbus*
G. rapanui
G. rollandi
G. starcki*

G. notialis*
G. talboti*
G. traceyi*
Lepidozygus tapeinosoma
Neopomacentrus metallicus*
Pomachromis spp.*
Paraglyphidodon behni
P. melas
P. polyacanthus
P. thoracotaeniatus*
Parma sp.*
Plectroglyphidodon dickii
P. flaviventris
P. johnstonianus*
P. lacrymatus
Pomacentrus amboinensis
P. australis
P. lepidogenys
P. sp.
P. melanopterus*
P. alexanderae
P. popei
P. vaiuli
Premnas biaculeatus

The majority of species listed above are chiefly confined to the upper portion of the slope, seldom penetrating below 15 to 20 meters. There are several forms, however, which are normally found below these depths. *Chromis* C and D, *C. analis*, *C. elerae*, *Glyphidodontops caeruleolineatus*, and *Pomacentrus reidi* were usually observed between 20 and 75 meters. *Chromis* A was recorded from 95 meters at Palau by Dr. Walter A. Starck II while diving with mixed-gas apparatus. Other species which were seen regularly below 20 meters include the following (maximum depth in meters shown in parentheses):

Acanthochromis polyacanthus (65)
Amblyglyphidodon aureus (35)
A. leucogaster (45)
Amphiprion clarkii (55)
A. latezonatus (45)
Chromis agilis (48)
C. amboinensis (65)
C. atripes (35)
C. flaviventris (48)
C. hypsilepis (46)
C. kennensis (35)
C. ovalis (45)
C. retrofasciata (65)
C. xanthochir (48)
C. xanthura (35)

Dascyllus reticulatus (50)
D. trimaculatus (55)
Glyphidodontops flavipinnis (38)
G. notialis (45)
G. rollandi (35)
G. starcki (40)
G. talboti (35)
Paraglyphidodon thoracotaeniatus (40)
Pomacentrus amboinensis (40)
P. australis (40)
P. sp. (35)
P. melanopterus (40)
P. alexanderae (60)
P. nigromarginatus (65)
P. vaiuli (40)

Chromis verater and *C. struhsakeri*, from the Hawaiian Islands, are found below depths frequented by most damselfishes. The former species is found in six to at least 160 meters, whereas *C. struhsakeri* is known only from specimens taken in a shrimp trawl between 99 and 183 meters.

It is emphasized that the habitat distributions outlined in this chapter represent generalizations, and it is not unusual to encounter isolated individuals outside of their normal environment. For example, *Chromis nitida* is exceedingly abundant on the outer reef at One Tree Island on the Great Barrier Reef. Small schools of juveniles and occasional adults appear in the lagoon, but their sporadic distribution and lack of permanence indicate they are not dwelling in normal habitat conditions.

El Torito anchored on the Great Barrier Reef off Cairns, Queensland.

A steep outer reef drop-off at Sandfly Passage, Florida Island, Solomon Islands. Yellow fish are *Chromis analis.*

Aerial view of One Tree Island, Capricorn Group, Great Barrier Reef. The shallow reef flat is well developed and occupies most of the photograph (F. Talbot photo).

Small freshwater stream near Luganville, Espiritu Santo, New Hebrides. Specimens of *Neopomacentrus taeniurus* were collected at this locality.

Chapter III

ZOOGEOGRAPHY

The term "South Seas" as used herein pertains to the region which includes Melanesia (except West Irian), the Great Barrier Reef, and most of the islands of the tropical West Pacific, which collectively are sometimes referred to as Oceania. Damselfishes occur throughout this vast province. The greatest abundance of species is found in the Indo-Malayan Archipelago. The farther one travels in any direction from this region, the fewer species are represented. Attenuation of this sort is exemplified by a wide assortment of tropical organisms and is generally believed to provide evidence that the Indo-Malayan region served as the center of development from which other tropical regions have recruited the main contingent of their fauna (Ekman, 1953). The rather classical pattern of diminution demonstrated by W. Pacific damselfishes is represented in the figures. At this time the exact limits of the Indo-Malayan "heartland" remain vague, but hopefully will be clarified by further collecting efforts. Likewise, the contours which appear west and north of the Moluccas remain to be verified. I have collected 103 species at New Guinea. It seems a logical assumption to expect a few additional forms at Indonesia, but probably not many. Essentially there is an unbroken chain of close-set islands extending from Indonesia to the Solomon Islands. However, as one travels away from the Solomon Islands the fauna diminishes in a somewhat predictable fashion. Going east the average rate of attenuation is about 14 species per 1,000 miles. The number of damselfish species at a given location in the Indo-West Pacific is thus dependent on several factors which include: (1) the distance from the Indo-Malayan "heartland"; (2) the degree of isolation from adjacent island areas; and (3) latitude (diminution is rapid outside the tropics).

The unequaled variety of habitats in the Indo-Malayan province and apparent environmental stability through past geologic ages has set the stage for evolutionary divergence. Many species are more or less restricted to this region, having evolved under rather specialized conditions which have no equal in the insular areas to the east or west. For example, the genus *Dischistodus*, which inhabits shallow coastal reefs, frequently subject to heavy silting, has failed to penetrate Oceania. On the other hand, species which exhibit certain preadaptations to oceanic island conditions have successfully pushed westward. Members of the genus *Plectroglyphidodon* and certain *Chromis* are notable in this respect. They typically frequent outer reef slope areas, a habitat which is extremely similar in both Indo-Malayan and Pacific regions. Other species which may possess the necessary preadaptations have no doubt failed to gain access to the area simply because the available niches were already filled. In other words, there is a certain degree of randomness as far as colonization patterns are concerned. Species which happen to arrive at the right place at the right time may have a better chance of establishing themselves than subsequent arrivals. This phenomenon of random distribution is often referred to by zoogeographers as "sweepstakes dispersal."

Greenfield (1968), in discussing the zoogeography of the squirrelfish genus *Myripristis*, suggested that the Indo-Pacific fauna may have originated in the island area east of the Indo-Australian region primarily because existing ocean currents do not favor dispersal from an Indo-Malayan center. He suggested that the greater number of species in the latter province was due to long term stability of environmental conditions which fostered the diversification of accumulated species from areas to the west and southwest. However, this notion fails to account for the strong Indo-Malayan affinities which exist in the fish faunas of the Hawaiian Islands, Marquesas Islands, and Easter Island, approximately forming the eastern boundary of the Indo-West Pacific faunal province. If existing current patterns are used as criteria for determining dispersal routes, these areas might be expected to exhibit a significant faunal element from the eastern Pacific. This component is totally lacking in the Hawaiian Islands and Marquesas Islands and represents an insignificant portion of the Easter Island fauna, where about 90% of the approximately 110 species of inshore fishes show Indo-Malayan relationships (personal observation). This appears to be ample evidence that colonization in the West Pacific has indeed progressed in an easterly direction, utilizing island "stepping stones." The probable routes of dispersal are indicated in the figure. Faunal evidence would also support the contention that current patterns during past geologic periods were different than existing ones. Even today it is likely that a certain amount of eastward dispersal is accomplished via equatorial countercurrent systems.

Factors which affect the distribution of pomacentrids include habitat availability, ocean currents, surface temperatures, local hydrographic features, and past and present land barriers. An additional factor, and perhaps the most important, is the ability of the larvae to survive in the pelagic realm for extended periods, at least long enough for the currents to carry them to suitable reef areas. Pomacentrid larvae are relatively advanced in their development at hatching, and previous studies on *Amphiprion* (Allen, 1972) and *Abudefduf* (Helfrich, 1958) indicate a larval life of only a few weeks duration. It seems likely that the pomacentrids have gradually spread out from the Indo-Malayan region via island "stepping stones" or along the shallows of continental land masses. For example, *Amphiprion* have been able to penetrate most of the islands of the tropical West Pacific, which are numerous and generally not isolated from neighboring islands. However, where vast stretches of open water exist, such as between the Marshall Islands and Hawaii or between the Tuamotu Islands and Easter Island, *Amphiprion* have failed to penetrate, while forms with extended pelagic larval stages, such as *Acanthurus*, have been able to make these crossings (Randall, 1956). No doubt the dispersal ability of larvae is variable among the many pomacentrid species. *Acanthochromis polyacanthus* seems to have lost this capacity altogether.

The present study incorporates 162 species, nearly all of which were collected or observed by either myself or Dr. John E. Randall. These are listed in Appendix Tables I and II which appear after Chapter XXV. The general localities where each species was taken is also indicated. The tables include 359 new locality records which are distributed as follows:

Solomon Islands	54	Lord Howe Island	16
New Hebrides	47	Marquesas Islands	12
Palau Islands	43	Rapa	10
New Caledonia-Loyalty Islands	41	Pitcairn Group	9
New Guinea	40	Line Islands	6
Fiji Islands	37	Tuamotu Islands	5
Australia	34	Marshall Islands	4
Mariana Islands	1		

Most of the specimens on which these records are based are deposited at either the Australian Museum, Sydney or the Bernice P. Bishop Museum, Honolulu.

An analysis of the zoogeography of "South Seas" pomacentrids is presented in Table 1. Approximately 80% of the species are either relatively widespread forms or residents of the habitat-rich Indo-Australian Archipelago (including Melanesia). About 12% of the total fauna is composed of elements which are restricted to the periphery of the Pacific distribution. This area includes the Hawaiian and Marquesas Islands and S.E. Oceania. It is characterized by a relatively high rate of endemism which is directly related to the degree of geographic isolation. The percentage of endemism for the pomacentrid fauna of selected areas is shown in Table 2.

Aerial view of the coast of New Georgia, Solomon Islands. The steep outer reef is situated close to shore and is penetrated by a deep passage. Coastal inlets such as those shown at the top of the picture are inhabited by *Dischistodus* and *Neopomacentrus*.

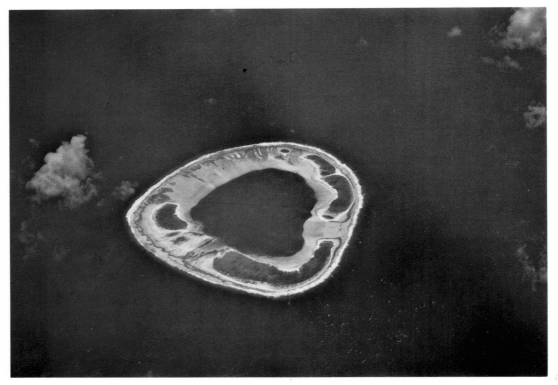

Oeno, Pitcairn Group exhibits a classic atoll structure with a circle of islets and shallow coral reefs surrounding a deep lagoon.

Coastal fringing reef at Raiatea, Society Islands.

A section of coastal reef at Bougainville, Solomon Islands. A thin ribbon of shallow reef separating the lagoon and outer slope is visible in the distance.

If S.E. Oceania is considered as a single unit, 12 of 46 or about one-fourth of the species are endemic. Thus, this region and the Hawaiian Islands constitute the primary "pockets" of endemism for the Pacific distribution. A secondary enclave exists in the South Coral Sea-North Tasman region, where nine endemic species occur. This area encompasses Whitley's (1932b) Phillipian and Montrouzierian provinces and also the southern portion of his Solanderian province. Two species from this region, *Chromis kennensis* and *Glyphidodontops starcki*, demonstrate disjunct distributions which include Taiwan and the Ryukyu Islands. It is possible that these species are relicts (i.e., isolated remnants of a formerly widespread species). Other possible relicts include *Amphiprion rubrocinctus* (Fiji and N.W. Australia) and *Chromis leucura* (Hawaiian Islands, Marquesas, and possibly Mauritius).

The Hawaiian Islands are particularly interesting from a zoogeographical standpoint. Gosline and Brock (1960) stated that 34% of the inshore fishes have endemic distributions. It is apparent that many of these forms have evolved relatively recently because of the morphological similarities they share with species farther west. For example, *Abudefduf abdominalis*, *Chromis hanui*, *Dascyllus albisella*, and *Plectroglyphidodon sindonis* have apparently evolved from the ancestral stocks of *A. saxatilis*, *C. margaritifer*, *D. trimaculatus*, and *P. leucozona*. These latter species are widely distributed in the Indo-West Pacific, except Hawaii.

Actually very few groups of fishes from the Indo-West Pacific have been collected and studied in great enough detail to allow the elucidation of their zoogeography. The present investigation is especially interesting because of the large number of species involved and the intensive collecting effort over a wide geographic area. However, this is certainly not the last word on the zoogeography of West Pacific pomacentrids. The overall picture will not be complete until further collections and underwater observations are obtained for adjacent regions, particularly Indonesia, Philippines, Ryukyu Islands, Red Sea, and Indian Ocean. The primary purpose of the present analysis is to provide a solid foundation for future studies of pomacentrid zoogeography and to provide comparative material for investigators of other faunal groups.

The "South Seas." The geographic area covered in this book is enclosed within the bold black line. The numbers on the map refer to the following localities:

1. Hawaiian Islands
2. Johnston Island
3. Line Islands
4. Marquesas Islands
5. Tuamotu Islands
6. Pitcairn Group
7. Easter Island
8. Rapa
9. Society Islands
10. Cook Islands
11. Samoa Islands
12. Fiji Islands
13. Phoenix Islands
14. Gilbert Islands
15. Marshall Islands
16. Caroline Islands
17. Mariana Islands
18. Palau Islands
19. Papua-New Guinea
20. Great Barrier Reef
21. Lord Howe Island
22. New Britain
23. Solomon Islands
24. New Hebrides
25. New Caledonia
26. Loyalty Islands

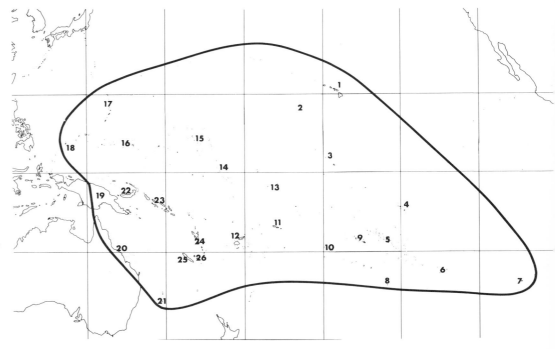

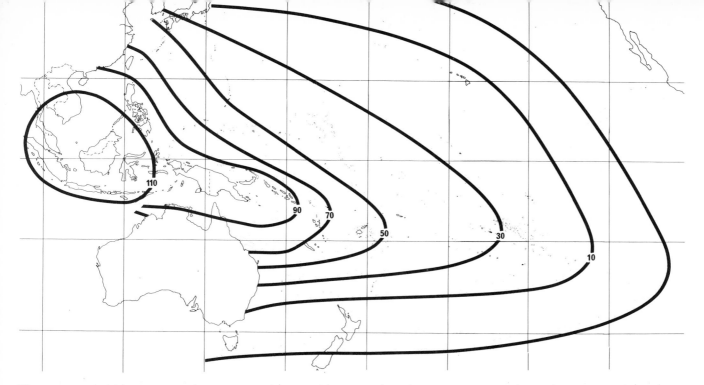

The pomacentrid fauna diminishes with increased distance from the Indo-Malayan region. Each successive contour represents an increase or decrease of 20 species, except the outermost which marks the approximate limit of distribution for Indo-West Pacific pomacentrids.

TABLE 1

ZOOGEOGRAPHIC ANALYSIS OF THE DAMSELFISHES
INHABITING THE "SOUTH SEAS"
(each distributional category mutually exclusive)

Distribution	No. species	% of S. Seas pomacentrid fauna
Indo-Austral. Arch. (incl. Palau)	50	30.9
Widespread Indo-W. Pacific	22	13.6
Far W. Pacific[1] and Indo-Austral. Arch.	17	10.5
Widespread W. Pacific	15	9.3
Indo-far W. Pacific[1]	10	6.2
S. Coral Sea-N. Tasman Sea	9	5.5
Hawaiian Islands	7	4.3
S.E. Oceania	6	3.7
Australia	5	3.1
Marquesas Islands	4	2.5
Marshall, Caroline, and Marianas Islands	4	2.5
New Caledonia, Fiji and Samoa Islands	3	1.9
Taiwan, Ryukyus, and S. Coral Sea	2	1.2
Easter Island	2	1.2
Widespread S. Oceania	1	.6
Central and S.E. Oceania	1	.6
Hawaii and Marquesas Islands	1	.6
N. Territory (Austral.) and Fiji Islands	1	.6
Lord Howe Island	1	.6
Circumtropical	1	.6
TOTAL	162	100.0

[1]primarily distributed west of 160°E longitude

Acropora coral dominates this scene on the Great Barrier Reef, off Cairns. This is the characteristic habitat of several members of the genus *Plectroglyphidodon.*

Rich staghorn coral beds are a typical feature of Indo-Pacific lagoons. This photo was taken at Alite Reef, off Malaita, Solomon Islands.

An aggregation of *Abudefduf whitleyi* hovers above a surge channel at One Tree Island, Great Barrier Reef.

TABLE 2

PERCENTAGE OF ENDEMISM IN POMACENTRID FAUNAS OF SELECTED LOCALITIES

Locality	Total Species	Endemic	%
Easter Island	3	2	66.6
Hawaiian Islands	15	7	46.6
Marquesas Islands	19	4	21.0
Pitcairn Group	16	2	12.5
Lord Howe Island	26	1	3.8
Marshall Islands	44	1	2.3

Distribution of genera and species of pomacentrids for certain localities in the South Pacific. The large numbers represent the total species recorded during the present study. The number of genera is indicated by smaller numbers.

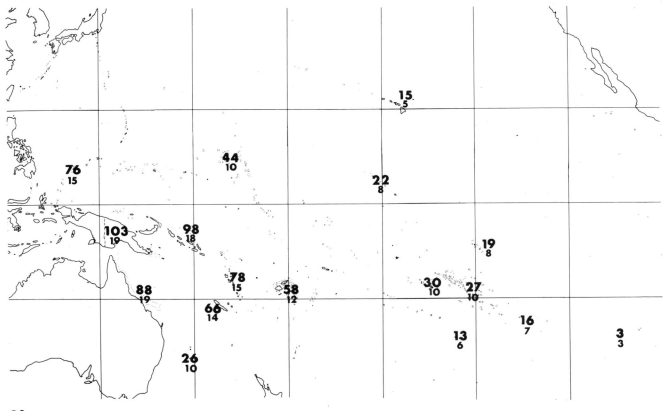

Chapter IV

A PROVISIONAL GENERIC CLASSIFICATION FOR THE POMACENTRIDAE OF THE TROPICAL INDO-WEST PACIFIC

In spite of their abundance and the bright colors and conspicuous habits exhibited by many of the species, the higher classification of the damselfishes remains an unsolved enigma. Certain groups such as *Amphiprion, Dascyllus,* and *Chromis* are more or less clearly definable, but the two largest "genera," *Abudefduf* and *Pomacentrus* as recognized by previous authors, obviously constitute artificial assemblages. *Abudefduf* in particular has served as a "catch-all" for a diversity of forms which are clearly polyphyletic. Most recent investigators (including myself) have been content to follow the classifications proposed by authors of regional monographs (i.e., Fowler and Bean, 1928; De Beaufort, 1940; Smith, 1948; Schultz, *et al.,* 1960; and Munro, 1967). However, these authors are usually unable to probe intra-familial relationships in detail because of their comprehensive faunal coverage.

Probable routes of colonization for pomacentrids in the western Pacific.

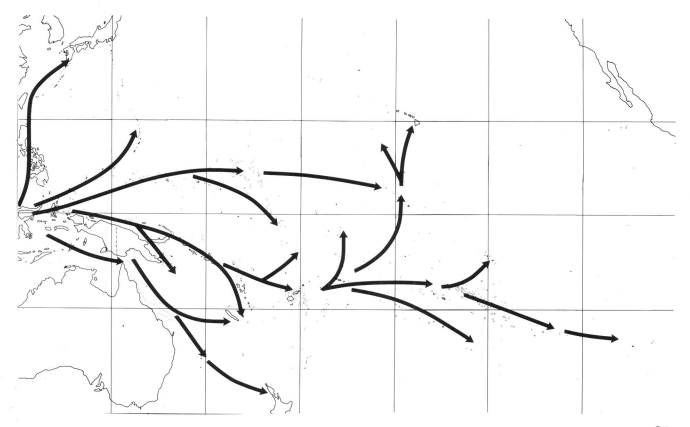

Mixed feeding aggregation of *Lepidozygus tapeinosoma* and *Chromis atripectoralis* on the outer edge of Pixie Reef, Great Barrier Reef.

An isolated patch of staghorn coral, *Acropora*, offers shelter to several pomacentrid species in the lagoon off Mala-kal, Palau Islands. Species shown here include *Pomacentrus popei*, *P. amboinensis*, *Dascyllus aruanus*, *Amblygly-phidodon curacao*, and *Chromis lepidolepis*.

Outer edge of the Great Barrier Reef off Cairns, Queensland.

A short time after I began serious study of the Pomacentridae at the Palau Islands, I realized that the generic scheme recognized by most taxonomists was inadequate. Two years later I had gathered enough material from the South Pacific to allow construction of a detailed generic framework. My personal collections were supplemented by numerous specimens at the Australian Museum taken at New Guinea and the Great Barrier Reef by Drs. Bruce Collette and Frank Talbot. In addition, specimens were borrowed from the Bishop Museum, Honolulu, and J. L. B. Smith Institute of Ichthyology in South Africa.

The generic classification proposed herein is summarized in Table 3 and in the figure. The scheme is briefly amplified in the remaining portion of the chapter, and keys to the subfamilies and genera (also subgenera of *Amphiprion* and *Pomacentrus*) are included. In addition, *Lepidopomacentrus* is proposed as a new subgenus of *Pomacentrus*, and other subgeneric groupings are suggested. Because the present classification is based entirely on external features and because of the regional treatment, it must be regarded as provisional. Hopefully this chapter will serve as a guide for several colleagues who have generic reviews in progress or are at least contemplating them. The subfamily classification presented below agrees with Norman (1966) except Premninae is included in Amphiprioninae and *Lepidozygus* represents a separate subfamily instead of being placed in the Chrominae.

KEY TO THE SUBFAMILIES OF POMACENTRIDAE
FROM THE INDO-WEST PACIFIC

1a. Scales small, usually more than 50 in a longitudinal series from rear edge of opercle to base of caudal fin; all the opercles usually serrate . . . . Amphiprioninae
1b. Scales relatively large, usually less than 45 in a longitudinal series; all the opercles not serrate . . 2
2a. Upper and lower edge of caudal base usually with two to three projecting spiniform procurrent rays; teeth conical, either biserial or multiserial; head usually entirely scaled except narrow region at front of snout and around each nostril . . . . Chrominae
2b. Upper and lower edge of caudal base without projecting spiniform rays; teeth conical or incisiform, uniserial or biserial; head scaled entirely or frequently without scales on snout, preorbital, and suborbital 3
3a. Body extremely elongate, 2.9 to 3.0 in SL; small papilla-like structures on inner edge of posterior circumorbitals . . . . Lepidozyginae
3b. Body orbiculate to elongate, usually 1.5 to 2.8 in SL; papilla-like structures on posterior circumorbitals absent . . . . Pomacentrinae

SUBFAMILY AMPHIPRIONINAE

This subfamily contains small to medium sized, brightly colored damselfishes which live commensally with large sea anemones. The classification used herein agrees with that presented in my 1972 revision of *Amphiprion* except for the following modifications: (1) *Premnas* is elevated to full generic ranking; and (2) the species "complexes" are accorded subgeneric ranking (except the *clarkii* and *ephippium* "complexes" are combined to form the subgenus *Amphiprion*).

KEY TO THE GENERA OF AMPHIPRIONINAE OF THE INDO-W. PACIFIC

1a. Suborbital usually armed with a pair of elongate spines; scales small, about 68 to 76 in a longitudinal series from upper edge of opercle to caudal base; two predorsal bones . . . . *Premnas* (Chapter VI)
1b. Suborbital without pair of elongate spines, although serrae present; scales moderate, usually about 50 to 60 in a longitudinal series; three predorsal bones . . . . *Amphiprion* (Chapter V)

Remarks—The genus *Premnas* is monotypic, containing only *P. biaculeatus*. *Amphiprion* includes 26 species which are divisable into four subgenera. A key to the subgenera and a brief diagnosis of each is presented below.

KEY TO THE SUBGENERA OF *AMPHIPRION*

1a. Occipital naked. . . . .*Actinicola*
1b. Occipital scaled 2
2a. Greatest body depth of adults usually greater than 2.0 in SL. 3
2b. Greatest body depth of adults usually less than 2.0 in SL. . . . .*Amphiprion*
3a. Interorbital naked; soft dorsal rays usually 14 to 16. . . . .*Paramphiprion*
3b. Interorbital scaly; soft dorsal rays usually 16 to 20. . . . .*Phalerebus*

Subgenus *Actinicola* Fowler, 1904: 533 (type species: *Lutjanus percula* Lacépède).

Diagnosis.—interorbital and occipital naked; body depth 2.1 to 2.4 in SL; dorsal rays usually X to XI, 14 to 16; soft dorsal junction with prominent notch; teeth incisiform to nearly conical; midbody bar with forward projection; ground color of body and fins orange, brown, or black; four middle hypural bones fused into two plates; pelvic axillary scale process usually weakly developed; caudal fin rounded.

Species.—*ocellaris* Cuvier; *percula* (Lacépède).

Subgenus *Paramphiprion* Wang, 1941: 89 (type species, *Paramphiprion hainanensis* Wang = *Amphiprion polymnus*).

Diagnosis.—interorbital naked; occipital scaled; body depth 2.1 to 2.4 in SL; dorsal rays usually X or XI, 14 to 16; soft dorsal junction usually with prominent notch; teeth conical; ground color of body and fins (except caudal) dark brown to blackish; caudal fin usually mostly dark; four middle hypural bones usually distinct; pelvic axillary scale process usually well-developed; caudal fin rounded or truncate.

Species.—*latezonatus* Waite; *polymnus* (Linnaeus); *sebae* Bleeker.

Subgenus *Phalerebus* Whitley, 1929: 216 (type species: *Amphiprion akallopisos* Bleeker).

Diagnosis.—interorbital and occipital scaled; body depth 2.0 to 2.4 in SL; dorsal rays usually IX to X, 16 to 20; soft dorsal junction obtusely notched; teeth conical or incisiform; one or no pale bars; ground color of body reddish, pinkish, or orange; four middle hypural bones fused into two plates; pelvic axillary scale process moderately or weakly developed; caudal fin rounded or slightly lobed.

Species.—*akallopisos* Bleeker; *leucokranos* Allen; *nigripes* Regan; *perideraion* Bleeker; *sandaracinos* Allen.

Subgenus *Amphiprion* Bloch and Schneider 1801: 200 (type species: *Lutjanus ephippium* Bloch).

Diagnosis.—interorbital naked or scaled; occipital scaled; body depth 1.7 to 2.0 in SL; dorsal rays usually IX to XI, 15 to 18; soft dorsal junction usually slightly notched or without notch; teeth conical; one to three pale bars, ground color of body usually orange, red, brown, or black; four middle hypural bones usually distinct; pelvic axillary scale process strongly developed; caudal fin either emarginate or rounded.

Species.—*akindynos* Allen; *allardi* Klausewitz; *bicinctus* Rüppell; *calliops* Schultz; *chagosensis* Allen; *chrysogaster* Cuvier; *chrysopterus* Cuvier; *clarkii* Bennett; *ephippium* (Bloch); *frenatus* Brevoort; *fuscocaudatus* Allen; *latifasciatus* Allen; *mccullochi* Whitley; *melanopus* Bleeker; *rubrocinctus* Richardson; and *tricinctus* Schultz and Welander.

Outer edge of the Great Barrier Reef off Port Douglas, Queensland.

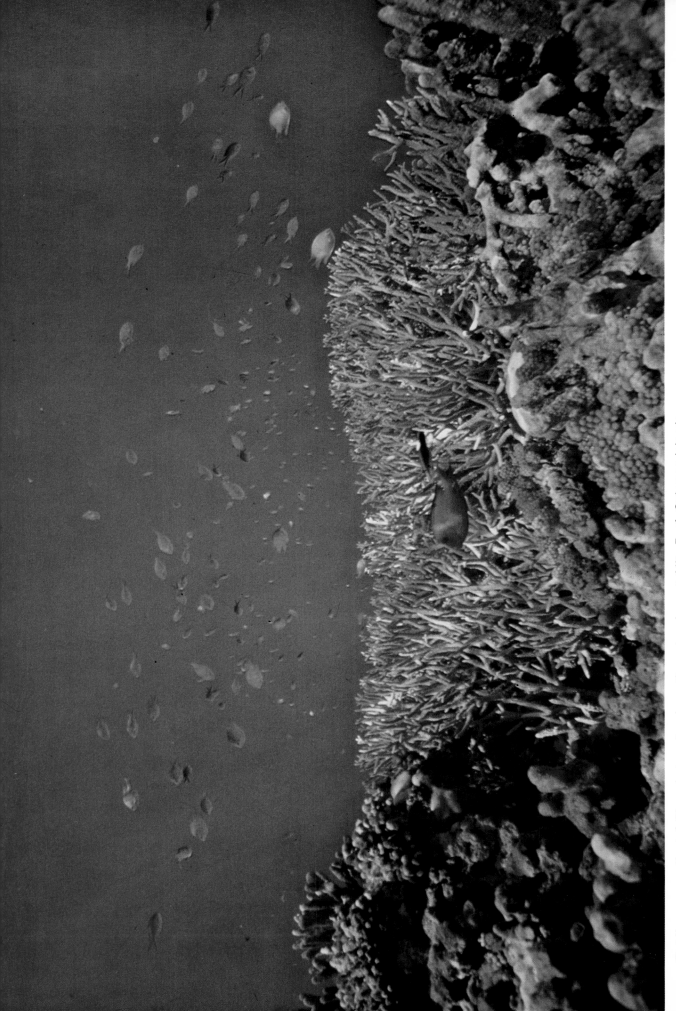

Feeding aggregation of *Chromis ternatensis* on the outer slope at Alite Reef, Solomon Islands.

SUBFAMILY CHROMINAE

This subfamily contains small to large pomacentrids which frequently form large feeding aggregations well above the bottom. Zooplankton comprises the major dietary component. The dentition of the jaws is conical, usually being comprised of an outer row of larger teeth and one or more rows of secondary teeth behind. Three genera in the Indo-West Pacific: *Acanthochromis*, *Chromis* and *Dascyllus*.

KEY TO THE GENERA OF CHROMINAE OF THE INDO-WEST PACIFIC

1a. Dorsal spines XII to XV..2
1b. Dorsal spines usually XVII.............................*Acanthochromis* (ChapterVIII)
2a. Suborbital and hind margin of preopercle finely serrate.............*Dascyllus* (Chapter VII)
2b. Suborbital entire or covered with scales; hind margin of preopercle usually entire
Chromis (Chapter IX)

Remarks.—*Chromis* is probably separable into several subgenera. However, I have not elaborated these because the genus will be treated in detail in a forthcoming revision by Dr. John E. Randall. A large share of the species belong to the *margaritifer* "complex" which is characterized by XII dorsal spines, an exposed suborbital margin, and prolonged bi-furcate filaments at the tips of the caudal lobes. Other distinct subgroups are typified by the following species (available subgeneric names indicated in parentheses): *analis* (*Dorychromis* Fowler and Bean, 1928); *caerulea* (*Hoplochromis* Fowler, 1918); *chrysura* (*Lepicephalochromis* Fowler, 1943); *lepidolepis* (*Lepidochromis* Fowler and Bean, 1928); *vanderbilti* (*Pycnochromis* Fowler, 1941); *ovalis* (*Thrissochromis* Fowler, 1941).

SUBFAMILY LEPIDOZYGINAE

The subfamily Lepidozyginae contains a single genus and species, *Lepidozygus tapeinosoma*. Refer to Chapter X for additional information on this widely distributed damselfish.

SUBFAMILY POMACENTRINAE

The subfamily Pomacentrinae is a diverse group containing many species in the tropical Indo-West Pacific and Atlantic. Bleeker (1877b) was the first person to accurately describe the polyphyletic nature of this assemblage. The basic framework which he proposed is presented in Table 4. Although the present study indicates that this scheme is generally a sound one, most recent investigators have lumped the majority of species in either *Abudefduf* or *Pomacentrus* depending on the condition of the preopercle margin (i.e., smooth in *Abudefduf* and serrate in *Pomacentrus*). This plan, however, is unsatisfactory as there are certain natural groupings which are characterized by an intermediate condition in which the preopercle is either crenulate or weakly serrate (for example, *Neopomacentrus* and *Pomachromis*). It is not practical to base a generic classification on a single character, especially one that is not entirely reliable in showing species relationships. It is far better, of course, to analyze several characters. Such features as general body shape (perhaps best quantified in terms of body depth in the SL), dentition, scalation, and counts must be given equal consideration.

The classification proposed below essentially agrees with Bleeker's, but with some modification. Seven of Bleeker's generic groups are recognized and four of his subgenera have been elevated to genera. *Parapomacentrus* is a synonym of *Pomacentrus*, and *Lepidozygus* has been placed in a separate subfamily. *Hypsypops*, restricted to the eastern Pacific, is not included in the present study. In addition, the subfamily contains the following five genera: *Cheiloprion, Neopomacentrus, Parma, Pomachromis,* and *Pristotis. Teixeirichthys* from the western Indian Ocean and Japan was not studied, but is probably allied to *Pristotis*.

KEY TO THE GENERA OF POMACENTRINAE OF THE INDO-WEST PACIFIC

1a. Scales small, usually about 44 to 46 in longitudinal series from upper edge of gill opening to caudal base; body depth 2.4 to 2.8 in SL..................................*Teixeirichthys*

1b. Scales large, usually about 26 to 35 (except 30–46 in *Parma*, which has body depth 1.6 to 1.9) in longitudinal series from upper edge of gill opening to caudal base; body depth 1.5 to 3.0 in SL...2

2a. Hind margin of preopercle crenulate or weakly to strongly serrate.................................3

2b. Hind margin of preopercle entire...12

3a. Lips normal, not greatly thickened and curled back over snout...................................4

3b. Lips greatly thickened, fimbriate, and curled back over snout......*Cheiloprion* (Chapter XIV)

4a. Teeth of jaws uniserial..5

4b. Teeth of jaws biserial (at least anteriorly)..8

5a. Edge of suboperculum entire...6

5b. Edge of suboperculum serrate.......................................*Pristotis* (Chapter XXV)

6a. Suborbital scaly; snout scaled to about level of nostrils........*Eupomacentrus* (Chapter XVI)

6b. Suborbital naked; snout naked; predorsal scales extending to about level of anterior edge of orbits..7

7a. Body elongate, depth 2.6 to 2.9 in SL; dorsal spines XIV........*Pomachromis* (Chapter XXIV)

7b. Body ovate, depth 2.1 to 2.3 in SL; dorsal spines XIII.....*Amblypomacentrus* (Chapter XIII)

8a. Suborbital naked (at least anteriorly); hind margin of preopercle distinctly serrate.........9

8b. Suborbital scaly; hind margin of preopercle crenulate or weakly serrate.....................10

9a. Snout mostly naked, predorsal scales extending to about front of orbits or slightly beyond; notch between preorbital and suborbital absent.....................*Dischistodus* (Chapter XV)

9b. Snout scaled to about level of nostrils or beyond; usually a prominent notch between preorbital and suborbital (much reduced in certain species).............*Pomacentrus* (Chapter XXIII)

10a. Body more or less elongate, depth usually 2.3 to 2.8 in SL; outer row of teeth with flattened tips; caudal lunate or strongly emarginate; posterior portion of dorsal and anal fins and outer caudal rays frequently produced into filaments..............*Neopomacentrus,* n. gen. (Chapter XIX)

10b. Body ovate, depth 2.0 to 2.3 in SL; outer row of teeth with conical tips; caudal rounded or slightly emarginate; outer caudal rays and posterior portion of dorsal and anal fins not produced into filaments..11

11a. Dorsal and anal rays 14 to 15; pectoral rays 18; slight notch between preorbital and suborbital; spinous dorsal without dark spot at base of hindmost spines.................................
................................*Pomacentrus* (*Lepidopomacentrus* n. subgenus) (Chapter XXIII)

11b. Dorsal and anal rays 11 to 13; pectoral rays 15 to 16; notch between preorbital and suborbital absent; spinous dorsal with prominent dark spot at base of hindmost spines................
....*Glyphidodontops* (*traceyi* and *talboti* only) (Chapter XVII)

12a. Vertical scale rows about 28; horizontal scale rows from lateral line to origin of anal fin less than 12 13

12b. Vertical scale rows in excess of 30; horizontal scale rows below lateral line to origin of anal fin more than 14...*Parma* (Chapter XXI)

13a. Horizontal scale rows above middle of lateral line usually 3 to 3½......*Abudefduf* (Chapter XI)

13b. Horizontal scale rows above middle of lateral line 1 to 2½ (usually 1½).........................14

14a. Gill rakers on first arch 10 to 35...15

14b. Gill rakers on first arch approximately 65 to 85..........*Hemiglyphidodon* (Chapter XVIII)

15a. Dorsal spines XIII or XIV...16

15b. Dorsal spines XII...*Plectroglyphidodon* (Chapter XXII)

16a. Body somewhat orbiculate, depth 1.5 to 1.8 in SL; longest dorsal spine about equal in length to distance from tip of snout to uppermost portion of preopercle border.................................
....*Amblyglyphidodon* (Chapter XII)

Dead coral rubble is frequently inhabited by *Pomacentrus coelestis*, the blue fish shown here. Taken at Guadalcanal, Solomon Islands.

Large boulders are the dominant feature of this section of Sandfly Passage, Florida Island, Solomon Islands. The black and white barred fish is *Abudefduf saxatilis*.

16b. Body moderately deep to elongate, depth usually 1.8 to 2.7 in SL; longest dorsal spine usually much shorter than distance from tip of snout to uppermost portion of preopercle border....17

17a. Body moderately deep, usually less than 2.0 in SL; preorbital and suborbital scaly (except mostly naked in *P. polyacanthus*); teeth biserial, at least anteriorly....*Paraglyphidodon* (Chapter XX)

17b. Body ovate to elongate, depth usually greater than 2.0 in SL; preorbital and suborbital scaly or naked; teeth biserial or uniserial....................*Glyphidodontops* (Chapter XVII)

Remarks.—Abudefduf: This genus corresponds with Bleeker's subgenus *Glyphidodon*. It contains relatively large pomacentrids, generally possessing dark transverse bars. Forskål (1775) introduced the generic name *Abudefduf* with *Chaetodon sordidus* Forskål as the type species. Jordan (1917) stated "It may receive objection as a barbarous name. It was probably a 'stop-gap' word for which Forskål intended to supply a Latin equivalent." Lacépède later introduced the name *Glyphisodon* (usually spelled *Glyphidodon*) which was accepted by Bleeker and others. However, nearly all recent authors prefer to use the earlier, but unorthodox, *Abudefduf*.

Amblyglyphidodon: A distinct group characterized by a relatively orbiculate shape. *A. ternatensis* differs from the other members of the genus by having an auxiliary row of buttress teeth at the front of the jaws.

Amblypomacentrus: Contains a single species, *A. breviceps*, which has been included in *Pomacentrus* by recent authors. However, it seems to more closely resemble certain members of *Glyphidodontops*.

Cheiloprion: Contains a single species, *C. labiatus*, distinguished by large, fleshy, lips.

Dischistodus: A close-knit group containing six species which are mainly restricted to the Indo-Australian Archipelago and Melanesia.

Eupomacentrus: The genus is probably divisible into at least two subgenera based on similarities of dorsal spine counts. *E. albifasciatus, E. lividus,* and *E. nigricans* possess XII spines, while the other Indo-West Pacific species, except *E. gascoynei*, characteristically have XIII spines. *E. gascoynei*, with XIV spines, is otherwise very similar to the XIII-spined forms, typified by the wide-ranging *E. fasciolatus*.

Glyphidodontops: This diverse group possesses some of the most serious problems for students of pomacentrid taxonomy. It is probable that some of the forms which are presently included in this genus will be placed elsewhere when osteological studies now in progress are completed. However, there are two "complexes" in the genus which are reasonably distinct. One contains *G. leucopomus, G. biocellatus, G. unimaculatus, G. glaucus,* and *G. niger*. The fin ray and gill raker counts, level of predorsal scalation, lack of scales on the preorbital and suborbital, elongate teeth of the jaws, shape of the head and profile of the dorsal fin indicate a close relationship among the members of this group. Likewise, *G. rollandi, G. azureopunctatus, G. hemicyaneus, G. traceyi,* and *G. talboti* comprise a "complex" which is characterized by low soft dorsal and pectoral ray counts, similar dentition (teeth not nearly as elongate as in the *leucopomus* complex), and a distinctive dorsal fin profile in which the membranes between the spines are deeply incised (at least anteriorly) and there is an obtuse notch at the soft dorsal junction. The relationship of *G. flavipinnis, G. rex, G. cyaneus,* and *G. tricinctus* is not clear. These species combine various characters from the two complexes just discussed. *G. caeruleolineatus* probably deserves at least separate subgeneric ranking on the strength of such characters as XIV dorsal spines, predorsal scalation which extends anteriorly to about the mid-interorbital level, and uniserial teeth. *G. galbus, G. notialis, G. rapanui,* and *G. starcki*, species which are mainly restricted to the southern periphery of Oceania, may be related. All except *G. rapanui* have uniserial teeth, which is atypical for *Glyphidodontops*.

Hemiglyphidodon: Contains a single species, *H. plagiometopon*, which is characterized by a unique body shape and nearly three times as many gill rakers on the first arch as other damselfishes.

Neopomacentrus: This new genus is described in Chapter XIX. Bleeker placed some of these fishes in *Parapomacentrus*, but the type species for that genus, *Pomacentrus polynema*, is a synonym of *P. pavo*. Therefore the name *Parapomacentrus* is not applicable.

Paraglyphidodon: These fishes are essentially deep bodied "*Glyphidodontops.*" They are easily distinguished in the field and appear to form a natural grouping.

Parma: Contains eight species which are generally restricted to the subtropical and temperate waters of Australia and New Zealand. However, *P. polylepis* penetrates the southern fringe of the tropics at the Capricorn Group, Queensland, and New Caledonia, and *P. oligolepis* occurs along the Queensland coast.

Plectroglyphidodon (Bleeker's *Stegastes*): *P. imparipennis*, whose relationship to this group has generally been overlooked, constitutes a separate subgenus *(Oliglyphisodon)*. It is more slender, has a different fin outline, and fewer gill rakers than other *Plectroglyphidodon*.

Pomacentrus: This genus is divisable into three subgenera: *Pomacentrus*, *Pseudopomacentrus* and *Lepidopomacentrus* n. subgen.

KEY TO THE SUBGENERA OF *POMACENTRUS* OF THE INDO-WEST PACIFIC

1a. Preorbital and suborbital usually naked (except suborbital scaled posteriorly in *P. philippinus* and preorbital with small patch of scales in *P. littoralis*)..................................2
1b. Preorbital and suborbital scaly........................*Lepidopomacentrus* new subgenus
2a. Greatest body depth usually in excess of 2.4 in SL; color in life blue...........*Pomacentrus*
2b. Greatest body depth usually 1.8 to 2.1 (occasionally 2.2 or 2.3) in SL; color in life not blue ....*Pseudopomacentrus*

Lepidopomacentrus, n. subgen. (type species, *Pomacentrus lepidogenys* Fowler and Bean, 1928). *Diagnosis.*—A subgenus of *Pomacentrus* distinguished by the following combination of characters: preorbital and suborbital scaled; dorsal spines XIII; body depth 2.0 to 2.3 in SL; margin of suborbital entire; margin of preopercle weakly serrate; color generally brown or greyish without distinguishing marks.

The subgenus *Pomacentrus* contains the following species from the "South Seas": *P. australis*, *P. coelestis*, and *P. pavo*. The other "South Seas" representatives of the genus are referable to *Pseudopomacentrus* except *P. lepidogenys*. *P. opisthostigma* and *P. reidi* differ from other *Pseudopomacentrus* by having XIV dorsal spines. *P. smithi* is also somewhat aberrant. It has a suborbital margin which is non-serrate, a weakly serrate preopercle, and only a slight notch between the preorbital and suborbital. *P. littoralis* (type species of *Pseudopomacentrus*) differs from all other *Pomacentrus* by the possession of a small patch of scales on the preorbital. I examined two specimens of *littoralis* at the Australian Museum which were collected at Darwin.

Pomachromis: This recently described genus contains four species which, except for *P. richardsoni*, are confined to the West Pacific. There are few differences between species except color.

Pristotis: I have united *Daya* Bleeker with *Pristotis* Rüppell for reasons given in Chapter XXV.

Amphiprion akindynos (about 75 mm TL), Heron Island, Great Barrier Reef in five meters (W. Deas photo).

A swarm of *Amphiprion tricinctus* swimming over a sea anemone *Radianthus simplex* at Eniwetok, Marshall Islands.

*Amphiprion
chrysopterus* (about
125 mm TL), Madang,
New Guinea in 10
meters.

Amphiprion clarkii
(about 125 mm TL),
Efate, New Hebrides
in 10 meters.

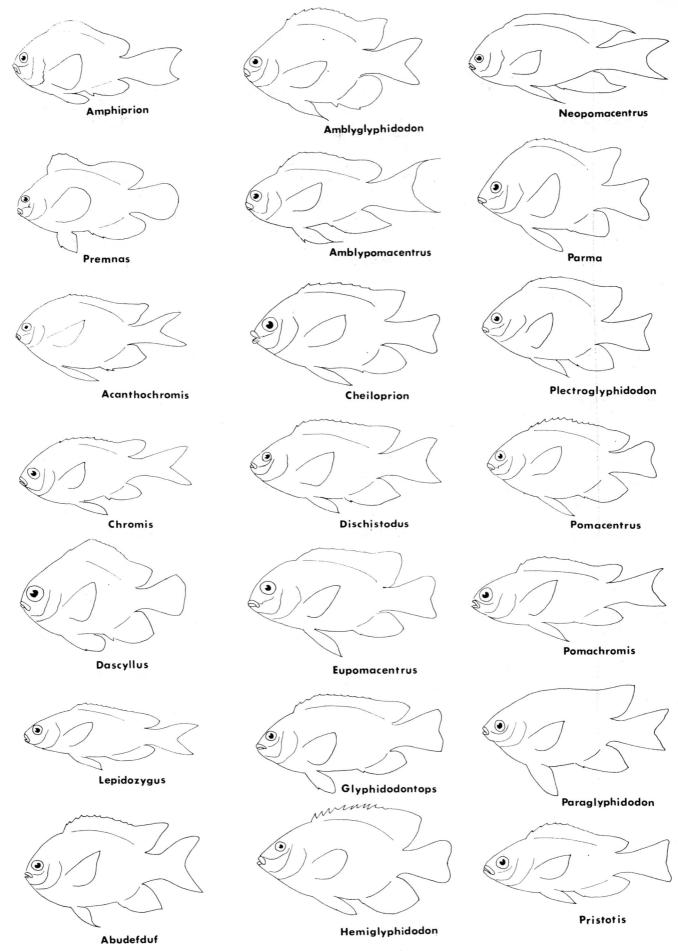

Amphiprion

Amblyglyphidodon

Neopomacentrus

Premnas

Amblypomacentrus

Parma

Acanthochromis

Cheiloprion

Plectroglyphidodon

Chromis

Dischistodus

Pomacentrus

Dascyllus

Eupomacentrus

Pomachromis

Lepidozygus

Glyphidodontops

Paraglyphidodon

Abudefduf

Hemiglyphidodon

Pristotis

Genera of Pomacentridae from the "South Seas."

TABLE 3

PROVISIONAL GENERIC CLASSIFICATION FOR THE POMACENTRIDAE OF THE TROPICAL INDO-WEST PACIFIC

Family: Pomacentridae
    Subfamily: Amphiprioninae
        Genus: *Amphiprion* Bloch and Schneider
        Genus: *Premnas* Cuvier
    Subfamily: Chrominae
        Genus: *Acanthochromis* Gill
        Genus: *Chromis* Cuvier
        Genus: *Dascyllus* Cuvier
    Subfamily: Lepidozyginae
        Genus: *Lepidozygus* Günther

    Subfamily: Pomacentrinae
        Genus: *Abudefduf* Forskål
        Genus: *Amblyglyphidodon* Bleeker
        Genus: *Amblypomacentrus* Bleeker
        Genus: *Cheiloprion* Weber
        Genus: *Dischistodus* Gill
        Genus: *Eupomacentrus* Bleeker
        Genus: *Glyphidodontops* Bleeker
        Genus: *Hemiglyphidodon* Bleeker
        Genus: *Neopomacentrus*, new genus
        Genus: *Paraglyphidodon* Bleeker
        Genus: *Parma* Günther
        Genus: *Plectroglyphidodon* Fowler and Ball
        Genus: *Pomacentrus* Lacépède
        Genus: *Pomachromis* Allen and Randall
        Genus: *Pristotis* Rüppell

TABLE 4

BLEEKER'S CLASSIFICATION OF THE POMACENTRINAE

Family: Pomacentridae
    Subfamily: Pomacentrinae
        Genus: *Pomacentrus*
           Subgenus: *Pomacentrus*
           Subgenus: *Pseudopomacentrus*
        Genus: *Parapomacentrus*
        Genus *Amblypomacentrus*
        Genus: *Lepidozygus*
        Genus: *Daya*
        Genus *Eupomacentrus*
           Subgenus: *Eupomacentrus*
           Subgenus: *Brachypomacentrus*

Genus: *Dischistodus*
Genus: *Glyphidodon*
    Subgenus: *Glyphidodon*
    Subgenus: *Hemiglyphidodon*
    Subgenus: *Amblyglyphidodon*
    Subgenus: *Stegastes*
    Subgenus: *Hypsypops*
Genus: *Paraglyphidodon*
Genus: *Glyphidodontops*

Amphiprion clarkii
(about 50 mm TL),
Madang, New Guinea
in 15 meters.

Amphiprion clarkii
(about 125 mm TL),
Rabaul, New Britain
in 18 meters.

Amphiprion latezonatus (about 125 mm TL), Lord Howe Island in 30 meters.

Amphiprion latezonatus (about 60 mm TL), Byron Bay, New South Wales in 18 meters (W. Deas photo).

Chapter V
AMPHIPRION

The anemonefishes of the genus *Amphiprion* are particularly well known because of their bright colors and interesting relationship with large tropical sea anemones. The genus was recently revised by the author (Allen, 1972) and includes 26 species from the Indo-West Pacific. There are 13 species known from the "South Seas" region. One of these, *Amphiprion leucokranos* from the Solomon Islands and New Guinea, remained undiscovered until 1972.

The genus contains small to medium sized damselfishes which characteristically feed on zooplankton a short distance above the host anemone. Most of the species also feed on benthic algae. Typically there is an adult pair and one or more juveniles present at each large anemone, but in situations where there are many anemones in close proximity the territory of the adult pair may include several actiniaria. Spawning takes place adjacent to the anemone in a location where the eggs are protected by the stinging tentacles. Generally between 300 and 700 eggs are attached to solid rock near the base of the anemone. Both parents assume an active role in guarding and caring for the eggs. The male, however, performs the bulk of these chores. Hatching occurs in six or seven days and the fry are pelagic for the first few weeks.

GENUS *AMPHIPRION* BLOCH AND SCHNEIDER

Amphiprion Bloch and Schneider, 1801: 200 (type species, *Lutjanus ephippium* Bloch).

Diagnostic features.—Body ovate or oblong; teeth conical or incisiform; preorbital and suborbital with one or more serrations; opercle, subopercle, and interopercle with strong serrae; opercular bones scaled; interorbital scaled or naked; pelvic axillary scale process weakly to strongly developed; scales small, 47 to 66 (usually 50 to 60) vertical rows between upper edge of opercle and caudal fin base; dorsal rays VIII to XI, 14 to 21; anal rays II, 11 to 15; pectoral and pelvic fins rounded to pointed; caudal fin rounded, truncate, or emarginate.

The key to species which appears below generally applies to specimens in excess of 40 mm SL. The young of *A. mccullochi; A. melanopus,* and *A. rubrocinctus* frequently exhibit two or three pale bars, but otherwise resemble the adult pattern.

KEY TO THE SPECIES OF *AMPHIPRION* FROM THE SOUTH SEAS

1a. Two or three pale bars present, midbody bar may form abbreviated saddle.............2
1b. One pale bar present or bar entirely absent.................................8
2a. Caudal fin mostly pale.....................................3
2b. Caudal fin mostly dark.....................................6
3a. Caudal and pectoral fins entirely pale; predorsal scales extending to interorbital region......4
3b. Caudal and pectoral fins with prominent black submarginal band; predorsal scales extending to level well behind rear of orbits (Melanesia and Queensland).......................*A. percula*
4a. Midbody bar usually 7 to 12 scales wide; three complete whitish bars present, usually with abrupt light-dark boundary (convex anteriorly at forward edge of caudal peduncle) (Indo-far West Pacific)....................................*A. clarkii*
4b. Midbody bar usually two to six scales wide; two complete whitish bars present, usually without abrupt light-dark boundary at forward edge of caudal peduncle......................5

5a. Color of sides brown to blackish; anal rays usually 14; pectoral rays usually 20; midbody bar usually two to three scales wide in adults; caudal fin tan or cream-colored in life (Tuamotus; Society Islands; Samoa Islands; Melanesia, except New Caledonia; Gilbert Islands; Micronesia)..*A. chrysopterus*

5b. Color of sides tannish to brown; anal rays usually 13; pectoral rays usually 19; midbody bar usually four to six scales wide; caudal fin white in life (Queensland and northern New So. Wales; New Caledonia; Loyalty Islands)..*A. akindynos*

6a. Dark portion of caudal fin tapering in width posteriorly and bordered by broad white margins on upper and lower lobes; midbody bar frequently forming abbreviated saddle; pale bar on caudal peduncle usually absent (Ryukyus; China; Taiwan; Philippines; East Indies; Northern Territory; New Guinea; New Britain; Solomon Islands......................*A. polymnus*

6b. Dark portion of caudal fin not tapering in width posteriorly; midbody bar not forming abbreviated saddle; pale bar on caudal peduncle usually present (occasionally absent in *A. tricinctus*)...7

7a. Midbody bar greater than 15 scales wide; caudal fin with broad pale posterior margin (Lord Howe Island; northern New So. Wales and southern Queensland).............*A. latezonatus*

7b. Midbody bar less than six scales wide; caudal fin with or without narrow pale margin (Marshall Islands)...*A. tricinctus*

8a. Body depth less than 2.0 in SL; a single pale bar present on head........................9

8b. Body depth greater than 2.1 in SL; a single pale bar on side of head or bar absent.........11

9a. Pelvic fins pale; ground color of body usually pale (red in life) (N.W. Australia; Fiji Islands; Samoa Islands; Tonga Islands; Society Islands)..............................*A. rubrocinctus*

9b. Pelvic fins entirely dark brown or black; ground color of body either uniformly dark brown or pale with intense blackish area on middle of sides..10

10a. Head bar of each side usually connected at dorsal midline; soft dorsal fin pale; length of tallest dorsal spine 2.7 to 3.2 in head length; pectoral rays usually 18 or 19; caudal fin rounded (West Pacific)..*A. melanopus*

10b. Head bar of each side not connected at dorsal midline; soft dorsal fin brown; length of tallest dorsal spine 1.6 to 2.3 in head length; pectoral rays usually 20; caudal fin emarginate (Lord Howe Island)..*A. mccullochi*

11a. Head bar present..12

11b. Head bar absent (Philippines; Solomon Islands; New Guinea)...............*A. sandaracinos*

12a. Head bar and predorsal stripe about equal or greater than eye diameter in width; soft dorsal rays usually 18; pectoral rays usually 19 (Solomon Islands; D'Entrecasteaux Islands; New Guinea)...*A. leucokranos*

12b. Head bar and predorsal stripe less than $\frac{1}{2}$ eye diameter in width; soft dorsal rays usually 16; pectoral rays usually 17 (Japan and Ryukyu Islands; Philippines; East Indies; Micronesia; Melanesia; Queensland)..*A. perideraion*

Amphiprion akindynos Allen
Barrier Reef Anemonefish

Illus. p. 44

Amphiprion akindynos Allen, 1972: 153 (Capricorn Group, Queensland).

Diagnosis.—Dorsal rays X, 15 to 17; anal rays II, 13 to 14; pectoral rays 19 to 20. Tubed lateral-line scales 31 to 40. Gill rakers on first arch 19 to 22. Body depth 1.8 to 2.0 in SL. Color in alcohol generally brown with two grey-white bars; dorsal and anal fins brown; remainder of fins mostly pale. Maximum size to about 85–90 mm SL.

Ecology.—Inhabits lagoons and outer reef slopes in one to 20 meters. Commensal with anemones, most frequently with *Radianthus* spp.

Distribution.—Northern New South Wales, southern Queensland, Great Barrier Reef, New Caledonia, and Loyalty Islands.

Amphiprion leuco-kranos (about 75 mm TL), Madang, New Guinea in six meters.

Amphiprion mccullochi (about 75 mm TL), Lord Howe Island in four meters.

Amphiprion melanopus (about 75 mm TL), Madang, New Guinea in 10 meters.

Amphiprion melanopus (about 50 mm TL), Efate, New Hebrides in 10 meters.

Amphiprion chrysopterus Cuvier
Orange-fin Anemonefish

Illus. p. 45

Amphiprion chrysopterus Cuvier, 1830: 396 (no locality given).

Diagnosis.—Dorsal rays X, 15 to 17 (occasionally XI, 15 to 17); anal rays II, 13 to 14; pectoral rays 20 to 21. Tubed lateral-line scales 35 to 42. Gill rakers on first arch 19 to 21. Body depth 1.8 to 1.9 in SL. Color in alcohol generally dark brown to black with two bluish-grey bars; fins pale, except pelvic and anal fins black in most specimens from Melanesia.

Ecology.—Inhabits passages and outer reef slopes in one to 20 meters. Feeds chiefly on planktonic copepods, algae, echuroid and sipunculoid worms, and pelagic tunicates (see Allen, 1972). Commensal with a variety of anemones; usually three to four fish per host, including an adult pair.

Distribution.—New Guinea, D'Entrecasteaux Islands, New Britain, Solomon Islands, New Hebrides, Fiji Islands, Caroline Islands, Mariana Islands, Marshall Islands, Gilbert Islands, Samoa Islands, Society Islands, and Tuamotu Islands.

Amphiprion clarkii (Bennett)
Clark's Anemonefish

Illus. pp. 45, 48

Anthias clarkii Bennett, 1830: 29 (Ceylon).
Amphiprion papuensis Macleay, 1883: 271 (D'Entrecasteaux Islands).

Diagnosis.—Dorsal rays X, 15 to 16; anal rays II, 13 to 14; pectoral rays 19 to 20. Tubed lateral-line scales 36 to 40. Gill rakers on first arch 18 to 20. Body depth 1.7 to 2.0 in SL. Color in alcohol generally tan to black with three white bars; caudal and pectoral fins pale; remainder of fins variable, either dark or pale.

Ecology.—Inhabits lagoons and outer reef slopes in one to 55 meters. The latter figure, recorded for one individual at Osprey Reef (Coral Sea), represents a new depth record for the genus. Commensal with a variety of anemones; usually one adult pair and several juveniles per host.

Distribution.—The most widespread species in the genus, occurring from the Persian Gulf eastward to the Caroline Islands and Melanesia (except Fiji Islands). The northern limit of distribution in the Pacific is southern Japan and the southern limit is New Caledonia. Two specimens at the Australian Museum collected off Mackay, Queensland represent a new record for eastern Australia.

Amphiprion latezonatus Waite
Wide-band Anemonefish

Illus. p. 49

Amphiprion latezonatus Waite, 1900: 201 (Lord Howe Island).

Diagnosis.—Dorsal rays XI, 15 to 16; anal rays II, 12 to 14; pectoral rays 19 to 20. Tubed lateral-line scales 34 to 36. Gill rakers on first arch 18 to 20. Body depth 1.9 to 2.0 in SL. Color in alcohol generally dark brown with three pale bars; midbody bar exceptionally broad; caudal brown with broad pale posterior margin. Maximum size to about 125 mm SL.

Ecology.—Inhabits rocky reefs in 15 to 45 meters. Commensal with anemones (usually *Radianthus* sp.).

Distribution.—Lord Howe Island, northern New So. Wales and southern Queensland.

Amphiprion leucokranos Allen
White-bonnet Anemonefish

Illus. p. 52

Amphiprion leucokranos Allen, 1973b: 319 (Madang, New Guinea).

Diagnosis.—Dorsal rays IX, 18 to 19; anal rays II, 13 to 14; pectoral rays 19 to 20. Tubed lateral-line scales 35 to 39. Gill rakers on first arch 18 to 20. Body depth 2.1 to 2.2 in SL. Color in alcohol generally tan, darker dorsally; broad whitish bar on side of head and whitish patch covering predorsal region behind orbits; fins pale. Maximum size to about 70 mm SL.

Ecology.—Inhabits lagoons and outer reef slopes in two to six meters. Commensal with sea anemones (usually *Radianthus malu*).

Distribution.—New Guinea, D'Entreceasteaux Islands, and Solomon Islands.

Amphiprion mccullochi Whitley
McCulloch's Anemonefish
Illus. p. 52

Amphiprion mccullochi Whitley, 1929: 213 (Lord Howe Island).

Diagnosis.—Dorsal rays X, 15 to 17; anal rays II, 13 to 14; pectoral rays 20 to 21. Tubed lateral-line scales 36 to 41. Gill rakers on first arch 18 to 20. Body depth 1.8 to 1.9 in SL. Color in alcohol generally dark brown with a single pale bar on the head; caudal fin pale; remainder of fins brown to dark brown. Maximum size to about 90 mm SL.

Ecology.—Inhabits the lagoon and rocky outer reefs of Lord Howe Island in two to 10 meters. Commensal with unidentified anemones.

Distribution.—Known only from Lord Howe Island.

Amphiprion melanopus Bleeker
Black Anemonefish
Illus. pp. 53, 56

Amphiprion melanopus Bleeker, 1852b: 561 (Amboina).
Amphiprion monofasciatus Thiolliere, 1856: 476 (Woodlark Island).
Amphiprion arion De Vis, 1884: 450 (South Seas).
Amphiprion verweyi Whitley, 1933: 85 (Queensland).

Diagnosis.—Dorsal rays X, 16 to 18; anal rays II, 13 to 14; pectoral rays 18 to 19. Tubed lateral-line scales 34 to 42. Gill rakers on first arch 17 to 19. Body depth 1.7 to 1.9 in SL. Color in alcohol generally dark reddish-brown, nearly black with single pale bar on head (certain individuals from Melanesia largely pale with reduced blackish area on sides); dorsal, pectoral, and caudal fins pale; pelvics blackish; anal fin pale or blackish. Maximum size to about 90 mm SL.

Ecology.—Inhabits lagoon and outer reef environments at depths between one and 10 meters. Feeds predominantly on planktonic copepods and algae (see Allen, 1972). Commensal with anemones (apparently host specific for *Physobrachia douglasi*); large numbers of *A. melanopus* are common in areas where this cluster-dwelling anemone is numerous.

Distribution.—East Indies, Queensland, Melanesia (except Fiji Islands), and Oceania in general as far east as the Paumotu Islands in the south and Marshall Islands in the north. Not yet reported from the Fiji Islands where it is apparently replaced by the closely related *Amphiprion rubrocinctus*.

Amphiprion percula (Lacépède)
Clown Anemonefish
Illus. p. 56

Lutjanus percula Lacépède, 1802: 194 (New Britain).
Amphiprion tunicatus Cuvier, 1830: 399 (Vanikoro).

Diagnosis.—Dorsal rays IX or X, 14 to 17; anal rays II, 11 to 13; pectoral rays 15 to 17. Tubed lateral-line scales usually 30 to 38. Gill rakers on first arch 15 to 17. Body depth 2.1 to 2.4 in SL. Color in alcohol generally pale yellow or tannish to brown with three pale bars bordered with black margins (these margins considerably expanded in some specimens); fins pale yellow or tannish to brown with prominent black trim, all except pelvics and spinous dorsal with broad whitish margins. Maximum size to about 60 mm SL.

Ecology.—Inhabits lagoons and outer reef slopes in one to 12 meters (more common in protected lagoons). Commensal with anemones (*Radianthus* and *Stoichactis*).

Distribution.—Queensland and Melanesia. Not encountered at New Caledonia and the Fiji Islands, although Fowler (1959) recorded it from the latter area.

Amphiprion melanopus (about 50 mm TL), Efate, New Hebrides in 10 meters. This unusual color variety lacks the characteristic black pigmentation.

Amphiprion percula
(about 75 mm TL),
Madang, New Guinea
in three meters.

Amphiprion perideraion (about 100 mm TL), Suva, Fiji Islands in three meters.

Amphiprion perideraion (about 75 mm TL), Madang, New Guinea in 18 meters.

Amphiprion perideraion Bleeker
Pink Anemonefish

Amphiprion perideraion Bleeker, 1855: 437 (Groot Oby).

Diagnosis.—Dorsal rays X, 16 to 17; anal rays II, 12 to 13; pectoral rays 16 to 18. Tubed lateral-line scales 32 to 43. Gill rakers on first arch 17 to 20. Body depth 2.1 to 2.7 in SL. Color in alcohol generally tan with one narrow pale bar on head; fins pale. Maximum size to about 75 mm SL.

Ecology.—Inhabits lagoons and outer reef slopes in three to 20 meters. Feeds predominately on benthic algae, but zooplankton (primarily copepods) is also taken. Commensal with *Radianthus ritteri*; usually one adult pair and several juveniles at each anemone.

Distribution.—Japan and Ryukyu Islands, Micronesia, Philippines, East Indies, Melanesia, and Great Barrier Reef.

Amphiprion polymnus (Linnaeus)
Saddleback Anemonefish

Perca polymnus Linnaeus, 1758: 291 (Indies).
Amphiprion laticlavius Cuvier, 1830: 394 (New Guinea).

Diagnosis.—Dorsal rays X or XI, 13 to 16; anal rays II, 12 to 14; pectoral rays 18 to 19. Tubed lateral-line scales 32 to 41. Gill rakers on first arch 16 to 19. Body depth 2.1 to 2.4 in SL. Color in alcohol generally brown (darker dorsally) with two to three pale bars; midbody bar frequently forming abbreviated saddle; caudal brown and broadly surrounded with white, the dark portion tapering to a point which is directed posteriorly; remainder of fins dark brown except most of soft dorsal pale. Maximum size to about 100 mm SL.

Ecology.—Inhabits silty lagoons and harbors in two to 30 meters. Commensal with large sand dwelling anemones.

Distribution.—Ryukyu Islands, China, Taiwan, Philippines, East Indies, New Guinea, Northern Territory, New Britain, and Solomon Islands.

Amphiprion rubrocinctus Richardson
Red Anemonefish

Amphiprion rubrocinctus Richardson, 1842: 391 (Depuch Island, Western Australia).
Amphiprion tricolor Günther, 1862: 8 (Port Essington, Australia).
Amphiprion ruppelii Castelnau, 1873: 91 (Darwin, Australia).

Diagnosis.—Dorsal rays X, 16 to 17; anal rays II, 13 to 15; pectoral rays 18 to 19. Tubed lateral-line scales 34 to 38. Gill rakers on first arch 18 to 19. Body depth 1.7 to 1.9 in SL. Color in alcohol generally tan (Fiji and Samoa) to dark brown (northern Australia) with a single pale bar on head; fins pale. Maximum size to about 100 mm SL.

Ecology.—Observed during the present study only at Suva, Fiji Islands where it is relatively common inside the barrier reef in one to eight meters. Commensal with *Radianthus* spp.

Distribution.—Northern Territory and Western Australia, Fiji Islands, Tonga Islands, Samoa Islands and Society Islands. The only known specimens from the latter locality were collected by Zane Grey in 1931.

Amphiprion sandaracinos Allen
Orange Anemonefish

Amphiprion sandaracinos Allen, 1972: 81 (Philippines).

Diagnosis.—Dorsal rays IX, 16 to 18; anal rays II, 12; pectoral rays 17 to 18. Tubed lateral-line scales 33 to 37. Gill rakers on first arch 17 to 18. Body depth 2.2 to 2.4 in SL. Color in alcohol generally pale tan to brown with whitish middorsal stripe extending from edge of upper lip to base of caudal fin (the whitish coloration encompassing the scaly basal sheath of the dorsal fin); fins pale. Maximum size to about 110 mm SL.

Ecology.—Inhabits lagoons and outer reef slopes in three to 12 meters. Commensal with *Stoichactis giganteum.*

Distribution.—Philippines, New Guinea, D'Entrecasteaux Islands, and Solomon Islands.

Amphiprion tricinctus Schultz and Welander
Three-band Anemonefish

Illus. pp. 44, 61

Amphiprion tricinctus Schultz and Welander (*In* Schultz, 1953): 195 (Bikini Atoll, Marshall Islands).

Diagnosis.—Dorsal rays X, 15 to 16 (occasionally XI, 15 to 16); anal rays II, 13 to 14; pectoral rays 19 to 20. Tubed lateral-line scales 38 to 43. Gill rakers on first arch 20 to 21. Body depth 1.7 to 1.9 in SL. Color in alcohol either entirely dark brown with two or three pale bars or dark brown with head, breast, pectoral, pelvic, and anal fins pale. Maximum size to about 100 mm SL.

Ecology.—Inhabits lagoons and outer reef slopes in three to 38 meters. Feeds primarily on planktonic copepods, a variety of algae, echiuroids, and sipunculoids (see Allen, 1972). Commensal with six species of anemones in the Marshall Islands.

Distribution.—Known only from the Marshall Islands.

Amphiprion polymnus (about 50 mm TL), Guadalcanal, Solomon Islands in 18 meters.

Amphiprion polymnus (about 100 mm TL), Rabaul, New Britain in six meters.

Amphiprion rubrocinctus (about 100 mm TL), Suva, Fiji Islands in three meters.

Amphiprion sandara-cinos (about 75 mm TL), Madang, New Guinea in 10 meters.

Amphiprion tricinctus (83 mm SL), Eniwetok Atoll, Marshall Islands (J. Randall photo).

Amphiprion tricinctus (78 mm SL), Eniwetok Atoll, Marshall Islands (J. Randall photo).

Chapter VI
PREMNAS

I included *Premnas* as a subgenus of *Amphiprion* in my 1972 revision of the anemonefishes. However, at the time it was emphasized that this arrangement was provisional, subject to change pending further investigation of the generic classification within the Pomacentridae. I now find it necessary to elevate *Premnas* to full generic status in order to maintain consistency in the familial classification introduced herein. The genus differs from *Amphiprion* primarily with regards to the smaller scale size, presence of two predorsal bones instead of three, the enlarged spines on the suborbital, and reduced serration of the opercle bones.

GENUS *PREMNAS* CUVIER

Premnas Cuvier, 1817: 345 (type species, *Chaetodon biaculeatus*).

Diagnostic features.—Body ovate; teeth incisiform; suborbital usually armed with two long spines; opercle and interopercle with few and rather feeble radiating striae or serrations; subopercle without serrations; opercle mostly naked; interorbital completely naked; pelvic axillary scale process absent or weakly developed; scales small, 68 to 76 vertical rows between upper edge of opercle and caudal fin base; dorsal rays X, 16 to 18 (usually X, 17); anal rays II, 13 to 15 (usually II, 14); pectoral and pelvic fins rounded; caudal fin rounded; two predorsal bones.

The genus contains a single species, *P. biaculeatus.*

Premnas biaculeatus (Bloch)
Spine-cheek Anemonefish

Illus. p. 64

Chaetodon biaculeatus Bloch, 1790: 11 (East Indies).
Premnas gibbosus Castelnau, 1875: 34 (Cape York, Australia).

Diagnosis.—Dorsal rays X, 17 to 18; anal rays II, 13 to 15; pectoral rays 17. Tubed lateral-line scales usually 40 to 48. Gill rakers of first arch 17 to 21. Body depth 1.9 to 2.3 in SL. Color in alcohol generally light brown or tan to dark brown, including fins, with two to three bars (usually paler than surrounding body color, but on certain tan individuals they may appear darker).

Maximum size to about 130 mm SL.

Ecology.—Inhabits lagoons and outer reef slopes in one to 16 meters. Feeds on zooplankton and benthic algae. Commensal with anemones (usually *Radianthus gelam?*). Pairs are commonly encountered in which the female is two to three times larger than the male.

Distribution.—East Indies; Philippines; New Guinea; northern Queensland; New Britain; Solomon Islands; and New Hebrides. In addition it has been recorded from Mauritius by Lacépède (1802) and Baissac (1956). Abe (1939) listed it from the Palau Islands, but I did not encounter it there during the present study.

Chapter VII
ACANTHOCHROMIS

The genus *Acanthochromis* contains a single species which inhabits reefs of the Indo-Australian Archipelago and immediately adjacent regions. These fish sometimes form large midwater feeding aggregations. Their reproductive biology is extremely interesting and unlike any other pomacentrid. Robertson (1973) reported that the young are non-pelagic. Instead they aggregate in the vicinity of the nest and depend on the parents for protection and possibly a part of their nutrition. Robertson and the present author have observed the tiny young make quick glancing blows and picking movements on the surface of the parents. It is possible they are feeding on mucus in the manner of certain cichlid fishes. At One Tree Island, on the southern Great Barrier Reef, I collected additional information on the early life history. Spawning occurs primarily between October and April, or approximately during the warmest portion of the year. Individual broods contain an average of about 100 young (range for 17 broods, 30–196). The members of a given brood are about the same size. The smallest observed were approximately 6.0 mm SL. As the young fish increase in size they become less dependent on the parents for protection and tend to form looser aggregations. After a few months, at a size of about 30–40 mm SL, the original broods tend to disband and merge with other groups from adjacent territories. Growth rates recorded for the young fish ranged from 3.6 to 4.6 mm per month. On one occasion I released a pair of slightly larger young (14 mm SL) among a brood of 9 mm SL fish. These were summarily driven away by the parents. On another occasion I speared the parents and almost immediately a number of young were devoured by predators which included wrasses and pseudochromids, thus emphasizing the importance of parental care. Both parents guard the brood and are particularly aggressive towards wrasses and other *Acanthochromis*.

During my first year of collecting fishes in New Guinea and Australia I was puzzled by the tremendous amount of color pattern variation exhibited by *A. polyacanthus*. I was familiar with the rather startling variation found in the juvenile to adult stages of certain damsel fishes, and the more subtle changes frequently associated with geographic locale. However, the pattern which emerged with *A. polyacanthus* was ridiculous! It was almost as though a different color variety existed for every location we visited, even if separated by only 20–30 miles, for example, the distance between Goodenough and Fergusson Islands in the D'Entrecasteaux Group, off the eastern tip of New Guinea. On the Great Barrier Reef there are at least five distinct color varieties. After meeting Ross Robertson and discussing his discovery of non-pelagic young in *Acanthochromis*, this pattern of color variation began to make sense. Variation of this sort is not surprising considering the fact that each population (which in the case of small islands and isolated reefs is clearly definable) is isolated because of the loss of the pelagic larval dispersing mechanism. What is surprising, however, is the apparent absence of morphological differences between the many isolated populations. Perhaps the loss of the pelagic larval stage was a relatively recent event in the evolution of *Acanthochromis*, and we are observing the first stages of speciation. A study of the genetic variation among several populations by Dr. M. Soulet of the University of California at San Diego is currently in progress.

Premnas biaculeatus
(50 mm SL),
Philippine Islands (J.
Randall photo).

Premnas biaculeatus
(about 50 mm TL),
Madang, New Guinea
in 12 meters.

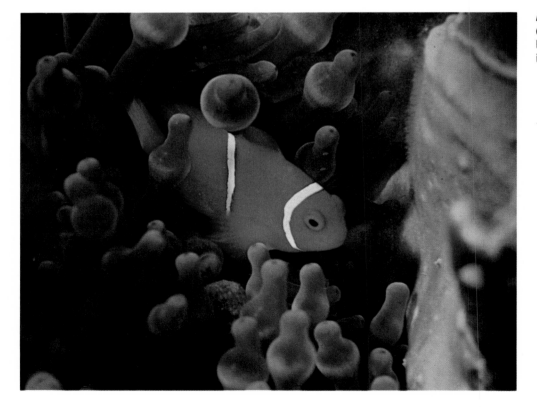

*Acanthochromis
polyacanthus* (about
150 mm TL), Great
Barrier Reef, off
Cairns, Queensland
in six meters.

*Acanthochromis
polyacanthus* with
several juveniles,
Great Barrier Reef, off
Cairns, Queensland.

*Acanthochromis
polyacanthus* (70 mm
SL), One Tree Island,
Great Barrier Reef
(J. Randall photo).

GENUS *ACANTHOCHROMIS* GILL

Acanthochromis Gill, 1863: 214 (type species, *Dascyllus polyacanthus* Bleeker).

Diagnostic features.—Dorsal spines XVII; a pair of spiniform procurrent rays on upper and lower edge of caudal fin; edge of preopercle and suborbital finely serrate; edge of suborbital distinct, not hidden by scales; teeth of jaws biserial (at least anteriorly), outer row of enlarged conical teeth, and inner row of slender buttress teeth; scale rows in longitudinal series from upper edge of operculum to base of caudal fin about 33.

Acanthochromis polyacanthus (Bleeker)
Spiny Chromis

Illus. p. 65

Dascyllus polyacanthus Bleeker, 1855: 503 (Batjan, Indonesia).

Diagnosis.—Dorsal rays XVII, 14 to 16; anal rays II, 14 to 16; pectoral rays 17 to 18. Tubed lateral-line scales 20 to 22. Gill rakers on first arch 21 to 23. Body depth 1.7 to 1.9 in SL. Color in alcohol extremely variable, usually uniformly dark brown or with caudal peduncle and fin mostly whitish. Maximum size to about 110 mm SL.

Ecology.—A ubiquitous species found in harbors, lagoons, and on outer reef slopes in one to 65 meters.

Distribution.—East Indies, Philippines, New Guinea, New Britain, Solomon Islands, New Hebrides, and northern Australia.

Acanthochromis polyacanthus (45 mm SL), Guadalcanal, Solomon Islands (J. Randall photo).

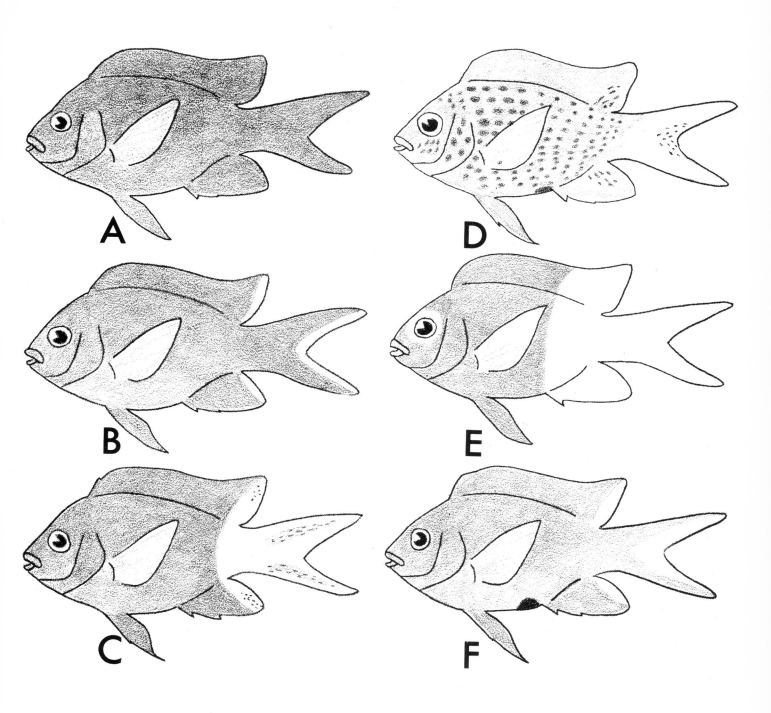

Geographical variants of *Acanthochromis polyacanthus*: (A) Madang, New Guinea; (B) Fergusson Island, D'Entrecasteaux Group; (C) Goodenough Island, D'Entrecasteaux Group; (D) Torres Strait; (E) Cape York Peninsula,
Queensland; (F) Hook Island, Queensland.

Chromis acares (about 50 mm TL), Egum Atoll, Solomon Sea in three meters.

Chromis agilis (about 100 mm TL), Noumea, New Caledonia in 20 meters.

Chromis agilis (about 75 mm TL), Oahu, Hawaiian Islands in 12 meters.

Chromis amboinensis (about 75 mm TL), Suva, Fiji Islands in 35 meters.

Chapter VIII
CHROMIS

The genus *Chromis* is comprised of approximately 50 species which inhabit both Atlantic and Indo-Pacific coral reefs; 36 species are known from the "South Seas." The elongate body, forked caudal fin, and relatively small mouth (with conical teeth) in many of the species represent specialized adaptations for plankton feeding and a more open-water mode of life. Similar adaptive features are found in other midwater-feeding fishes which belong to families comprised mainly of benthic forms.

In the Indo-Pacific at least, these fishes probably form the bulk of the pomacentrid fauna of outer reef slopes, with regard to both number of species and biomass. Huge "swarms" of *Chromis* were a typical feature of nearly every outer reef visited during the present study. Most of the species are confined to the upper edge of the slope in about three to 12 meters, but several regularly penetrate below 30 meters. On the outer reef slope at Agulupelu Reef in the Palau Islands the only pomacentrids observed regularly below 30 meters were two species of *Chromis* (undescribed, referred to as "A" and "D" in the subsequent text). *C. struhsakeri* from the Hawaiian Islands is only known from depths between 99 and 183 meters.

Although outer reefs and passage areas must be regarded as the primary habitat for the genus, at least two species, the closely related *C. atripectoralis* and *C. caerulea*, have successfully invaded the shallow lagoon environment. Large aggregations of these fishes feeding in midwater above isolated coral heads are a characteristic feature of this habitat. *C. amboinensis*, *C. lepidolepis*, *C. margaritifer*, and *C. ternatensis* also frequent lagoons in certain localities.

The reproductive behavior of *Chromis* appears to be rather stereotyped on the basis of several species which have been studied to date. Typically up to several thousand eggs are deposited on rocky substratum, dead coral branches, or on vegetation. The male may spawn with several females and assumes an aggressive role in guarding and caring for the eggs, which hatch in two to four days. The fry are pelagic for an unknown period before permanently settling on the reef.

Dr. J. Randall of the Bishop Museum, Honolulu is currently preparing a revision of *Chromis* which will include descriptions of several new species treated at the end of this chapter. These are referred to as A, B, C, etc. and will be listed as such in the synonymy sections of Randall's forthcoming revision.

GENUS *CHROMIS* CUVIER

Chromis Cuvier, 1814: 88 (type species, *Sparus chromis* Linnaeus).

Diagnostic features.—Dorsal spines XII to XIV; two to three spiniform procurrent caudal rays; hind edge of preopercle usually entire, occasionally with minute serrations (visible under magnification); teeth of jaws small and conical, outer row of enlarged teeth and irregular band of villiform teeth behind; edge of suborbital entire or hidden by scales; scale rows in longitudinal series from upper edge of operculum to base of caudal fin less than 30.

Note.—A. Emery (in press) has shown that the name *Chromis* is of variable gender, but because it was first used for a proper genus as a feminine name, subsequent authors are required to follow this precedent. Therefore, the following specific names which usually appear with *-us* endings are affected: *caerulea, chrysura, leucura, lineata, nitida, retrofasciata,* and *xanthura.*

KEY TO THE SPECIES OF *CHROMIS* FROM THE SOUTH SEAS

1a. Dorsal spines XII to XIII..2
1b. Dorsal spines XIV to XV..32
2a. Dorsal spines XII..3
2b. Dorsal spines XIII..23
3a. Color mostly dark brown to blackish with posterior portion of body and/or caudal fin more or less abruptly pale or anterior half of body dark and posterior half abruptly pale.............4
3b. Color not as in 3a..11
4a. Line of demarcation between light and dark area at about middle of sides (Great Barrier Reef; Melanesia; Samoa Islands; Society Islands)........................*C. iomelas*
4b. Line of demarcation between light and dark area on posterior portion of body...............5
5a. Caudal peduncle dark (Marquesas Islands).....................................species "F"
5b. Caudal peduncle pale..6
6a. Pectoral rays usually 16 (occasionally 17); tubed lateral-line scales usually 14 or less..........7
6b. Pectoral rays usually 17 to 18; tubed lateral-line scales usually 15 or more..................8
7a. Pelvic fins pale (Hawaiian Islands; Marquesas Islands).........................*C. leucura*
7b. Pelvic fins dark (Palau Islands; Melanesia) ....species "D"
8a. Tubed lateral-line scales usually 15.......................................9
8b. Tubed lateral-line scales usually 16 to 17.................................10
9a. Dorsal and anal rays usually 12 (last ray branched near base); body depth 1.8 to 1.9 in SL (Marquesas Islands)..species "G"
9b. Dorsal and anal rays usually 13 (last ray branched near base); body depth 2.0 to 2.1 in SL (Pitcairn Group)..species "E"
10a. Dorsal rays usually 12 (last ray branched near base); gill rakers on first arch 24 to 27; color generally dark brown to blackish (W. Pacific)........................*C. margaritifer*
10b. Dorsal rays usually 13 (last ray branched near base); gill rakers on first arch 26 to 32; color generally brown (Hawaiian Islands)........................*C. hanui*
11a. Body with several longitudinal lines.....................................12
11b. Body without longitudinal lines..13
12a. Lower lobe of caudal fin with broad black band; tubed lateral-line scales usually 17 (W. Pacific, including Hawaiian Islands)....................................*C. vanderbilti*
12b. Lower lobe of caudal fin pale; tubed lateral-line scales usually 15 (Philippines; Palau Islands; New Guinea; New Britain; Solomon Islands)..............................*C. lineata*
13a. Scales of body each with about one to three basal axillary scales (Indo-W. Pacific)...*C. lepidolepis*
13b. Scales of body without axillary scales....................................14
14a. Caudal fin with dark streak on upper and lower lobes..........................15
14b. Caudal fin without dark streak on upper and lower lobes........................16
15a. Body depth 1.8 to 1.9 in SL; pectoral rays usually 17 to 18; tubed lateral-line scales usually 15 to 16 (Indo-W. Pacific)......................................*C. ternatensis*
15b. Body depth 1.5 to 1.7 in SL; pectoral rays usually 16; tubed lateral-line scales usually 13 (W. Pacific)..*C. amboinensis*
16a. Pectorals with prominent dark spot covering most of fin base.......................17
16b. Pectorals without prominent dark spot covering most of fin base.....................18
17a. Dark spot covering nearly all of pectoral fin base; pectoral rays usually 16; pelvics dark brown (Indo-W. Pacific)..*C. agilis*
17b. Dark spot covering upper half of pectoral base; pectoral rays usually 17; pelvics dusky (Solomon Islands; Palau Islands)....................................species "C"
18a. Body depth greater than 2.3 in SL; color generally pale with large black area on anal fin (W. Pacific, including Hawaiian Islands)..................................*C. acares*

71

Chromis analis (about 125 mm TL), Rabaul, New Britain in 20 meters.

Chromis atripectoralis (about 100 mm TL), Heron Island, Great Barrier Reef in six meters.

Chromis atripes (about 50 mm TL), Efate, New Hebrides in 10 meters.

Chromis atripes (about 50 mm TL), Augulpelu Reef, Palau Islands in 20 meters.

18b. Body depth less than 2.3 in SL; color not as in 18a...................................19
19a. Dorsal and anal fins pale to slightly dusky..20
19b. Dorsal and anal fins mostly dark brown to blackish................................22
20a. Posterior portion of body with prominent black bar; pectoral rays 15 to 16; tubed lateral-line scales usually 12 (East Indies; Philippines; Palau Islands; Great Barrier Reef; Melanesia)....
....*C. retrofasciata*
20b. Posterior portion of body without black bar; pectoral rays usually 18 to 20; tubed lateral-line scales usually 15 to 16...21
21a. Pectoral rays usually 19 to 20; axil of pectoral fin black (W. Pacific)..........*C. atripectoralis*
21b. Pectoral rays usually 18; axil of pectoral fin pale or slightly dusky (Indo-W. Pacific)..*C. caerulea*
22a. Body color generally light brown; body depth 1.8 to 1.9 in SL; pectoral rays usually 16 (Philippines; Palau Islands; Melanesia; Great Barrier Reef; Gilbert Islands).......*C. atripes*
22b. Body color generally dark brown; body depth 2.1 to 2.2 in SL; pectoral rays usually 18 to 19 (Philippines; Palau Islands; Melanesia)....................................*C. elerae*
23a. Body depth usually 1.6 to 1.9 in SL...24
23b. Body depth usually 2.0 to 2.3 in SL...27
24a. Color generally brown with caudal fin and peduncle more or less abruptly pale; body depth usually 1.6 to 1.8 in SL; dorsal rays usually 14 to 15; tubed lateral-line scales usually 18 to 19 (Mauritius; Japan and Ryukyu Islands; eastern Australia; southeastern Melanesia)..*C. chrysura*
24b. Color not as in 24a; body depth usually 1.7 to 1.9; dorsal rays usually 11 to 13; tubed lateral-line scales usually 14 to 17...25
25a. Pectorals with black spot covering most of fin base (Marquesas Islands)..........species "B"
25b. Pectorals without black spot covering most of fin base................................26
26a. Caudal and anal fins pale; tubed lateral-line scales usually 17 (E. Africa; Japan; Ryukyu Islands; China; Philippines; Palau Islands; E. Indies; Melanesia).........................*C. analis*
26b. Caudal and anal fins brown; tubed lateral-line scales usually 14 to 15 (Palau Islands; Melanesia; Samoa Islands; Society Islands)..species "A"
27a. Pectorals with dark spot covering most of fin base; caudal fin without dark streak on upper and lower lobes..28
27b. Pectorals without dark spot covering most of fin base; caudal fin with dark streak on upper and lower lobes..30
28a. Color generally dark with caudal fin and peduncle more or less abruptly pale; pectoral rays usually 18 to 19 (Indo-W. Pacific)...*C. xanthura*
28b. Color generally dark with caudal fin and peduncle about same color as adjacent body region or gradually becoming paler posteriorly; pectoral rays usually 20 to 21....................29
29a. Body depth usually 2.0 to 2.1 in SL; tubed lateral-line scales usually 19 to 20 (S.E. Australia; Lord Howe Island; Norfolk Island; northern New Zealand)................*C. hypsilepis*
29b. Body depth usually 2.2 to 2.3 in SL; tubed lateral-line scales usually 17 to 18 (S.E. Australia; Lord Howe Island; New Caledonia; Ryukyu Islands)..........................*C. kennensis*
30a. Color generally pale with oblique dark stripe extending from snout to hindmost dorsal spines, area above stripe brown (E. Australia)..*C. nitida*
30b. Color not as in 30a...31
31a. Pectoral base and axil yellowish; tips of caudal lobes not noticeably darker than adjacent part of fin; tubed lateral-line scales usually 16 to 17 (Philippines; Palau Is.; Melanesia)..*C. xanthochir*
31b. Pectoral base and axil brown; tips of caudal lobes noticeably darker than adjacent part of fin; tubed lateral-line scales usually 18 to 19 (Indo-W. Pacific).........................*C. weberi*
32a. Dorsal spines XIV..33
32b. Dorsal spines XV..35

33a. Dorsal rays usually 12; tubed lateral-line scales usually 20; gill rakers 33 to 37; body depth 2.0 to 2.4 in SL; caudal fin deeply forked, the caudal concavity 1.3 to 1.7 in head length (Hawaiian Islands)..*C. ovalis*

33b. Dorsal rays usually 13 to 14; tubed lateral-line scales usually 17 to 18; gill rakers 28 to 34; body depth 1.8 to 2.1 in SL; caudal fin not deeply forked, the caudal concavity of adults 1.8 to 2.6 in head length...34

34a. Three spiniform procurrent caudal rays; dorsal rays usually 13; lower-limb gill rakers 19 to 23 (excluding raker at angle); color dark grey to dark brown with large black spot at upper pectoral base (Hawaiian Islands)...*C. verater*

34b. Two spiniform procurrent caudal rays; dorsal rays 14; lower-limb gill rakers 22 to 25 (excluding raker at angle); color light brown without black spot at upper pectoral base (Hawaiian Islands) ....*C. struhsakeri*

35a. Pectorals with dark spot covering base of fin; body depth usually 2.7 to 3.0 in SL (Gambier Islands; Rapa; Pitcairn Group)..................................species "H"

35b. Pectorals without dark spot covering base of fin (only upper half of axil dark); body depth usually about 2.5 in SL (Easter Island)...*C. randalli*

Chromis acares Randall and Swerdloff
Midget Chromis

Illus. p. 68

Chromis acares Randall and Swerdloff, 1973: 331 (Rarotonga, Cook Islands).

Diagnosis.—Dorsal rays XII, 11; anal rays II, 10 to 11; pectoral rays 17, occasionally 16 or 18. Tubed lateral-line scales 15 to 17. Gill rakers on first arch 21 to 25. Body depth 2.4 to 2.6 in SL. Color in alcohol generally light brown, paler ventrally; small whitish spot at rear base of dorsal fin; dorsal fin dusky; anal fin with large black area over most of central and basal portion of fin; remainder of fins pale. Maximum size to about 40 mm SL.

Ecology.—Inhabits outer reef slopes in two to 37 meters. Usually seen on the upper edge of the slope over live coral or rubble. Occurs in small to large aggregations.

Distribution.—Cook Islands, Austral Islands, Society Islands, Samoa Islands, Line Islands, Marshall Islands, Mariana Islands, Egum Atoll (Solomon Sea), New Hebrides, Johnston Island, and Oahu, Hawaiian Islands. The last record is based on an underwater observation. In addition, specimens were recently collected at the Gilbert Islands by D. Hoese of the Australian Museum.

Chromis agilis Smith
Reef Chromis

Illus. pp. 68, 69

Chromis agilis Smith, 1960: 324 (Astove Island, western Indian Ocean).

Diagnosis.—Dorsal rays XII, 13 to 14; anal rays II, 13 to 14; pectoral rays 16, occasionally 17. Tubed lateral-line scales 14 to 15. Gill rakers on first arch 27 to 30. Body depth 1.7 to 1.9 in SL. Color in alcohol generally brownish, pale brown ventrally and on caudal peduncle; dorsal and anal fins mostly brown, abruptly pale on posterior edge; pelvics dark brown; pectorals pale with black spot covering base and axil of fin; caudal light brown to dusky-white. Maximum size to about 75 mm SL.

Ecology.—Inhabits inshore rocky areas and outer reef slopes in three to 56 meters. Frequently occurs in large aggregations. It was very common on the Kona coast of Hawaii.

Distribution.—Widespread in the tropical Indo-West Pacific from East Africa to the Hawaiian Islands and Pitcairn Group. In the Pacific at least, this species appears to be largely restricted to island areas, although it does occur on the Great Barrier Reef.

Chromis chrysurua (about 100 mm TL), Great Barrier Reef, off Cairns, Queensland in 14 meters.

Chromis caerulea (about 75 mm TL) Malakal Island, Palau Islands in two meters.

Chromis elerae (about 75 mm TL), Guadalcanal, Solomon Islands in 28 meters.

Chromis hypsilepis (about 125 mm TL), Lord Howe Island in 10 meters.

Chromis amboinensis (Bleeker)
Ambon Chromis

Illus. p. 69

Heliases amboinensis Bleeker, 1873: 111 (Amboina).
Glyphidodon bimaculatus Macleay, 1883: 271 (New Guinea).
Chromis fragoris Whitley, 1964: 185 (Lihou Atoll, Coral Sea).

Diagnosis.—Dorsal rays XII, 12 to 13; anal rays II, 12 to 13; pectoral rays 16. Tubed lateral-line scales 13, occasionally 14. Gill rakers on first arch 26 to 29. Body depth 1.5 to 1.7 in SL. Color in alcohol generally yellowish-brown, darker brown dorsally; dorsal fin brown except hindmost portion pale; remainder of fins mostly pale; caudal with broad bar which tapers posteriorly on upper and lower margins. Maximum size to about 60 mm SL.

Ecology.—Inhabits lagoons, passages, and outer reef slopes in five to 65 meters. Occurs solitarily or in small to large aggregations.

Distribution.—Widespread in the Indo-Australian Archipelago and western Pacific as far east as the Samoa Islands to the south and the Marshall Islands in the north.

Remarks.—The type of *Glyphidodon bimaculatus* Macleay was examined at the Australian Museum (catalog number I.9236). The fin ray counts and body shape agree with *C. amboinensis*. It has typical *Chromis* teeth and spiniform procurrent caudal rays.

Chromis analis (Cuvier)
Yellow Chromis

Illus. p. 72

Heliases analis Cuvier, 1830: 496 (Amboina).

Diagnosis.—Dorsal rays XIII, 11 to 12; anal rays II, 11 to 12; pectoral rays 18. Tubed lateral-line scales 17. Gill rakers on first arch 25 to 28. Body depth 1.8 to 1.9 in SL. Color in alcohol generally pale yellowish to tan grading to dark grey above lateral-line; fins pale except spinous dorsal dark grey on basal half; small dark spot on upper portion of pectoral base. Maximum size to about 100 mm SL.

Ecology.—Usually inhabits steep outer reef slopes at depths between 18 and 70 meters. Occurs solitarily or in small to large aggregations.

Distribution.—East Africa, southern Japan, Ryukyu Islands, China, Philippines, Palau Islands, East Indies, New Guinea, New Britain, Solomon Islands, New Hebrides, Loyalty Islands, New Caledonia and Fiji Islands.

Chromis atripectoralis Welander and Schultz
Black-axil Chromis

Illus. p. 72

Chromis atripectoralis Welander and Schultz, 1951: 107 (central and western tropical Pacific).

Diagnosis.—Dorsal rays XII, 10 to 11; anal rays II, 10 to 11; pectoral rays 19 to 20. Tubed lateral-line scales 15 to 16. Gill rakers on first arch 29 to 30. Body depth about 2.0 in SL. Color in alcohol generally greyish; fins pale to dusky. Maximum size to about 85 mm SL.

Ecology.—Inhabits lagoons, passages, and outer reef slopes in two to 15 meters. Occurs in large aggregations which feed high above the bottom. The stomachs of several individuals examined contained mainly copepods, amphipods, and zoea.

Distribution.—Widespread in the tropical western Pacific as far east as the Tuamotu Islands to the south and Marshall Islands to the north. Probably also occurs throughout the Indo-Malayan region, but previously confused with *C. caerulea*. J. E. Randall recently collected several individuals at the Dampier Archipelago, Western Australia, which constitutes a new record for the Indian Ocean.

Remarks.—This species is very similar in appearance to *C. caerulea*. However, it can be easily separated from that species when encountered in the sea by virtue of the black pectoral axil and larger size of adults.

Chromis atripes Fowler and Bean
Dark-fin Chromis

Illus. p. 73

Chromis atripes Fowler and Bean, 1928: 43 (Philippines).

Diagnosis.—Dorsal rays XII, 12 to 14; anal rays II, 12 to 13; pectoral rays 16. Tubed lateral-line scales 14 to 16. Gill rakers on first arch 25 to 27. Body depth 1.8 to 1.9 in SL. Color in alcohol generally light brown grading to dark brown dorsally; dorsal and anal fins dark brown except posterior edge of these fins pale; pelvics pale; pectorals pale with blackish triangular spot on upper portion of fin base and axil; caudal pale with dark streak at base on dorsal and ventral surface.

Ecology.—Inhabits passages and outer reef slopes in two to 35 meters. Occurs solitarily or in small groups.

Distribution.—Philippines, Palau Islands, New Guinea, New Britain, Solomon Islands, New Hebrides, Loyalty Islands, New Caledonia, and the Great Barrier Reef. In addition, it was recently taken at the Gilbert Islands by D. Hoese.

Chromis caerulea (Cuvier)
Blue-green Chromis

Illus. p. 76

Heliases caeruleus Cuvier, 1830: 497 (New Guinea; Ulea).

Diagnosis.—Dorsal rays XII, 10 to 11; anal rays II, 10 to 11; pectoral rays 18. Tubed lateral-line scales 15 to 16. Gill rakers on first arch 29 to 30. Body depth 2.0 to 2.1 in SL. Color in alcohol generally light brown to yellowish on sides, dark grey to brownish dorsally; fins pale. Maximum size to about 60–65 mm SL.

Ecology.—Inhabits lagoons, passages, and outer reef slopes in 1.5 to 12 meters. Huge aggregations characteristically feed above rich beds of live coral, into which they suddenly retreat at the approach of danger.

Distribution.—Widespread in the tropical Indo-West Pacific from East Africa to the Tuamotu Islands in the South Pacific and the Line Islands in the North Pacific.

Chromis chrysura (Bliss)
Stout-body Chromis

Illus. p. 76

Heliastes chrysurus Bliss, 1883: 56 (Mauritius).
Chromis isharae Schmidt, 1930: 67 (Ryukyu Islands).
Siphonochromis lepidostethicus Fowler, 1946: 145 (Ryukyu Islands).
Lepicephalochromis westalli Whitley, 1964: 180 (Kenn Reef, Coral Sea).

Diagnosis.—Dorsal rays XIII, 14 to 15; anal rays II, 13 to 14; pectoral rays 19. Tubed lateral-line scales 18 to 19. Gill rakers on first arch 29 to 32. Body depth 1.6 to 1.8 in SL. Color in alcohol generally dark brown; dorsal and anal fins dark brown to blackish except most of soft dorsal and hindmost anal rays pale; pelvics brown; pectorals pale; caudal peduncle and fin pale, sometimes with narrow dark upper and lower margins. Maximum size to about 105 mm SL.

Ecology.—Inhabits outer reef slopes and passages in six to 20 meters. Very common off Noumea, New Caledonia.

Distribution.—Mauritius, southern Japan, Ryukyu Islands, Great Barrier Reef, Coral Sea, New Hebrides, Loyalty Islands, New Caledonia, and Fiji Islands. R. Kuiter recently collected specimens near Sydney, Australia.

Chromis hanui (about 75 mm TL), Oahu, Hawaiian Islands

Chromis iomelas
(about 75 mm TL),
Osprey Reef, Coral
Sea in 10 meters.

Chromis kennensis (about 100 mm TL), Noumea, New Caledonia in 16 meters.

Chromis lepidolepis (about 75 mm TL), Malakal Island, Palau Islands in three meters.

Chromis elerae Fowler and Bean
Twin-spot Chromis

Illus. p. 77

Chromis elerae Fowler and Bean, 1928: 52 (Philippines).

Diagnosis.—Dorsal rays XII, 11 to 12; anal rays II, 10 to 11; pectoral rays 18 to 19. Tubed lateral-line scales 16. Gill rakers on first arch 29 to 30. Body depth 2.1 to 2.2 in SL. Color in alcohol generally dark brown, except chin, breast, and abdomen tannish; dorsal and anal fins blackish except hindmost rays abruptly pale; small white spot sometimes apparent at base of hindmost dorsal and anal rays; anterior portion of caudal fin brown grading to pale on posterior part; pelvic and pectoral fins pale. Maximum size to about 55 mm SL.

Ecology.—Inhabits steep outer reef slopes in 12 to 70 meters. This species typically inhabits crevices and caves or similar areas of low light intensity. Large numbers of these fishes were associated with black coral beds in the Palau Islands.

Distribution.—Philippines, Palau Islands, New Guinea, Solomon Islands, and Fiji Islands.

Chromis hanui Randall and Swerdloff
Hawaiian Bicolor Chromis

Illus. p. 80

Chromis hanui Randall and Swerdloff, 1973: 338 (Oahu, Hawaiian Islands).

Diagnosis.—Dorsal rays XII, 13; anal rays II, 13, occasionally 14; pectoral rays 17, occasionally 18. Tubed lateral-line scales usually 16 or 17. Gill rakers on first arch 26 to 32. Body depth 1.9 to 2.0 in SL. Color in alcohol generally brown; dorsal, anal and pelvic fins darker; caudal peduncle and fin, and posterior dorsal rays, abruptly pale; dark spot covering base of pectoral fin. Maximum size to about 60 mm SL.

Ecology.—Forms small to large aggregations in six to 50 meters, sometimes mixed with *C. agilis*. This species stays close to protective cover and is particularly abundant in rich coral areas such as those off Kahe Point, Oahu. Feeds on a variety of zooplankton which includes copepods, fish eggs, and malacostracan larvae.

Distribution.—Endemic to the Hawaiian Islands where it replaces the closely related *C. margaritifer*.

Remarks.—This species has been erroneously referred to as *C. leucurus* by most previous authors.

Chromis hypsilepis (Günther)
Brown Puller

Illus. p. 77

Heliastes hypsilepis Günther, 1867: 66 (New So. Wales).

Diagnosis.—Dorsal rays XIII, 13 to 14; anal rays II, 12 to 13; pectoral rays 20 to 21. Tubed lateral-line scales 19 to 20. Gill rakers on first arch 32 to 34. Body depth 2.0 to 2.1 in SL. Color in alcohol dark brown, tan ventrally; fins dark brown except pectorals pale; black spot covering most of pectoral fin base.

Ecology.—Inhabits rocky reefs in three to 46 meters. Occurs in small to large aggregations.

Distribution.—Southeastern Australia, Lord Howe Island, Norfolk Island, and northern New Zealand.

Chromis iomelas Jordan and Seale
Half and Half Chromis

Illus. p. 80

Chromis iomelas Jordan and Seale, 1906: 292 (Pago Pago, Samoa Islands).

Diagnosis.—Dorsal rays XII, 13 to 14; anal rays II, 13 to 14; pectoral rays 17. Tubed lateral-line scales 15. Gill rakers on first arch 26 to 27. Body depth 1.9 in SL. Color in alcohol generally dark brown on anterior half and abruptly whitish on posterior half. Maximum size to about 55 mm SL.

Ecology.—Inhabits passages and outer reef slopes in three to 35 meters. Occurs solitarily or in small groups. The species is sometimes seen in mixed aggregations with the closely related *C. margaritifer*.

82

Distribution.—Great Barrier Reef, New Hebrides, New Caledonia, Fiji Islands, Samoa Islands, and Society Islands. In addition, it is recorded from New Guinea on the basis of one individual observed by the author off Port Moresby.

Chromis kennensis Whitley
Kenn Reef Chromis

Illus. p. 81

Chromis kennensis Whitley, 1964: 182 (Kenn Reef, Coral Sea).

Diagnosis.—Dorsal rays XIII, 12 to 13; anal rays II, 11 to 13; pectoral rays 20. Tubed lateral-line scales 17 to 18. Gill rakers on first arch 31 to 32. Body depth 2.2 to 2.3 in SL. Color in alcohol generally dark brown; breast and abdomen may have slight silvery sheen; dorsal and anal fins mostly blackish; caudal and pelvic fins dusky, pectorals pale with distinct black spot covering base of fin. Maximum size to about 90 mm SL.

Ecology.—Inhabits outer reef slopes in six to 35 meters. Occurs in small to large aggregations. Very common off Noumea, New Caledonia.

Distribution.—Described from Kenn Reef, Coral Sea, but recently collected by the author at Lord Howe Island, New Caledonia, and Uvea, Loyalty Islands. Also taken at Sydney, Australia by R. Kuiter and at the Ryukyu Islands by J. Randall.

Chromis lepidolepis Bleeker
Scaly Chromis

Illus. pp. 81, 84

Chromis lepidolepis Bleeker, 1877a: 389 (Timor).

Diagnosis.—Dorsal rays XII, 11 to 12; anal rays II, 11 to 12; pectoral rays 18. Tubed lateral-line scales 17. Gill rakers on first arch 27 to 30. Body depth 2.0 to 2.2 in SL. Color in alcohol generally brownish, darker dorsally; dorsal and anal fins dark brown, lighter on hindmost rays; pelvics dusky; pectorals pale with small dark spot on upper portion of fin base; caudal pale with dark streak on upper and lower margins; intense black spot at tip of caudal lobes. Maximum size to about 65 mm SL.

Ecology.—Inhabits harbors, lagoons, and outer reef areas in two to 20 meters. Occurs solitarily or in small to large groups.

Distribution.—Widespread in the tropical Indo-West Pacific as far east as the Fiji Islands to the south and the Line Islands to the north.

Chromis leucura Gilbert
White-tail Chromis

Illus. p. 84

Chromis leucurus Gilbert, 1905 (in part): 620 (Avau Channel between Maui and Lanai, Hawaiian Islands).

Diagnosis.—Dorsal rays XII, 14; anal rays II, 13; pectoral rays 16. Tubed lateral-line scales 13 to 14. Gill rakers on first arch 26. Body depth 1.9 to 2.2 in SL. Color in alcohol generally dark brown with caudal fin and peduncle and hindmost portion of soft dorsal and anal fins abruptly pale; pelvics and pectorals pale with dark spot covering base of pectoral fin. Maximum size to about 50 mm SL.

Ecology.—Known only from a few specimens, but extremely abundant off the Kona coast of Hawaii below a depth of about 25 meters.

Distribution.—Known previously only from the Hawaiian Islands, but recently collected by J. Randall at the Marquesas Islands.

Remarks.—Most specimens previously reported as *C. leucura* from Hawaii are actually *C. hanui*.

Chromis leucura (about 50 mm TL), Hawaii, Hawaiian Islands.

Chromis lepidolepis (about 60 mm TL), Malakal Island, Palau Islands.

Chromis margaritifer (about 75 mm TL), Augulpelu Reef, Palau Islands in 10 meters.

Chromis lineata (about 50 mm TL), Savo, Solomon Islands in 10 meters.

Chromis lineata Fowler and Bean
Lined Chromis
Illus. p. 85

Chromis lineatus Fowler and Bean, 1928: 50 (Philippines).

Diagnosis.—Dorsal rays XII, 11 to 12; anal rays II, 11 to 12; pectoral rays 17. Tubed lateral-line scales 14 to 15. Gill rakers on first arch 22 to 24. Body depth 2.2 in SL. Color in alcohol brown with five to six dark stripes below lateral-line; lower portion of body tannish; small pale spot at base of hindmost dorsal rays on some specimens; fins pale. Maximum size to about 40 mm SL.

Ecology.—Inhabits the upper edge of outer reef slopes, usually around live coral heads in two to ten meters. Occurs in small to large aggregations.

Distribution.—Philippines, Palau Islands, New Guinea, New Britain, and Solomon Islands. It is apparently replaced by the closely related *C. vanderbilti* throughout most of Oceania.

Chromis margaritifer Fowler
Bicolor Chromis
Illus. p. 85

Chromis dimidiatus margaritifer Fowler, 1946: 140 (Ryukyu Islands).

Diagnosis.—Dorsal rays XII, 12 to 13; anal rays II, 12 to 13; pectoral rays 17. Tubed lateral-line scales 17, occasionally 18. Gill rakers on first arch 24 to 27. Body depth 1.9 to 2.0 in SL. Color in alcohol generally dark brown, except posterior portion of dorsal and anal fins; caudal fin and peduncle abruptly whitish. Maximum size to about 60 mm SL.

Ecology.—Inhabits lagoons, passages, and outer reef slopes in 1.5 to 15 meters, usually in areas of abundant coral growth. Occurs solitarily or in small to large groups.

Distribution.—Widely distributed throughout the tropical western Pacific as far east as the Tuamotu Islands to the south and the Line Islands to the north. Specimens recently collected at the Dampier Archipelago, Western Australia by J. E. Randall represent a new record for the Indian Ocean.

Remarks.—Specimens from the western Pacific have previously been reported as *C. dimidiatus*, but J. E. Randall, who is presently revising *Chromis*, informed the author that *dimidiatus* is confined to the Red Sea and western Indian Ocean.

Chromis nitida (Whitley)
Barrier Reef Chromis
Illus. p. 88

Tetradrachmum nitidum Whitley, 1928: 219 (Hayman Island, Queensland).

Diagnosis.—Dorsal rays XIII, 11 to 13; anal rays II, 10 to 11; pectoral rays 19. Tubed lateral-line scales 17 to 18. Gill rakers on first arch 28 to 31. Body depth 2.2 to 2.3 in SL. Color in alcohol generally silvery-whitish with oblique dark stripe extending from tip of snout to posterior spines of dorsal fin; spinous dorsal and anterior portion of soft dorsal brown, posterior soft rays pale; anal spines and first few soft rays blackish; posterior anal rays and remainder of fins pale. Maximum size to about 70 mm SL.

Ecology.—Common on the outer edge of certain reefs in rich coraliferous areas in five to 25 meters. Juveniles and occasional adults are sometimes observed in lagoon habitats. Occurs in small to large aggregations.

Distribution.—Previously known only from the Great Barrier Reef, but specimens have recently been observed or collected at Lord Howe Island and Sydney, Australia. It is very abundant in the Capricorn Group at the southern extremity of the Barrier Reef, but rare to the north off Cairns.

Chromis weberi Fowler and Bean
Weber's Chromis
Illus. p. 89

Chromis weberi Fowler and Bean, 1928: 41 (Philippines).

Diagnosis.—Dorsal rays XIII, 11 to 12; anal rays II, 11 to 12; pectoral rays 19 to 20. Tubed lateral-line scales 18 to 19. Gill rakers on first arch 28 to 32. Body depth 2.1 to 2.3 in SL. Color in alcohol generally brown, darker dorsally; edge of preopercle and upper edge of opercle with black bar; dorsal and anal fins dark brown except posterior edge abruptly pale; pelvics dusky; pectorals pale with dark spot on upper portion of fin base; caudal fin base brown, each lobe of caudal with broad brown streak, posterior margin of fin pale. Maximum size to about 95 mm SL.

Ecology.—Inhabits passages and outer reef slopes in three to 25 meters. Occurs solitarily or in small to large aggregations.

Distribution.—Widespread in the tropical Indo-West Pacific from East Africa to the Pitcairn Group in the South Pacific and the Line Islands in the North Pacific.

Chromis ovalis (Steindachner)
Hawaiian Chromis

Illus. p. 89

Heliastes ovalis Steindachner, 1900: 502 (Honolulu).
Chromis velox Jenkins, 1901: 393 (Honolulu).

Diagnosis.—Dorsal rays XIV, 11 to 13; anal rays II, 12 to 13; pectoral rays 20 to 22. Tubed lateral-line scales 19 to 21. Gill rakers on first arch 33 to 39. Body depth 2.0 to 2.4 in SL. Color in alcohol generally brown, darker dorsally; fins dusky to brownish except pectorals pale with dark spot on upper portion of fin base. Maximum size to about 150 mm SL.

Ecology.—Inhabits rocky areas in seven to 45 meters. Occurs in small to large aggregations. According to Swerdloff (1970), the diet consists mainly of calanoid and cyclopoid copepods, but tunicates, mysids, euphausids, crustacean larvae, larval polychaetes, siphonophores, and fish eggs are also taken.

Distribution.—Endemic to the Hawaiian Islands.

Remarks.—Swerdloff (1970) reported that the spawning season extends from February to May.

Chromis randalli Greenfield and Hensley
Randall's Chromis

Illus. p. 89

Chromis randalli Greenfield and Hensley, 1970: 689 (Easter Island).

Diagnosis.—Dorsal rays XV, 10; anal rays II, 10 to 11; pectoral rays 21 to 22. Tubed lateral-line scales 21 to 22. Gill rakers on first arch 33 to 37. Body depth 2.3 to 3.0 in SL. Color in alcohol brown, dark brown on upper half of head and body; fins brown to dusky except pectorals and margin inside caudal fork pale; dark spot on upper half of pectoral axil. Maximum size to about 130 mm SL.

Ecology.—Inhabits rocky reefs in five to 30 meters. Occurs in small to large aggregations.
Distribution.—Endemic to Easter Island.

Chromis retrofasciata Weber
Black-bar Chromis

Illus. p. 96

Chromis retrofasciatus Weber, 1913: 359 (Kur Island, Indonesia).

Diagnosis.—Dorsal rays XII, 12 to 13; anal rays II, 12 to 13; pectoral rays 15 to 16. Tubed lateral-line scales 12. Gill rakers on first arch 24 to 26. Body depth 1.8 to 2.0 in SL. Color in alcohol generally yellowish-brown or tan; prominent black bar extending across caudal peduncle onto posterior portion of soft dorsal and anal fins; fins pale, except pelvics dusky. Maximum size to about 40 mm SL.

Ecology.—Inhabits lagoon and outer reef environments in five to 65 meters. It is more common on the outer reef slope usually around small heads of live coral. Occurs solitarily or in small groups. The diet consists mainly of copepods, but some algae are taken.

Distribution.—East Indies, Philippines, Palau Islands, New Guinea, New Britain, Solomon Islands, New Hebrides, New Caledonia, Loyalty Islands, Fiji Islands, and the Great Barrier Reef.

Remarks.—A very small species. I have examined a 34 mm SL female with ripe eggs.

Chromis nitida (about 75 mm TL), One Tree Island, Great Barrier Reef in 15 meters.

Chromis nitida (about 60 mm TL), One Tree Island, Great Barrier Reef in 15 meters.

Chromis weberi
(about 100 mm TL),
Heron Island, Great
Barrier Reef in 12
meters.

Chromis ovalis (about
100 mm TL), Oahu,
Hawaiian Islands in
10 meters.

Chromis randalli
(101.6 mm SL),
Easter Island
(J. Randall photo).

Chromis struhsakeri (27 mm SL), Molokai, Hawaiian Islands (J. Randall photo).

Chromis struhsakeri Randall and Swerdloff
Struhsaker's Chromis

Chromis struhsakeri Randall and Swerdloff, 1973: 344 (Oahu, Hawaiian Islands).

Diagnosis.—Dorsal rays XIV, 13 to 14; anal rays II, 13 to 14; pectoral rays 19 to 20. Tubed lateral-line scales 16 to 18. Gill rakers on first arch 29 to 34. Body depth 1.8 to 1.9 in SL. Color in alcohol light brown grading to blackish posteriorly; within blackish zone a large pale spot on upper anterior caudal peduncle and rear base of dorsal fin; dorsal and anal fins dusky yellowish, caudal and paired fins pale. Maximum size to about 85 mm SL.

Ecology.—A deep-dwelling species known on the basis of specimens captured by a shrimp trawl in 99–183 meters.

Distribution.—Apparently endemic to the Hawaiian Islands.

Chromis ternatensis (Bleeker)
Ternate Chromis

Illus. p. 92

Heliases ternatensis Bleeker, 1856c: 377 (Ternate, Indonesia).

Diagnosis.—Dorsal rays XII, 10 to 12; anal rays II, 10 to 12; pectoral rays 17 to 18. Tubed lateral-line scales 14 to 16. Gill rakers on first arch 28 to 30. Body depth 1.8 to 1.9 in SL. Color in alcohol generally dark brown grading to light brown on ventral half of body, scale edges dusky giving overall reticulated appearance; dorsal fin brown, remainder of fins pale; caudal with dark streaks near upper and lower margins of fin. Maximum size to about 65 mm SL.

Ecology.—Inhabits lagoons and outer reef slopes in two to 15 meters. Occurs in small to large aggregations.

Distribution.—Widespread in the tropical Indo-West Pacific from East Africa to the Fiji Islands in the South Pacific and the Marshall Islands in the North Pacific.

Chromis vanderbilti (Fowler)
Vanderbilt's Chromis

Illus. p. 92

Pycnochromis vanderbilti Fowler, 1941: 260 (Oahu, Hawaiian Islands).

Diagnosis.—Dorsal rays XII, 11; anal rays II, 11; pectoral rays 17, occasionally 16 or 18. Tubed lateral-line scales 16 to 18. Gill rakers on first arch 23 to 27. Body depth 2.3 to 2.7 in SL. Color in alcohol generally brown with five to six faint stripes on sides; head and body pale ventrally; fins pale except most of anal fin dark and lower lobe of caudal fin with broad black band. Maximum size to about 50 mm SL.

Ecology.—Inhabits outer reef slopes and rocky inshore reefs in two to 20 meters. Occurs in small to large aggregations. Feeds on a variety of zooplankton, but especially fond of copepods.

Distribution.—Primarily an insular species recorded from widely scattered localities in the western Pacific as far east as the Hawaiian Islands and Pitcairn Group. Specimens recently collected by the author at the Capricorn Group, Great Barrier Reef represent a new record.

Chromis verater Jordan and Metz
Three-spot Chromis

Illus. p. 93

Chromis verater Jordan and Metz, 1912: 526 (Honolulu).

Diagnosis.—Dorsal rays XIV, 12 to 14; anal rays II, 12 to 14; pectoral rays 19 to 20. Tubed lateral-line scales 17 to 19. Gill rakers on first arch 27 to 33. Body depth 1.8 to 2.1 in SL. Color in alcohol generally dark brown; fins blackish except pectorals pale with large black spot covering base of fin; pale spot sometimes present at base of hindmost dorsal and anal rays, and also at base of middle caudal rays. Maximum size to about 160 mm SL.

Ecology.—Forms large feeding aggregations high above the bottom in rocky areas, around caves and ledges. According to Brock and Chamberlain (1968) this species was the most abundant fish associated with reef outcrops at a depth of 70 meters off Oahu. The known depth range extends from six to 160 meters.

Distribution.—Known only from the Hawaiian Islands and Johnston Island.

Remarks.—Swerdloff (1970) reported that the spawning season extends from December to June.

Chromis xanthochir (Bleeker)
Yellow-Axil Chromis

Illus. p. 93

Heliases xanthochir Bleeker, 1851: 248 (E. Indies)

Diagnosis.—Dorsal rays XIII, 11; anal rays II, 11 to 12; pectoral rays 19. Tubed lateral-line scales 16 to 17. Gill rakers on first arch 30 to 32. Body depth 2.0 to 2.2 in SL. Color in alcohol generally dark brown; pale yellowish-brown on side of head and ventral portion of body; dorsal and anal fins dark brown to blackish except last few rays pale; pectoral and pelvic fins pale; broad blackish streak on upper and lower margin of caudal fin. Maximum size to about 100 mm SL.

Ecology.—Inhabits outer reef slopes in 10 to 48 meters. Occurs solitarily or in small groups.

Distribution.—Known only from Indonesia, Philippines, Palau Islands, New Guinea, New Britain, and the Solomon Islands, but probably widespread in the Indo-Malayan region.

Chromis xanthura (Bleeker)
Pale-tail Chromis

Illus. p. 96

Heliases xanthurus Bleeker, 1854a: 107 (Banda, Indonesia).

Diagnosis.—Dorsal rays XIII, 11 to 12; anal rays II, 11 to 12; pectoral rays 18 to 19. Tubed

Chromis ternatensis
(about 75 mm TL),
Heron Island, Great
Barrier Reef in six
Meters.

Chromis vanderbilti (about 50 mm TL), Noumea, New Caledonia in 20 meters.

Chromis verater
(about 125 mm TL),
Oahu, Hawaiian
Islands at Sea Life
Park.

Chromis xanthochir (about 125 mm TL), Alite Reef, Solomon Islands in 16 meters.

lateral-line scales 17 to 18. Gill rakers on first arch 26 to 28. Body depth 2.1 to 2.3 in SL. Color in alcohol generally dark brown (nearly black); posterior edge of dorsal and anal fins, caudal peduncle and caudal fin abruptly whitish; pelvics blackish; pectorals pale with black spot covering base and axil of fin. Maximum size to about 110 mm SL.

Ecology.—Inhabits outer reef slopes in three to 35 meters, sometimes forming large aggregations which feed on zooplankton up to several meters above the bottom.

Distribution.—Widespread in the tropical Indo-West Pacific as far east as the Fiji Islands to the south and the Marshall Islands to the north.

Chromis sp. "A"
Yellow-speckled Chromis
Illus. p. 96

Diagnosis.—Dorsal rays XIII, 12 to 13; anal rays II, 12 to 13; pectoral rays 17 to 18. Tubed lateral-line scales 14 to 15. Gill rakers on first arch 27 to 28. Body depth 1.7 to 1.8 in SL. Color in alcohol generally brownish; scales of antero-dorsal region of body frequently with pale centers; dorsal fin brown except distal half of soft rays pale; anal fin brown except posterior edge narrowly translucent; pelvics light brown; pectorals pale, with small dark spot on upper portion of fin base; caudal mostly brown except posterior margin pale. Maximum size to about 90 mm SL.

Ecology.—Inhabits steep outer reef slopes in 18 to 95 meters. The latter depth was recorded at Palau Islands by W. Starck II while using mixed-gas SCUBA.

Distribution.—Palau Islands, New Guinea, Solomon Islands, New Hebrides, Loyalty Islands, New Caledonia, Fiji Islands, Samoa Islands, and the Society Islands.

Remarks.—Possibly an undescribed species which will be treated in more detail by J. Randall in his forthcoming revision of the genus.

Chromis sp. "B"
Marquesan Chromis
Illus. p. 97

Diagnosis.—Dorsal rays XIII, 11 to 12; anal rays II, 11 to 12; pectoral rays 18 to 19. Tubed lateral line scales 16 to 17. Gill rakers on first arch 28. Body depth 1.8 to 1.9 in SL. Color in alcohol generally brown; pectorals pale; remainder of fins dark brown except posterior portion of dorsal and anal fins, and hind margin of caudal fin pale; large dark blotch at pectoral base. Maximum size to about 110 mm SL.

Ecology.—Collected from rocky outer reefs in the Marquesas Islands in 15 to 25 meters.

Distribution.—Apparently endemic to the Marquesas Islands.

Remarks.—This species, which is new, will be described by J. Randall, who collected several specimens in 1971.

Chromis sp. "C"
Dusky Chromis
Illus. p. 97

Diagnosis.—Dorsal rays XII, 13 to 14; anal rays II, 13 to 14; pectoral rays 17, occasionally 18. Tubed lateral-line scales 14. Gill rakers on first arch 28 to 32. Body depth 1.6 to 1.8 in SL. Color in alcohol generally dark brown, paler ventrally; dorsal and anal fins blackish except posterior half of soft dorsal and last three to four anal rays pale; pelvics, caudal fin, and peduncle dusky; pectorals pale with distinct black spot covering upper half of base and most of pectoral fin axil. Maximum size to about 65 mm SL.

Ecology.—Known from only a few specimens collected from steep outer reef areas in 35 to 48 meters. However, it was relatively common at these depths at Alite Reef, off Malaita Island, Solomon Islands.

Distribution.—Known only from Alite Reef, Solomon Islands and the Palau Islands.

Remarks.—This new species will be described by J. Randall.

Chromis sp. "D"
Deep-reef Chromis

Illus. p. 100

Diagnosis.—Dorsal rays XII, 13 to 14; anal rays II, 13 to 14; pectoral rays 16, occasionally 17. Tubed lateral-line scales 12 to 14. Gill rakers on first arch 26 to 27. Body depth 1.7 to 1.9 in SL. Color in alcohol generally dark brown; caudal fin and peduncle dirty-white; dorsal, anal, and pelvic fins dark brown to blackish except last few dorsal rays pale; pectorals pale with distinct black spot covering base and axil of fin. Maximum size to about 55–60 mm SL.

Ecology.—Inhabits steep outer reef slopes in 20 to 80 meters. Occurs solitarily or in small to large groups. At Palau Islands it was the most common pomacentrid at a depth of 60–70 meters.

Distribution.—Palau Islands, New Guinea, New Britain, Solomon Islands, New Hebrides, and Fiji Islands.

Remarks.—Another new species which will be described by J. Randall.

Chromis sp. "E"
Pitcairn Chromis

Illus. p. 100

Diagnosis.—Dorsal rays XII, 13 to 14; anal rays II, 13 to 14; pectoral rays 17 to 18. Tubed lateral-line scales 15. Gill rakers on first arch 29 to 31. Body depth 2.0 to 2.1 in SL. Color in alcohol generally brown, darker dorsally; caudal fin and peduncle more or less abruptly pale; dorsal and anal fins dark brown except hindmost soft rays pale; pelvics dusky; pectorals pale with black spot covering base. Maximum size to about 60 mm SL.

Ecology.—Collected in 12 to 40 meters at Pitcairn Island and Oeno.

Distribution.—Apparently restricted to the Pitcairn Group.

Remarks.—This species, which is probably new, was collected by J. Randall in 1970.

Chromis sp. "F"
Marquesan White-tail Chromis

Illus. p. 101

Diagnosis.—Dorsal rays XII, 11 to 12; anal rays II, 11 to 12; pectoral rays 16 to 17. Tubed lateral-line scales 17. Gill rakers on first arch 26 to 27. Body depth 1.9 to 2.0 in SL. Color in alcohol generally dark brown with caudal fin abruptly pale; pectorals pale with black spot covering base. Maximum size to about 55–60 mm SL.

Ecology.—Collected at depths ranging from 0.3 to 22 meters.

Distribution.—Apparently restricted to the Marquesas Islands.

Remarks.—This species is closely related to *C. margaritifer* and, in fact, may represent a color variant of *margaritifer* which has a dark caudal peduncle. It is represented in the Bishop Museum collection by 14 specimens collected by J. Randall and the crew of *Charles H. Gilbert*.

Chromis sp. "G"
Fatu Hiva Chromis

Illus. p. 101

Diagnosis.—Dorsal rays XII, 12 to 13; anal rays II, 12 to 13; pectoral rays 17. Tubed lateral-line scales 15. Gill rakers on first arch 28 to 31. Body depth 1.8 to 1.9 in SL. Color in alcohol generally brown, darker dorsally, more or less abruptly pale at level of anterior soft dorsal rays; dorsal and anal fins brown, except posterior portion pale; caudal pale; pelvics dusky; pectorals pale with dark spot covering base. Maximum size to about 65 mm SL.

Ecology.—Collected at Hanauu Bay, Fatu Hiva, Marquesas Islands in 20 to 25 meters.

Distribution.—Apparently endemic to the Marquesas Islands.

Remarks.—This new species will be described by J. Randall, who collected the four known specimens in 1971.

Chromis xanthura (about 125 mm TL), Espiritu Santo, New Hebrides in 10 meters.

Chromis sp. "A" about (125 mm TL), Efate, New Hebrides in 25 meters.

Chromis retrofasciata (about 40 mm TL), Augulpelu Reef, Palau Islands in 15 meters.

Chromis sp. "B"
(98 mm SL),
Marquesas Islands
(J. Randall photo).

Chromis sp. "C" (about 100 mm TL), Alite Reef, Solomon Islands in 35 meters.

Chromis sp. "H"
Slender Chromis

Diagnosis.—Dorsal rays XV, 10 to 12; anal rays II, 11 to 12; pectoral rays 21. Tubed lateral-line scales 20. Gill rakers on first arch 35 to 36. Body depth 2.7 to 3.0 in SL. Color in alcohol generally dark brown shading to light brown ventrally; dorsal and anal fins dark brown except posteriormost rays pale; caudal mostly dark brown with hind margin pale; pelvics pale; pectorals pale with dark spot covering base. Maximum size to about 100 mm SL.

Ecology.—Collected in depths ranging from five to 20 meters.

Distribution.—Gambier Islands, Rapa, Pitcairn Island, and Oeno.

Remarks.—Another species to be described by J. Randall, who collected most of the known specimens. Apparently a close relative of *C. randalli* from Easter Island.

Chapter IX
DASCYLLUS

The genus *Dascyllus* is comprised of seven species which are confined to the Indo-West Pacific; six are known from the "South Seas." *D. aruanus* is the most widespread representative, occurring nearly everywhere in the Indo-West Pacific except Easter Island and the Hawaiian and Pitcairn Groups. Aggregations of about 50 or more *D. aruanus* are commonly encountered feeding in mid-water a short distance above isolated coral heads. At the approach of danger the fish draw closer to the coral, finally retreating among the branches. Collectors frequently take advantage of this behavior by bringing the entire coral head to the surface where the fish are shaken into a container. *D. aruanus* and *D. melanurus* are usually seen in shallow lagoon and coastal environments, whereas the other species also frequent passages and outer reef slopes. The young and occasional adults of *D. albisella* and *D. trimaculatus* are frequently commensal with sea anemones and behave much the same as *Amphiprion*. The dominant food source of *Dascyllus* consists of current-borne zooplankton, but a significant amount of benthic algae is also taken.

The author has studied the similar reproductive patterns of *D. reticulatus* and *D. trimaculatus* at Eniwetok Atoll in the Marshall Islands. The eggs, which usually number more than 1,000, are laid on dead coral branches, bare rock, or other suitable substrata. The sequence of photos shows a spawning which took place on an abandoned section of cable. The male aggressively guards the nest until hatching, which takes about three days. The fry are only about 2.0 mm TL, but after one week they are nearly double this figure. The young are pelagic for the first few weeks.

GENUS *DASCYLLUS* CUVIER

Dascyllus Cuvier, 1829: 179 (type species, *Chaetodon aruanus* Linnaeus).

Diagnostic features.—Body highly orbiculate, depth usually 1.5 to 1.7 in SL; preorbital and suborbital scaly, lower edges serrate; edge of preopercle and other opercle bones more or less serrate; teeth of jaws small and conical, outer row of enlarged teeth and irregular band of villiform teeth behind; dorsal spines usually XII; scale rows in a longitudinal series from upper edge of operculum to base of caudal fin less than 30.

KEY TO THE SPECIES OF *DASCYLLUS* FROM THE SOUTH SEAS

1a. Dorsal rays usually 12 (last ray frequently branched near base); color of head and body pale with three black bars 2
1b. Dorsal rays 14 to 16; color not as in 1a 3
2a. Caudal fin pale (Indo-W. Pacific) . . . .*D. aruanus*
2b. Caudal fin mostly dark (E. Indies; Philippines; Melanesia; Queensland; Caroline Islands). . . .
. . . . *D. melanurus*
3a. Color generally yellowish to brown, each scale with darker submarginal band; frequently with dark bar extending from dorsal fin origin to base of pelvics; upper portion of sides without isolated pale spot; gill rakers 25 to 28 (Indo-W. Pacific) . . . .*D. reticulatus*
3b. Color generally brown to blackish without dark bar extending from dorsal fin origin to base of pelvics; upper portion of sides frequently with isolated pale spot, especially in smaller individuals (less than about 50 mm SL); gill rakers 21 to 25 4
4a. Dorsal rays usually 16; anal rays 15 to 16 (Hawaiian Islands) . . . .*D. albisella*
4b. Dorsal rays usually 15; anal rays usually 14 (last ray frequently branched near base) 5
5a. Color generally dark brown to blackish; fins dark (Indo-W. Pacific) . . . .*D. trimaculatus*
5b. Color generally light brown to brown; fins pale to dusky (Marquesas Islands) . . . .*D. strasburgi*

Chromis sp. "D" (about 70 mm TL), Suva, Fiji Islands in 35 meters.

Chromis sp. "E"
(about 70 mm TL),
Pitcairn Group.

Chromis sp. "F" (about 70 mm TL), Marquesas Islands.

Chromis sp. "G" (about 70 mm TL), Fatu Hiva, Marquesas Islands.

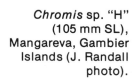

Chromis sp. "H" (105 mm SL), Mangareva, Gambier Islands (J. Randall photo).

Sequence of photos showing *Dascyllus trimaculatus* spawning at Eniwetok Atoll, Marshall Islands. The eggs are being deposited on an abandoned section of four-inch cable. The male fish fertilizes the eggs while following close behind the female in the upper and lower photos. In the center photo the fertilizing male and egg depositing female swim in opposite directions, but with their abdominal regions in close proximity. The male fish (left in upper photo, right in others) is characteristically lighter colored than the female during spawning activities.

Dascyllus albisella Gill
Hawaiian Dascyllus

Illus. p. 105

Dascyllus albisella Gill, 1862: 149 (Hawaii).
Dascyllus edmondsoni Pietschmann, 1934: 100 (Hawaii).

Diagnosis.—Dorsal rays XII, 15 to 16; anal rays II, 15 to 16; pectoral rays 19 to 20. Tubed lateral-line scales 19 to 20. Gill rakers on first arch 24 to 25. Body depth 1.5 to 1.7 in SL. Color in alcohol brown, each scale with dark submarginal band; fins generally brown to black except pectorals and hindmost dorsal rays pale; juveniles black with white spot on forehead and middle of sides. Maximum size to about 110 mm SL.

Ecology.—A relatively common species in rocky areas around the Hawaiian Islands to a depth of at least 46 meters. Occurs in small to large aggregations. Juveniles are usually associated with small heads of *Pocillopora* coral or occasionally with sand-dwelling anemones.

Distribution.—Known only from the Hawaiian Islands and Johnston Island, where it replaces the closely related *D. trimaculatus*, from which it was probably derived.

Dascyllus aruanus (Linnaeus)
Humbug Dascyllus

Illus. pp. 104, 105

Chaetodon aruanus Linnaeus, 1758: 275 (Indies).

Diagnosis.—Dorsal rays XII, 12 to 13; anal rays II, 12 to 13; pectoral rays 17 to 18. Tubed lateral-line scales 17 to 18. Gill rakers on first arch 23 to 24. Body depth 1.5 to 1.7 in SL. Color in alcohol generally whitish with three black bars; pelvics black. Maximum size to about 60 mm SL.

Ecology.—Inhabits lagoon and coastal reefs in one to 12 meters. Usually found in aggregations around small coral heads.

Distribution.—Widespread in the tropical Indo-West Pacific as far east as Rapa and the Marquesas Islands to the south and the Line Islands to the north.

Dascyllus melanurus Bleeker
Black-tail Dascyllus

Illus. p. 104

Dascyllus melanurus Bleeker, 1854a: 100 (Neiva and Banda, Indonesia).

Diagnosis.—Dorsal rays XII, 12 to 13; anal rays II, 12 to 13; pectoral rays 18. Tubed lateral-line scales 16 to 17. Gill rakers on first arch 25 to 27. Body depth 1.5 to 1.6 in SL. Color in alcohol generally whitish with black bar on head and two black bars on sides; pelvic and caudal fins mostly black. Maximum size to about 65 mm SL.

Ecology.—Inhabits sheltered lagoons, harbors, and inlets in one to 10 meters. Commonly occurs in aggregations associated with small coral heads. Feeds on a variety of plankton which includes larval shrimps and crabs, algae, ostracods, amphipods, pelagic tunicates, copepods, and fish eggs. Usually not as common as *D. aruanus*.

Distribution.—Largely restricted to the Indo-Australian Archipelago, Philippines, and Melanesia, but also occurs in the Caroline Islands as far east as Ponape.

Dascyllus reticulatus (Richardson)
Reticulated Dascyllus

Illus. p. 108

Heliases reticulatus Richardson, 1846: 245 (China and Japan).

Diagnosis.—Dorsal rays XII, 14 to 15; anal rays II, 14 to 15; pectoral rays 18. Tubed lateral-line scales 20. Gill rakers on first arch 25 to 28. Body depth 1.5 to 1.6 in SL. Color in alcohol generally yellowish to brown, each scale with dark submarginal band, specimens below about 50 mm SL with one or two dark bars on side; spinous dorsal fin pale basally and blackish distally; soft dorsal and anal fin dusky; pelvics mostly black; pectorals pale with dusky rays and small dark spot on upper portion of fin base; caudal dusky. Maximum size to about 65 mm SL.

Aggregation of
Dascyllus aruanus
around isolated coral
head at Eniwetok
Atoll, Marshall
Islands.

Dascyllus melanurus
(about 50 mm TL),
Port Moresby, New
Guinea in eight
meters.

Dascyllus albisella
(about 75 mm TL),
Oahu, Hawaiian
Islands at Waikiki
Aquarium.

Dascyllus aruanus
(about 40 mm TL),
Malakal Island, Palau
Islands in two meters.

Ecology.—Inhabits lagoons, passages, and outer reef slopes in one to 50 meters. Occurs in small to large aggregations which are frequently associated with live coral heads.

Distribution.—Widespread in the tropical Indo-West Pacific as far east as the Pitcairn Group to the south and the Marshall and Gilbert Islands to the north.

Dascyllus strasburgi Klausewitz
Strasburg's Dascyllus

Illus. p. 108

Dascyllus strasburgi Klausewitz, 1960: 45 (Marquesas Islands).

Diagnosis.—Dorsal rays XII, 15 to 16; anal rays II, 14 to 15; pectoral rays 19 to 20. Tubed lateral-line scales 18 to 19. Gill rakers on first arch 21 to 24. Body depth 1.5 to 1.7 in SL. Color in alcohol generally brownish with reticulated appearance due to darker scale centers; fins dusky to pale; pectoral base with small black spot on upper portion; small specimens with pale spot on sides below middle of spinous dorsal fin. Maximum size to about 90 mm SL.

Ecology.—Two specimens at Bishop Museum were collected off Matahumu Point, Fatu Hiva, Marquesas Islands by J. Randall in six to 12 meters.

Distribution.—Known only from the Marquesas Islands.

Dascyllus trimaculatus (Rüppell)
Three-spot Dascyllus

Illus. pp. 108, 109

Pomacentrus trimaculatus Rüppell, 1828: 39 (Massaua, Red Sea.)

Diagnosis.—Dorsal rays XII, 15 to 16; anal rays II, 14 to 15; pectoral rays 19 to 20. Tubed lateral-line scales 18 to 19. Gill rakers on first arch 23 to 25. Body depth 1.4 to 1.6 in SL. Color in alcohol usually entirely dark brown to blackish with small pale spot above lateral-line below middle of spinous dorsal fin; large adults frequently lacking pale spot and juveniles with additional pale spot on forehead. Maximum size to about 100 mm SL.

Ecology.—Inhabits lagoon and outer reef environments in one to 55 meters. Occurs in small to large aggregations. The stomachs of several specimens from the Palau Islands contained about 40 percent algae and 60 percent copepods and other planktonic crustacea.

Distribution.—Widespread in the tropical Indo-West Pacific as far east as the Pitcairn Group to the south and the Line Islands to the north.

Chapter X
LEPIDOZYGUS

The genus *Lepidozygus* contains a single species, *tapeinosoma*, which has been reported from scattered localities throughout the vast Indo-West Pacific region. Randall (in press) has shown that *L. anthioides* Smith from the Indian Ocean is a junior synonym of *L. tapeinosoma*. These fish form small to large schools which may include several hundred individuals. Unlike most pomacentrids, they frequently range widely over a particular section of reef. They exhibit the typical midwater adaptations which are also found in many *Chromis*. These include a slender-body, forked caudal fin, and a small mouth which opens forward. Zooplankton forms the major dietary component.

GENUS *LEPIDOZYGUS* GUNTHER

Lepidozygus Günther, 1862: 15 (type species, *Pomacentrus tapeinosoma* Bleeker).

Diagnostic features.—Body extremely elongate, depth about 2.9 to 3.0 in SL; dorsal spines XII; row of papilla-like structures on inner edge of posterior circumorbitals; preopercle finely serrate; teeth of jaws uniserial; edge of suborbital hidden by scales; scale rows in longitudinal series from upper edge of operculum to base of caudal fin 33 to 36.

Lepidozygus tapeinosoma (Bleeker)
Fusilier Damsel
Illus. pp. 109, 112

Pomacentrus tapeinosoma Bleeker, 1856c: 376 (Ternate, Indonesia).

Diagnosis.—Dorsal rays XII, 14 to 15; anal rays II, 15 to 16; pectoral rays 21 to 22. Tubed lateral-line scales 19 to 20. Gill rakers on first arch 26 to 28. Body depth 2.9 to 3.0 in SL. Color in alcohol generally brown to dark grey grading to tannish ventrally; dorsal fin dark grey; anal and caudal fins pale to dusky; remainder of fins pale. Maximum size to about 70 mm SL.

Ecology.—Usually inhabits the upper edge of outer reef slopes, but occasionally collected on lagoon reefs. Most common in areas of rich coral growth.

Distribution.—Widespread in the tropical Indo-West Pacific as far east as the Tuamotu, Marquesas, and Line Islands.

Dascyllus trimaculatus (about 75 mm TL), Augulpelu Reef, Palau Islands in 20 meters. This individual is being "inspected" for external parasites by a small cleaner wrasse, *Labroides dimidiatus*.

Dascyllus reticulatus (about 50 mm TL), Malakal Island, Palau Islands in six meters.

Dascyllus strasburgi (80 mm SL), Ua Huka, Marquesas Islands (J. Randall photo).

Dascyllus trimaculatus (about 75 mm TL), Suva, Fiji Islands in six meters.

Lepidozygus tapeinosoma (about 75 mm TL), Maldive Islands (H.R. Axelrod photo).

Chapter XI
ABUDEFDUF

The genus *Abudefduf* contains relatively large pomacentrids which frequently exhibit a pattern of dark bars. There are approximately 15 species which inhabit the tropical Atlantic and Indo-Pacific; nine are found in the "South Seas." Aggregations of these fishes are often a conspicuous feature of the fauna which is associated with wharf pilings, boat moorings, and breakwaters. All of the species dwell in relatively shallow water, although the maomao, *A. abdominalis*, is found down to at least 30 meters. Two species, *A. septemfasciatus* and *A. sordidus*, are inhabitants of the shallow surge zone. Algae seem to be the main dietary component of *Abudefduf*, although several of the species take zooplankton in midwater feeding aggregations.

Spawning generally takes place on bare rock, wharf pilings, etc., which have previously been cleared of algae by the male. The eggs which hatch in five to six days are guarded throughout the incubation period by the male. The fry are pelagic for several weeks.

GENUS *ABUDEFDUF* FORSKÅL

Abudefduf Forskål, 1775: 59 (type species, *Chaetodon sordidus* Forskål).

Diagnostic features.—Margin of preopercle and suborbital entire; notch between preorbital and suborbital absent; dorsal spines XIII; pectoral rays usually 18 to 20; gill rakers usually 21 to 27; tubed lateral-lined scales usually 20 to 22; preorbital and suborbital scaled or naked; teeth uniserial, usually with notched or flattened tips (at least at front of jaws); snout scaled at least to front of orbits, frequently to about level of nostrils or slightly beyond; body depth 1.6 to 1.9 in SL; color pattern usually composed of a series of dark cross bars on sides.

KEY TO THE SPECIES OF *ABUDEFDUF* FROM THE SOUTH SEAS

1a. Caudal peduncle with large black spot on dorsal surface on individuals of all sizes; dorsal rays 15 to 16 (Indo-W. Pacific)..*A. sordidus*

1b. Caudal peduncle without large black spot on dorsal surface (except dark saddle present on specimens of *A. septemfasciatus* under about 50 mm SL); dorsal rays usually 12 to 14 (last ray sometimes branched near base)...2

2a. Color of body dark with one to four narrow (about one to two scales wide) pale bars on sides; caudal fin pale (Japan; E. Indies; Philippines; Melanesia)........................*A. notatus*

2b. Color of body not as in 2a; usually pale to brown with four to seven dark bars on sides; caudal fin pale to black..3

3a. Each caudal lobe with median longitudinal dark band (Indo-W. Pacific)........*A. coelestinus*

3b. Each caudal lobe without median longitudinal dark band...............................4

4a. Anal and caudal fins mostly black (Great Barrier Reef; New Caledonia)...........*A. whitleyi*

4b. Anal and caudal fins pale to dusky..5

5a. Dorsal rays 14 (last branched near base)..6

5b. Dorsal rays 12 to 13...7

6a. Sides with four to five dark bars; large dark spot at base of hindmost soft dorsal and anal rays (Hawaiian Islands)...*A. abdominalis*

6b. Sides with six to seven dark bars; large dark spot at base of hindmost soft dorsal and anal rays absent (N. Australia; E. Indies; China Sea)...*A. bengalensis*

7a. Head and body with five dark bars on sides; suborbital scaly (circumtropical)......*A. saxatilis*

7b. Head and body with six to seven dark bars on sides; suborbital naked...................8

8a. Sides with seven prominent dark bars; caudal peduncle mostly blackish (E. Indies; Melanesia; Palau Islands)...*A.* sp.

8b. Sides with six diffuse bars; caudal peduncle with diffuse bar on anterior half (Indo-West Pacific)..*A. septemfasciatus*

Abudefduf abdominalis (Quoy and Gaimard)
Maomao

Illus. p. 112

Glyphisodon abdominalis Quoy and Gaimard, 1824: 390 (Hawaiian Islands).

Diagnosis.—Dorsal rays XIII, 14 to 15; anal rays II, 13 to 15; pectoral rays 19. Tubed lateral-line scales 21 to 22. Gill rakers on first arch 28 to 30. Body depth 1.7 to 1.9 in SL. Color in alcohol generally mottled whitish; head and predorsal region greyish-brown; body with four dark bars on upper half of sides; fins dusky except pectorals and pelvics pale; dark spot present at base of hindmost dorsal and anal rays. Maximum size to about 150 mm SL.

Ecology.—Found in a wide range of habitats in the Hawaiian Islands. Most common in rocky areas to a depth of at least 30 meters. The young are sometimes found in surge pools. Occurs in small to large aggregations. Feeds on a variety of algae and zooplankton.

Distribution.—Known only from the Hawaiian Islands where it replaces the circumtropical species *A. saxatilis*.

Abudefduf bengalensis (Bloch)
Bengal Sergeant

Illus. p. 113

Chaetodon bengalensis Bloch, 1787: 110 (Bengal).
Glyphidodon affinis Günther, 1862: 41 (China).
Glyphisodon palmeri Ogilby, 1913: 87 (Moreton Bay, Queensland).

Diagnosis.—Dorsal rays XIII, 14 to 15; anal rays II, 13 to 15; pectoral rays 19 to 20. Tubed lateral-line scales 20 to 21. Gill rakers on first arch 23 to 25. Body depth 1.7 to 1.9 in SL. Color in alcohol generally grey with seven dark bars; fins dusky. Maximum size to about 130 mm SL.

Ecology.—Inhabits inshore reefs along the Australian coastline and lagoon environments in one to six meters on the Great Barrier Reef. Occurs solitarily or in small group. Feeds on algae, gastropods and small crabs.

Distribution.—China, Viet Nam, Indonesia, E. Indian Ocean, Malaysia and tropical Australia.

Remarks.—Australian specimens have been invariably referred to as *A. palmeri*. However, I suspected there might be an older name after having discovered a specimen at the Australian Museum collected in the last century by Bleeker at Sumatra. The earliest available name for this species appears to be *A. bengalensis*, described by **Bloch** on the basis of an adult specimen from India. I have examined specimens from the South China Sea (Hong Kong and the coast of Viet Nam) at the California Academy of Sciences which agree perfectly with Australian specimens.

Aggregation of *Lepidozygus tapeinosoma* at Pulu Iwa Reef, New Hebrides in seven meters.

Abudefduf abdominalis
(about 125 mm TL), Oahu,
Hawaiian Islands at Sea Life Park.

Abudefduf bengalensis (about 150 mm TL), One Tree Island, Great Barrier Reef in two meters.

Abudefduf species (about 125 mm TL), Florida Island, Solomon Islands in one meter.

Abudefduf species
Black-tail Sergeant

Diagnosis.—Dorsal rays XIII, 12 to 13; anal rays II, 12 to 13; pectoral rays 18. Tubed lateral line scales 20 to 22. Gill rakers on first arch 22 to 24. Body depth 1.6 to 1.9 in SL. Color in alcohol generally greyish, paler ventrally; six dark bars on sides, last covering most of caudal peduncle; fins pale to dusky. Maximum size to about 150 mm SL.

Ecology.—Inhabits protected lagoon areas and sheltered coastal reefs in 0.5 to six meters. Also common around docks and breakwaters. Large numbers were encountered along the shoreline among the sheltered rock-islands of the southern Palau Group. Occurs in small to large aggregations.

Distribution.—Philippine Islands, Palau Islands, Molucca Islands, New Guinea, New Britain, and Solomon Islands.

Remarks.—This species has been confused by earlier authors with *A. bengalensis*. However, the two species are distinct, being clearly separable on the basis of fin-ray counts and coloration. In addition, the two exhibit an apparent allopatric pattern of distribution. Although *A. bengalensis* penetrates the islands of western Indonesia, it appears to be more of a continental form; whereas *Abudefduf* sp. is strictly an island dweller. The large black spot covering most of the caudal peduncle is a useful feature for separating this species from *bengalensis* and other close relatives. The species appears to be undescribed.

Abudefduf coelestinus (Cuvier)
Scissor-tail Sergeant

Glyphisodon coelestinus Cuvier, 1830: 464 (Indies; Mauritius; Malabar; Ulietea; Society Islands).

Diagnosis.—Dorsal rays XIII, 13 to 14; anal rays II, 12 to 14; pectoral rays 18. Tubed lateral-line scales 21. Gill rakers on first arch 24 to 27. Body depth 1.8 to 2.0 in SL. Color in alcohol generally dark grey grading to whitish on breast and abdomen; five black bars on sides; fins dusky to pale, caudal lobes with prominent longitudinal dark band. Maximum size to about 130 mm SL.

Ecology.—Inhabits lagoons, sheltered harbors, reef passages, and occasionally encountered on the upper edge of outer reef slopes in one to eight meters. Feeds in large aggregations on zooplankton and algae.

Distribution.—Widespread in the tropical Indo-West Pacific as far east as Rapa and the Marshall Islands.

Remarks.—Many authors have used the name *sexfasciatus* (Lacépède) for this species. However, as De Beaufort (1940) has pointed out, there was no mention in Lacépède's original description of the distinctive black margins on the caudal fin. Hence, *sexfasciatus* is most likely a synonym of *A. saxatilis*.

Abudefduf notatus (Day)
Yellow-tail Sergeant

Glyphidodon notatus Day 1869: 521 (Andaman Islands).

Diagnosis.—Dorsal rays XIII, 13 to 14; anal rays II, 13 to 14; pectoral rays 18. Tubed lateral-line scales 19 to 21. Gill rakers on first arch 26 to 27. Body depth 1.7 to 1.9 in SL. Color in alcohol generally brown with one to four narrow pale bars on sides; fins brownish, except caudal dull yellowish. Maximum size to about 130 mm SL.

Ecology.—Observed only on the upper edge of a sheer outer reef dropoff at Rabaul, New Britain. Six individuals were present in one to 12 meters.

Distribution.—East Africa, Seychelles Islands, Andaman Islands, East Indies, Philippines, Japan, and New Britain. The record by Fowler (1927) from Howland Island in the Phoenix Group is questionable.

Remarks.—No specimens were collected. The above diagnosis was compiled from Fowler and Bean (1928) and Smith (1960).

Abudefduf saxatilis (Linnaeus)
Sergeant Major

Illus. pp. 41, 117

Chaetodon saxatilis Linnaeus, 1758: 276 (India).

Diagnosis.—Dorsal rays XIII, 12 to 13; anal rays II, 11 to 13; pectoral rays 19. Tubed lateral-line scales 20 to 21. Gill rakers on first arch 25 to 26. Body depth 1.7 to 1.9 in SL. Color in alcohol generally dark grey to brownish grading to whitish ventrally; five black bars on sides; fins pale to dusky. Maximum size to about 150 mm SL.

Ecology.—Generally inhabits the upper edge of outer reef slopes in one to 12 meters. However, the young are sometimes common on lagoon reefs or in the vicinity of docks, wharf pilings, moorings, etc. Adults frequently form large feeding aggregations which include several hundred individuals.

Distribution.—Circumtropical.

Remarks.—I am following most previous authors in using the name *saxatilis* for this species. However, De Beaufort (1940) pointed out that the type of *saxatilis* is from America and thus resurrected a subspecific name, *vaigiensis* (Quoy and Gaimard) for the Indo-Pacific form. Therefore, should the Indo-Pacific and Atlantic varieties eventually be separated, the name *vaigiensis* would be applicable.

Abudefduf septemfasciatus (Cuvier)
Banded Sergeant

Illus. p. 117

Glyphisodon septemfasciatus Cuvier, 1830: 463 (Mauritius).

Diagnosis.—Dorsal rays XIII, 12 to 13; anal rays II, 12 to 13; pectoral rays 18. Tubed lateral-line scales 20 to 22. Gill rakers on first arch 23 to 25. Body depth 1.8 to 2.1 in SL. Color in alcohol generally grey to brown with six dark bars on sides; fins dusky; juveniles similar to *A. sordidus*, but readily distinguished from that species on the basis of dorsal and anal fin ray counts. Maximum size to about 150 mm SL.

Ecology.—Inhabits lagoon and outer reefs in shallow (0.2 to three meters) areas exposed to mild or moderate surge. Feeds almost exclusively on benthic algae.

Distribution.—Widespread in the tropical Indo-West Pacific as far east as the Tuamotu and Line Islands.

Abudefduf sordidus (Forskål)
Black-spot Sergeant

Illus. p. 120

Chaetodon sordidus Forskål, 1775: 62 (Djedda, Red Sea).

Diagnosis.—Dorsal rays XIII, 15 to 16; anal rays II, 14 to 15; pectoral rays 19. Tubed lateral-line scales 21 to 22. Gill rakers on first arch 26 to 28. Body depth 1.6 to 1.8 in SL. Color in alcohol grey to brown with five dark bars on sides, more distinct in juveniles; prominent black spot on upper caudal peduncle; fins pale to dusky; juveniles under about 40 mm SL with black spot on anterior dorsal spines. Maximum size to about 150 mm SL.

Ecology.—Generally restricted to areas of mild to moderate surge in 0.2 to three meters. Juveniles are common inhabitants of rocky surge pools in the Hawaiian Islands. Feeds mainly on benthic algae.

Distribution.—Widespread in the tropical Indo-West Pacific as far east as the Pitcairn Group and the Hawaiian Islands.

Abudefduf whitleyi Allen and Robertson
Whitley's Sergeant

Illus. pp. 29, 120

Abudefduf whitleyi Allen and Robertson, 1974: 154 (Great Barrier Reef).

Diagnosis.—Dorsal rays XIII, 13; anal rays II, 12; pectoral rays 19 to 20. Tubed lateral-line scales 20 to 22. Gill rakers on first arch 22 to 24. Body depth 1.7 to 1.9 in SL. Color in alcohol uniformly dark except for pale abdominal region; juveniles light brown to whitish with three to five narrow dark bars on sides. Maximum size to about 135 mm SL.

Ecology.—A very common species on the Great Barrier Reef. It generally lives in relatively shallow water (to a depth of about five meters) along the outer periphery of individual reef complexes. Feeding aggregations composed of a hundred or more individuals are frequently observed swimming high above the substratum.

Distribution.—Great Barrier Reef and New Caledonia.

Abudefduf coelestinus (about 40 mm TL), Malakal Island, Palau Islands in two meters.

Abudefduf notatus, painting based on individual observed off Rabaul, New Britain.

Abudefduf saxatilis (about 125 mm TL), Florida Island, Solomon Islands in 10 meters.

Abudefduf septemfasciatus (about 150 mm TL), Florida Island, Solomon Islands in two meters.

Chapter XII

AMBLYGLYPHIDODON

The genus *Amblyglyphidodon* is composed of six species which inhabit the Indo-West Pacific; four are found in the "South Seas." *A. curacao* is probably the most abundant member of the genus, and large midwater aggregations of this species are a common sight on both lagoon and outer reef slopes throughout the West Pacific. *A. ternatensis* is confined to lagoon areas, but *A. aureus* and *A. leucogaster* commonly inhabit steep outer reef slopes to depths of at least 34–45 meters. The diet of these fishes consists mostly of zooplankton and benthic algae.

Little is known about the reproductive activities of *Amblyglyphidodon*. I have observed nests of *A. curacao* and *A. aureus* which were guarded by an aggressive parent presumed to be the male. In both cases the nests were located on tubular structures of small diameter. The eggs of *A. curacao* were attached to a small dead tree branch and those of *A. aureus* on a dead gorgonian branch.

GENUS *AMBLYGLYPHIDODON* BLEEKER

Amblyglyphidodon Bleeker, 1877b: 92 (type species, *Glyphisodon aureus* Cuvier).

Diagnostic features.—Body highly orbiculate, depth usually 1.5 to 1.8 in SL; margin of preopercle and suborbital entire; dorsal spines XIII; pectoral rays usually 15 to 18; gill rakers usually 25 to 30; lateral-line scales usually 15 to 17; suborbital usually scaled (except naked in *aureus*); teeth usually uniserial with flattened or notched tips (*A. ternatensis* has a second row of slender, nearly inconspicuous buttress teeth anteriorly); predorsal scales extend to snout or beyond; dorsal spines elongate, the longest usually about equal in length to distance from tip of snout to upper edge of preopercle.

KEY TO THE SPECIES OF *AMBLYGLYPHIDODON* FROM THE SOUTH SEAS

1a. Tubed lateral-line scales usually 13 to 14; pectoral rays 15 to 16; dorsal rays 11 (last ray frequently branched near base); teeth biserial at front of jaws (Palau Islands; East Indies; New Guinea; Solomon Islands)....................................*A. ternatensis*

1b. Tubed lateral-line scales usually 16 to 17; pectoral rays 16 to 18; dorsal rays 12 to 14; teeth uniserial at front of jaws...2

2a. Suborbital naked; dorsal spines increasing in length posteriorly; body and fins uniformly pale (yellow in life) (Philippines; East Indies; northern Australia; Melanesia; Micronesia)..*A. aureus*

2b. Suborbital scaly; dorsal spines not increasing in length posteriorly (median spines longest); body and fins usually partly dark (caudal fin at least with dark upper and lower margins) or body with several dark bars..3

3a. Body with several dark bars; caudal fin without prominent dark upper and lower margins (although margins dusky, especially in Great Barrier Reef specimens); dorsal and anal fins dusky (East Indies; W. Pacific generally to the Marshall and Samoa Islands)............*A. curacao*

3b. Body without dark bars; caudal fin with prominent dark upper and lower margins; dorsal and anal frequently blackish on anterior half (pale in specimens from Fiji and Samoa) (East Indies; W. Pacific generally to the Marshall and Samoa Islands).....................*A. leucogaster*

Amblyglyphidodon aureus (Cuvier)
Golden Damsel

Illus. p. 121, 128

Glyphisodon aureus Cuvier, 1830: 479 (Java).

Diagnosis.—Dorsal rays XIII, 12 to 14; anal rays II, 14 to 15; pectoral rays 17. Tubed lateral-line scales 16. Gill rakers on first arch 25 to 29. Body depth 1.5 to 1.7 in SL. Color in alcohol generally pale brown to yellowish; predorsal region dusky; diffuse dark blotches sometimes present on sides; fins pale. Maximum size to about 100 mm SL.

Ecology.—Inhabits steep outer reef slopes in 12 to 35 meters. Solitary individuals or small groups feed on plankton up to several meters above the substratum.

Distribution.—Indo-Australian Archipelago and tropical West Pacific as far east as the Fiji Islands and the Marshall Islands.

Amblyglyphidodon curacao (Bloch)
Staghorn Damsel

Illus. p. 124

Chaetodon curacao Bloch, 1787: 106 ("Curacao Island", off Venezuela—error).

Diagnosis.—Dorsal rays XIII, 12 to 13; anal rays II, 13 to 15; pectoral rays 17 to 18. Tubed lateral-line scales 16 to 17. Gill rakers on first arch 25 to 27. Body depth 1.6 to 1.7 in SL. Color in alcohol generally olive to brown, whitish ventrally with five bars on sides (these may be obscure in large adults); fins dusky except pectorals and pelvics pale. Maximum size to about 90 mm SL.

Ecology.—A ubiquitous species which inhabits lagoons, outer reefs, coastal embayments and reef passages. Forms large feeding aggregations, frequently over growths of staghorn *Acropora* coral in one to 15 meters. The stomach of a specimen from Palau contained larval crabs and shrimps, fish eggs, and algae.

Distribution.—Ryukyu Islands, China, Philippines, East Indies, Melanesia, and Oceania in general as far east as the Samoa, Marshall, and Gilbert Islands.

Amblyglyphidodon leucogaster (Bleeker)
White-belly Damsel

Illus. p. 124

Glyphisodon leucogaster Bleeker, 1847: 26 (Java).

Diagnosis.—Dorsal rays XIII, 12 to 13; anal rays II, 13 to 14; pectoral rays 16 to 17. Tubed lateral-line scales 16. Gill rakers on first arch 25 to 27. Body depth 1.5 to 1.7 in SL. Color in alcohol generally grey to blackish with faint horizontal stripes; ventral portion of body pale; spinous dorsal and anterior half of anal fin black (pale in specimens from Fiji and Samoa Islands), most of soft dorsal and posterior half of anal fin pale; pelvics and pectorals pale with black spot on upper part of pectoral base; caudal fin pale with black upper and lower margins. Maximum size to about 100 mm SL.

Ecology.—Inhabits lagoons, reef passages, and the outer reef slope in five to 45 meters. Solitary individuals or small groups feed on plankton well above the bottom. The stomachs of several specimens contained copepods, amphipods, mysids, fish eggs, crustacean larvae, and a small portion of algae.

Distribution.—Ryukyu Islands, China Sea, Philippines, East Indies, Melanesia, Great Barrier Reef, Micronesia, and Samoa Islands. Records of *A. leucogaster* from the Indian Ocean and Red Sea are probably attributable to another species.

Abudefduf whitleyi (about 150 mm TL), Great Barrier Reef off Cairns, Queensland in three meters.

Abudefduf sordidus (about 150 mm TL), Florida Island, Solomon Islands in two meters.

Amblyglyphidodon aureus (about 125 mm TL), Augulpelu Reef, Palau Islands in 12 meters.

Amblyglyphidodon aureus (about 100 mm TL), Florida Island, Solomon Islands in 18 meters.

Amblyglyphidodon ternatensis (Bleeker)
Ternate Damsel

Glyphisodon ternatensis Bleeker, 1853a: 137 (Ternate).
Glyphidodon nigrifrons Macleay, 1883: 271 (New Guinea).

Diagnosis.—Dorsal rays XIII, 11 to 12; anal rays II, 12 to 13; pectoral rays 15 to 16. Tubed lateral-line scales 13 to 14. Gill rakers on first arch 27 to 30. Body depth 1.6 to 1.8 in SL. Color in alcohol dark brown antero-dorsally; remainder of body and fins pale. Maximum size to about 100 mm SL.

Ecology.—Inhabits sheltered coastal reefs and embayments in one to 12 meters. Common among the rock-islands of the southern Palau Group. Frequently forms mixed aggregations with *A. curacao*.

Distribution.—Palau Islands, East Indies, New Guinea, and Solomon Islands.

Remarks.—This species has been included as a synonym of *A. curacao* by several previous authors. In the sea it is easily distinguished from that species by the absence of bars and a marked duskiness on the dorsal surface of the caudal peduncle. The type of *Glyphidodon nigrifrons* was examined at the Australian Museum. It agrees with specimens of *A. ternatensis* which I collected at Palau and New Guinea. The low counts for the lateral-line and pectoral rays are particularly diagnostic.

Chapter XIII
AMBLYPOMACENTRUS

The genus *Amblypomacentrus* contains a single species which is restricted to the East Indies and immediately adjacent regions. *A. breviceps* is a conspicuous fish which dwells in sandy or silty areas. On the lagoon bottom at Egum Atoll in 35 meters it was found with *Pristotis jerdoni* in the vicinity of certain sponges which occasionally interrupted an otherwise featureless substratum. Normally the species was encountered in harbors or mud-bottom inlets. In the latter environment it frequently shelters inside bottles, tin cans, and wreckage.

The reproductive habits are poorly known. A single nest was located in the yacht harbor at Honiara, Guadalcanal. Several hundred eggs were attached inside a tin-can with an aggressive parent in attendance.

GENUS *AMBLYPOMACENTRUS* BLEEKER

Amblypomacentrus Bleeker, 1877b: 68 (type species, *Glyphisodon breviceps*, Schlegel and Müller).

Diagnostic features.—Margin of preopercle and suborbital weakly serrate (anterior section of suborbital frequently entire); notch between preorbital and suborbital absent; dorsal spines XIII, preorbital and suborbital naked; teeth uniserial, somewhat incisiform; snout mostly naked; greatest body depth 2.1 to 2.3 in SL.

Amblypomacentrus breviceps (Schlegel and Müller)
Black-banded Demoiselle   Illus. p. 125

Glyphisodon breviceps Schlegel and Müller, 1839–44: 23 (Sumatra).

Diagnosis.—Dorsal rays XIII, 11 to 12; anal rays II, 12 to 13; pectoral rays 16 to 17. Tubed lateral-line scales 17. Gill rakers on first arch 18 to 20. Body depth 2.1 to 2.3 in SL. Color in alcohol generally pale with black bar through eye and two black saddles on upper sides extending onto dorsal fin; soft dorsal, anal, and caudal fins sometimes with faint spots. Maximum size to about 50 mm SL.

Ecology.—Inhabits sandy or silty areas in two to 35 meters. Occurs solitarily or in small groups. Common at Blanche Bay, near Rabaul, New Britain.

Distribution.—East Indies, Philippines, New Guinea, New Britain, Solomon Islands, and Egum Atoll (Solomon Sea).

Remarks.—A mature female, 39 mm SL, with eggs was collected at Egum Atoll; thus indicative of the small size of the species.

Amblyglyphidodon leucogaster (about 125 mm TL), Augulpelu Reef, Palau Islands in 16 meters.

Amblyglyphidodon curacao (about 100 mm TL), Malakal Island, Palau Islands in six meters.

Amblyglyphidodon leucogaster (about 100 mm TL), Suva, Fiji Islands in 10 meters.

Amblypomacentrus breviceps (about 60 mm TL), Rabaul, New Britain in two meters.

Amblyglyphidodon ternatensis (about 75 mm TL), Madang, New Guinea in seven meters.

Chapter XIV
CHEILOPRION

The genus *Cheiloprion* contains only a single species which is confined to the Indo-Australian Archipelago and adjacent regions. It somewhat resembles certain members of the genus *Pomacentrus* with one important exception. The lips are greatly enlarged and curled back over the snout and chin. This is perhaps an adaptation for feeding on live coral polyps. It is possible that the thick lips represent a form of insulation which affords protection from stinging nematocysts. The fish are invariably found among live coral in shallow water. Several individuals which I observed at Madang, New Guinea, repeatedly "picked" at coral polyps. During the same dive a nest containing approximately 400 eggs was discovered by J. Randall and R. Steene. The eggs were attached on all sides of a dead coral branch, although the outer end of the branch was covered with live polyps. These were attended by a particularly aggressive parent presumed to be a male.

GENUS *CHEILOPRION* WEBER

Cheiloprion Weber 1913: 342 (type species, *Pomacentrus labiatus* Day).

Diagnostic features.—Lips greatly thickened, fimbriate, and curled back over snout; margin of preopercle and suborbital finely serrate; notch between preorbital and suborbital absent; dorsal spines XIII; preorbital and suborbital naked; teeth biserial (at least anteriorly); snout scaled to about level of nostrils or beyond; greatest body depth 1.7 to 1.9 in SL.

Note: Refer to the beginning of Chapter XXII for additional discussion regarding the taxonomy of *Cheiloprion*.

Cheiloprion labiatus (Day)
Big-lip Damsel

Illus. p. 129

Pomacentrus labiatus Day, 1877: 384 (Andaman and Nicobar Islands).

Diagnosis.—Dorsal rays XIII, 13 to 14; anal rays II, 13 to 14; pectoral rays 17. Tubed lateral line scales 18. Gill rakers on first arch 16 to 17. Body depth 1.7 to 1.9 in SL. Color in alcohol generally uniform dark brown, slightly lighter on breast. Maximum size to about 60 mm SL.

Ecology.—Inhabits beds of branching *Acropora* corals in lagoons and passages in 0.5 to three meters. Occurs solitarily or in small groups.

Distribution.—Andaman Islands, Nicobar Islands, East Indies, Philippines, Palau Islands, New Guinea, northern Australia, Solomon Islands, and New Hebrides.

Chapter XV
DISCHISTODUS

The genus *Dischistodus* consists of six species which are restricted to the Indo-Australian Archipelago and immediately adjacent areas. The members of the genus are relatively large herbivorous pomacentrids which inhabit protected lagoon and coastal reefs, frequently in sandy or silty areas. Large adults tend to be wary and hence are difficult to approach at close range. There is no information available on the reproductive habits of these fishes.

GENUS *DISCHISTODUS* GILL

Dischistodus Gill, 1863: 214 (type species, *Pomacentrus fasciatus* Cuvier and Valenciennes).

Diagnostic features.—Margin of preopercle and suborbital with distinct serrae; notch between preorbital and suborbital absent; dorsal spines XIII; preorbital and suborbital naked; teeth biserial anteriorly; snout mostly naked, predorsal scales extending to about front of orbits or slightly beyond; greatest body depth 2.0 to 2.3 in SL.

KEY TO THE SPECIES OF *DISCHISTODUS* FROM THE SOUTH SEAS

1a. Color of body pale, usually with two to three dark patches on back; gill rakers on first arch 33 to 35 (East Indies; Philippines; Palau Islands; Mariana Islands; Melanesia; northern Australia)..*D. perspicillatus*
1b. Color of body not as in 1a; gill rakers on first arch 18 to 32.............................2
2a. Anal region covered with large dark patch; color of body generally pale, except region above line extending from snout to end of spinous dorsal dark brown (East Indies; Philippines; Palau Islands; New Guinea; Solomon Islands; Queensland)...............*D. notopthalmus*
2b. Anal region without large dark patch; color of body not as in 2a.........................3
3a. Anus black; gill rakers 29 to 32 (East Indies; Philippines; N.W. Melanesia; Queensland)....
.... *D. prosopotaenia*
3b. Anus same color as surrounding area; gill rakers 18 to 24................................4
4a. Color of body mostly dark brown with pale spot between lateral-line and base of dorsal fin; gill rakers 22 to 24 (East Indies; Philippines; Palau Islands; New Guinea; Solomon Islands)....
.... *D. chrysopoecilus*
4b. Color of body not as in 4a, sometimes similar but with white spot extending at least 1½ scales below lateral-line; gill rakers 18 to 22...5
5a. Color generally dark brown with one or two whitish bars on upper portion of sides; scales behind superior part of opercle without black dots (Philippines; Solomon Sea; Queensland; Solomon Islands)...*D. pseudochrysopoecilus*
5b. Color not as in 5a; either entirely brown or with three or four pale bars on sides; scales behind superior part of opercle frequently with prominent black dots (East Indies; Philippines; northern Australia)...*D. fasciatus*

A nearly vertical drop-off on the outer slope at Alite Reef, Solomon Islands. The small yellow fish is *Amblyglyphidodon aureus.*

Cheiloprion labiatus (about 60 mm TL), Madang, New Guinea in two meters.

Amblyglyphidodon ternatensis (about 75 mm TL), Koror, Palau Islands in three meters.

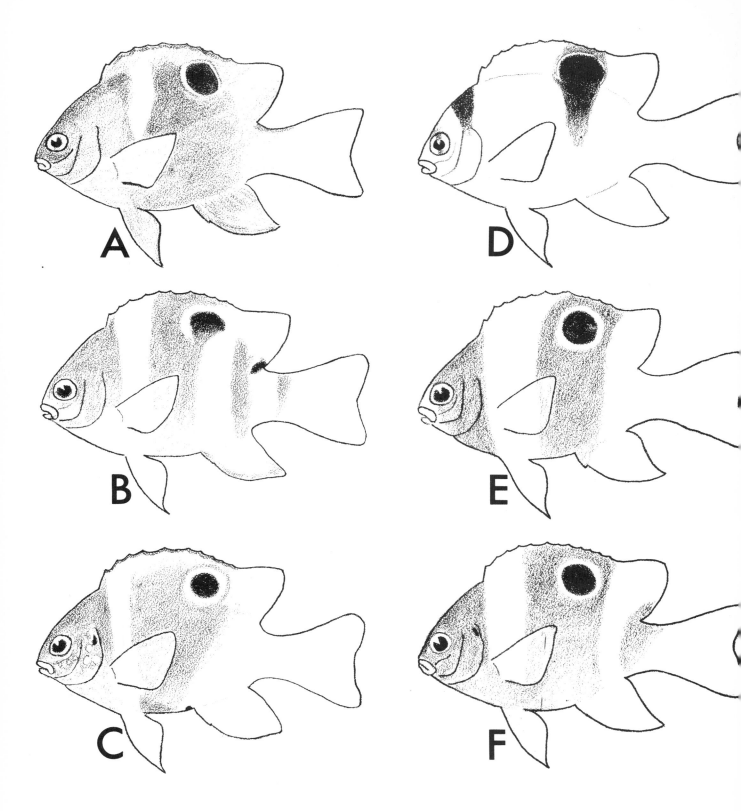

Juvenile color patterns of certain species of *Dischistodus:* (A) *D. chrysopoecilus*; (B) *D. fasciatus*; (C) *D. notopthalmus*; (D) *D. perspicillatus*; (E) *D. prosopotaenia*; (F) *D. pseudochrysopoecilus*.

Dischistodus chrysopoecilus (Schlegel and Müller)
White-spot Damsel

Illus. p. 132

Pomacentrus chrysopoecilus Schlegel and Müller, 1839–44: 21 (Java).

Diagnosis.—Dorsal rays XIII, 14 to 15; anal rays II, 13 to 14; pectoral rays 17. Tubed lateral-line scales 17. Gill rakers on first arch 22 to 24. Body depth 2.1 to 2.2 in SL. Color in alcohol generally dark brown with white spot below middle of dorsal fin, extending to lateral-line; dorsal fin dusky; anal and pelvic fins brown; remainder of fins pale. Maximum size to about 120 mm SL.

Ecology.—Inhabits lagoon and coastal reefs in 1.5 to five meters, usually in silty areas.

Distribution.—East Indies, Philippines, Palau Islands, New Guinea, and Solomon Islands.

Dischistodus fasciatus (Cuvier)
Banded Damsel

Illus. p. 132

Pomacentrus fasciatus Cuvier, 1830: 426 (Java).
Dascyllus fasciatus Macleay, 1878: 361 (Darwin, Australia).
Pomacentrus darwiniensis Whitley, 1928: 297 (Darwin, Australia).

Diagnosis.—Dorsal rays XIII, 13 to 14; anal rays II, 13 to 14; pectoral rays 18. Tubed lateral-line scales 17 to 18. Gill rakers on first arch 18 to 21. Body depth 2.1 to 2.2 in SL. Color in alcohol generally brown, darker dorsally; dark spot at origin of lateral-line and frequently similar spots scattered below lateral-line on anterior portion of body; fins brown except pectorals pale. Maximum size to about 115 mm SL.

Ecology.—Inhabits lagoon and coastal reefs in one to eight meters.

Distribution.—East Indies, Philippines, and northern Australia.

Remarks.—By coincidence, the species Macleay (1878) described as *Dascyllus fasciatus* was synonymous with *Pomacentrus fasciatus* Cuvier. Unaware of this synonymy, Whitley (1928) assigned the substitute name *Pomacentrus darwiniensis* to Macleay's species, thinking that *P. fasciatus* was preoccupied. I have examined the type of *Dascyllus fasciatus* at the Australian Museum. It represents a juvenile *Dischistodus fasciatus*.

Dischistodus notopthalmus (Bleeker)
Black-vent Damsel

Illus. p. 132

Pomacentrus notopthalmus Bleeker, 1853a: 137 (Ternate, Indonesia).

Diagnosis.—Dorsal rays XIII, 13 to 15; anal rays II, 13 to 14; pectoral rays 17. Tubed lateral-line scales 15 to 17. Gill rakers on first arch 21 to 23. Body depth 2.0 to 2.1 in SL. Color in alcohol generally light brown to whitish except region above an imaginary oblique line extending from eye to end of spinous dorsal dark brown; large black patch covering anal region; spinous dorsal mostly dark brown; remainder of fins pale. Maximum size to about 130 mm SL.

Ecology.—Inhabits lagoon and coastal reefs in one to 10 meters, usually around outcrops of live coral.

Distribution.—East Indies, Philippines, Palau Islands, New Guinea, Solomon Islands, and the Great Barrier Reef.

Dischistodus perspicillatus (Cuvier)
White Damsel

Illus. p. 133

Pomacentrus perspicillatus Cuvier, 1830: 417 (no locality given).
Pomacentrus bifasciatus Bleeker, 1854b: 330 (Flores, Indonesia).
Pomacentrus frenatus De Vis, 1885: 874 (Cardwell, Queensland).
Chromis humbug Whitley, 1954: 23 (Green Island, Queensland).

Diagnosis.—Dorsal rays XIII, 14 to 15; anal rays II, 14 to 15; pectoral rays 17 to 18. Tubed lateral-line scales 17 to 18. Gill rakers on first arch 33 to 35. Body depth 2.1 to 2.3 in SL. Color in alcohol generally pale, frequently with two or three black saddles on dorsal portion of body (especially specimens under about 70 mm SL); anus black; fins pale to dusky. Maximum size to about 160 mm SL.

Dischistodus chrysopoecilus (about 100 mm TL), Malakal Island, Palau Islands in two meters.

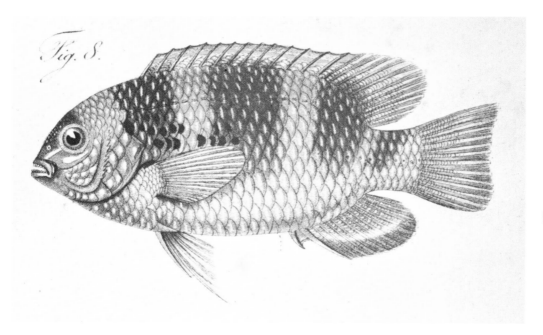

Dischistodus fasciatus, from Bleeker (1877c).

Dischistodus notopthalmus (about 100 mm TL), One Tree Island, Great Barrier Reef in two meters.

Dischistodus perspicillatus (about 100 mm TL), Malakal Island, Palau Islands in two meters.

Dischistodus perspicillatus (about 30 mm TL), Malakal Island, Palau Islands in three meters.

Dischistodus prosopotaenia (about 125 mm TL), Efate, New Hebrides in two meters.

Ecology.—Inhabits lagoon and coastal reefs in sandy areas in one to ten meters. The stomach contents of several specimens consisted mainly of algae and detritus mixed with sand grains.

Distribution.—Andaman and Nicobar Islands, East Indies, China, Philippines, Palau Islands, Mariana Islands, New Guinea, New Britain, Solomon Islands, New Hebrides, and the Great Barrier Reef.

Remarks.—*Pomacentrus bifasciatus* Bleeker represents the juvenile stage of *D. perspicillatus. Chromis humbug* Whitley is also a juvenile which possesses an aberrant dorsal spine count of XII. The 18 mm SL type was examined at the Australian Museum. I also examined the type of *P. frenatus* De Vis at the Queensland Museum. It is clearly synonymous with *D. perspicillatus.*

Dischistodus prosopotaenia (Bleeker)
Honey-head Damsel

Illus. pp. 133, 136

Pomacentrus prosopotaenia Bleeker, 1852a: 67 (Singapore).

Diagnosis.—Dorsal rays XIII, 14 to 16; anal rays II, 14 to 15; pectoral rays 17. Tubed lateral line scales 16 to 17. Gill rakers on first arch 29 to 32. Body depth 2.1 to 2.2 in SL. Color in alcohol generally pale with head brown, and blackish to brownish bar dorsally on sides; dorsal fin pale brown with pale submarginal band; remainder of fins pale to dusky; anus and axil of pectoral fin black. Maximum size to about 150 mm SL.

Ecology.—Inhabits lagoons and coastal reefs in 0.5 to 12 meters, usually in silty areas.

Distribution.—Nicobar Islands, East Indies, Hainan Island, Philippines, New Guinea, New Britain, Solomon Islands, New Hebrides, and the Great Barrier Reef.

Dischistodus pseudochrysopoecilus (Allen and Robertson)
Monarch Damsel

Illus. p. 136

Pomacentrus pseudochrysopoecilus Allen and Robertson, 1974: 160 (D'Entrecasteaux Group).

Diagnosis.—Dorsal rays XIII, 13 to 15; anal rays II, 13 to 14; pectoral rays 17. Tubed lateral-line scales 16 to 18. Gill rakers on first arch 20 to 22. Body depth 2.0 to 2.3 in SL. Color in alcohol generally brown, darker antero-dorsally; single whitish bar or saddle dorsally at middle of body; anus black; dorsal, anal, pelvic, and caudal fins dusky; pectorals pale with small black spot superiorly at pectoral base; juveniles with two white bars on sides and prominent, yellow-ringed, black ocellus between the two bars on the dorsal fin; large adults may be entirely dark brown without distinctive markings. Maximum size to about 140–150 mm SL.

Ecology.—Inhabits lagoon reefs in areas of scattered live coral thickets interspersed with open areas of sand and dead coral in one to five meters.

Distribution.—Philippines, D'Entrecasteux Group, Egum Atoll (Solomon Sea), Great Barrier Reef, and Solomon Islands.

Chapter XVI
EUPOMACENTRUS

The genus *Eupomacentrus* is comprised of less than 20 species which inhabit both Atlantic and Pacific reefs; eight are resident in the "South Seas." These fishes commonly inhabit shallow water where they feed on a variety of benthic algae. They usually occur solitarily or in small groups. The Indo-West Pacific species are mostly drab brown in color with the exception of *E. aureus* and *E. emeryi*. *E. nigricans* and *E. lividus* are among the most pugnacious and territorial of the pomacentrids. They frequently charge human intruders, sometimes taking painful nips, which can be mildly alarming if unexpected.

The eggs of *E. nigricans* are usually laid on a dead coral branch which has previously been cleared of algae by the male. During incubation, which lasts several days, the male is extremely territorial and will chase away fishes many times larger than itself. During these aggressive charges the fish emit a clicking noise which is clearly audible to the human ear. Little information is available regarding the reproductive activities of the other species.

GENUS *EUPOMACENTRUS* BLEEKER

Eupomacentrus Bleeker, 1877b: 40 (type species, *Chaetodon lividus* Bloch and Schneider).

Diagnostic features.—Margin of preopercle and suborbital with distinct serrae; notch between preorbital and suborbital absent; dorsal spines XII to XIII; preorbital mostly naked; suborbital scaled; teeth uniserial, relatively elongate with flattened tips; snout scaled to about level of nostrils; greatest body depth usually 1.9 to 2.2 in SL.

KEY TO THE SPECIES OF *EUPOMACENTRUS* FROM THE SOUTH SEAS

1a. Dorsal spines XII...2
1b. Dorsal spines XIII to XIV...5
2a. Preorbital wide, its least width nearly equal to eye in adults; black spot on upper portion of pectoral base absent; body without distinguishing marks on dorsal fin (except small juveniles) or caudal peduncle (Indo-W. Pacific)............................*E. lividus*
2b. Preorbital relatively narrow, its least width 1/2 to 2/3 eye in adults; small black spot on upper pectoral base; body with either dark spot at base of hindmost dorsal rays, ocellus on hindmost dorsal rays, or black spot on dorsal surface of caudal peduncle..........................3
3a. Color of body uniformly pale (yellowish) with black spot on upper caudal peduncle; gill rakers 31 to 33 (Line Islands; Phoenix Islands; Samoa Islands; Tuamotus; Marquesas Islands). *E. aureus*
3b. Color not as in 3a; mostly brown; gill rakers 22 to 25...4
4a. Soft dorsal fin with pale rimmed ocellus (or half ocellus) at base of hindmost rays; dorsal rays usually 15 (last ray branched near base) (W. Pacific)........................*E. albifasciatus*
4b. Soft dorsal fin with black spot (ocellus in small juveniles only) at base of hindmost rays; dorsal rays usually 16 (last ray branched near base) (Indo-W. Pacific)...............*E. nigricans*
5a. Dorsal spines XIV (South Coral Sea; northern New Zealand)..................*E. gascoynei*
5b. Dorsal spines XIII...6

Dischistodus pseudochrysopoecilus (about 60 mm TL), One Tree Island, Great Barrier Reef in two meters.

Dischistodus pseudochrysopoecilus (about 125 mm TL), One Tree Island, Great Barrier Reef in two meters.

Dischistodus prosopotaenia (about 35 mm TL), Port Moresby, New Guinea in six meters.

Eupomacentrus albifasciatus (about 100 mm TL), Augulpelu Reef, Palau Islands in one meter.

Eupomacentrus apicalis (about 90 mm TL), Heron Island, Great Barrier Reef in two meters (D.R. Robertson photo).

6a. Color of body brown except posterior third abruptly pale (yellowish); isolated dark spot below posterior portion of lateral-line; caudal fin pale; gill rakers 21 to 22 (Tuamotus; Pitcairn Group) . . . .*E. emeryi*

6b. Color of body not as in 6a; usually entirely brown; isolated dark spot below posterior portion of lateral-line absent; caudal fin dark; gill rakers 17 to 20. 7

7a. Tip of upper lobe of caudal fin abruptly pale (red-orange in life); dorsal fin with pale submarginal band about pupil width; spinous dorsal fin with black spot between second and third spines (northern Australia). . . . .*E. apicalis*

7b. Tip of upper lobe of caudal fin not abruptly pale, same color as surrounding part of fin; dorsal fin without black spot between second and third spines of adults (W. Pacific). . . . .*E. fasciolatus*

Eupomacentrus albifasciatus (Schlegel and Müller)
White-bar Gregory

Illus. p. 137

Pomacentrus albifasciatus Schlegel and Müller, 1839–44: 21 (Celebes).
Pomacentrus eclipticus Jordan and Seale, 1906: 282 (Samoa).

Diagnosis.—Dorsal rays XII, 15 to 16; anal rays II, 12 to 14; pectoral rays 18 to 19. Tubed lateral-line scales 18 to 19. Gill rakers on first arch 22 to 23. Body depth 1.9 to 2.1 in SL. Color in alcohol generally dark brown, frequently with broad grey to white bar on sides at level of hindmost dorsal spines; fins dusky to dark brown with half ocellus at base of hindmost soft dorsal rays; pectorals with black spot on upper portion of fin base. Maximum size to about 85 mm SL.

Ecology.—Inhabits areas of mild to moderate surge around rubble and boulders in 0.2 to two meters.

Distribution.—Widespread in the western Pacific from Indonesia as far east as the Tuamotu and Line Islands.

Eupomacentrus apicalis (De Vis)
Australian Gregory

Illus. p. 137

Pomacentrus apicalis De Vis, 1885: 874 (Queensland).

Diagnosis.—Dorsal rays XIII, 15 to 16; anal rays II, 13 to 14; pectoral rays 20. Tubed lateral-line scales 19 to 20. Gill rakers on first arch 17 to 20. Body depth 1.6 to 1.8 in SL. Color in alcohol generally dark brown to blackish; dorsal fin dark brown with black spot on distal portion of membrane between second and third dorsal spines and pale submarginal band about pupil width; anal and pelvic fins blackish; caudal blackish with tip of upper lobe pale; pectorals dusky. Maximum size to about 110 mm SL.

Ecology.—Inhabits dead coral outcrops and occasionally rubble areas in lagoons and the outer edges of individual reefs of the Great Barrier Reef complex in 1.5 to five meters.

Distribution.—Queensland and Northern Territory, Australia.

Eupomacentrus aureus (Fowler)
Golden Gregory

Illus. p. 140

Pomacentrus aureus Fowler, 1927: 22 (Howland Island).

Diagnosis.—Dorsal rays XII, 15 to 16; anal rays II, 12 to 14; pectoral rays 20. Tubed lateral-line scales 19 to 20. Gill rakers on first arch 31 to 33. Body depth 2.1 to 2.2 in SL. Color in alcohol generally yellowish-tan with large black spot on dorsal surface of caudal peduncle and small black spot at upper pectoral base; anus black; fins pale. Maximum size to about 85–90 mm SL.

Ecology.—Usually inhabits shallow reef-flat areas in one to two meters or less.

Distribution.—Gilbert, Line, Phoenix, Samoa, Tuamotu and Marquesas Islands.

Eupomacentrus emeryi Allen and Randall
Emery's Gregory

Illus. p. 140

Eupomacentrus emeryi Allen and Randall, 1974: 37 (Pitcairn Island).

Diagnosis.—Dorsal rays XIII, 15 to 17; anal rays II, 13 to 14; pectoral rays 18 to 20. Tubed lateral-line scales 20. Gill rakers on first arch 21 to 22. Body depth 1.9 to 2.0 in SL. Color in alcohol generally brown anteriorly with darker scale margins, abruptly pale on posterior third of body and caudal fin; pale area with dark spot directly below 15th-16th tubed lateral-line scales; spinous dorsal fin brown basally and pale distally; remainder of fins pale; pectorals with small dark spot on upper portion of fin base. Maximum size to about 75 mm SL.

Ecology.—Generally inhabits rocky outer reef areas in six to 18 meters, but collected by J. Randall in only one meter depth at Ducie Atoll. Occurs solitarily or in small groups.

Distribution.—Duke of Gloucester Group (Tuamotu Islands) and the Pitcairn Group.

Eupomacentrus fasciolatus (Ogilby)
Pacific Gregory

Illus. p. 140

Pomacentrus fasciolatus Ogilby, 1889: 16 (Lord Howe Island).
Eupomacentrus marginatus Jenkins, 1901: 391 (Hawaiian Islands).
Pomacentrus jenkinsi Jordan and Evermann, 1903: 189 (Hawaiian Islands).
Eupomacentrus paschalis Whitley, 1929: 225 (Easter Island).
Pomacentrus atrilabiatus Fowler, 1946: 146 (Ryukyu Islands).
Pseudopomacentrus navalis Whitley, 1964: 174 (Kenn Reef, Coral Sea).

Diagnosis.—Dorsal rays XIII, 16 to 17; anal rays II, 13 to 14; pectoral rays 20. Tubed lateral-line scales 20. Gill rakers on first arch 18 to 20. Body depth 1.9 to 2.0 in SL. Color in alcohol generally dark brown, slightly paler on breast; fins dark brown to blackish except pectorals pale with black axil and small dark spot on upper portion of fin base. Maximum size to about 90 mm SL.

Ecology.—Very common throughout most of its range, usually in shallow areas exhibiting mild to moderate surge conditions at depths between 0.5 and three meters. However, at Lord Howe and Easter Islands the species is more or less ubiquitous, occurring in rocky habitats from shallow surge pools down to at least 30 meters.

Distribution.—Widespread in the West Pacific as far east as the Hawaiian Islands and Easter Island.

Remarks.—This species has previously been referred to as *Pomacentrus jenkinsi* by many authors. However, *P. fasciolatus* Ogilby is an earlier name. I have examined the type specimens of *fasciolatus* at the Australian Museum and have also observed and collected numerous individuals at Lord Howe Island, the type locality. This material is essentially identical with specimens from other Pacific localities. The live coloration is variable, ranging from very pale brown or whitish to nearly black.

Eupomacentrus gascoynei (Whitley)
Coral Sea Gregory

Illus. p. 141

Pseudopomacentrus gascoynei Whitley, 1964: 173 (Kenn Reef, Coral Sea).

Diagnosis.—Dorsal rays XIV, 15 to 16; anal rays II, 13 to 14; pectoral rays 20 to 21. Tubed lateral-line scales 19 to 20. Gill rakers on first arch 17 to 19. Body depth 1.9 to 2.0 in SL. Color in alcohol generally brown, scale edges darker; fins brown except pelvics and pectorals pale; pectorals with dark spot on upper portion of fin base and axil. Maximum size to about 110 mm SL.

Ecology.—Inhabits outer reefs, just below the surge zone in two to five meters at the Capricorn Group, Great Barrier Reef. Found in all rocky habitats down to 30 meters at Lord Howe Island.

Distribution.—Capricorn Group, Kenn Reef, New Caledonia, Lord Howe Island, and northern New Zealand (Doak, 1972; photo of unidentified pomacentrid on plate 25).

Eupomacentrus aureus (72 mm SL), Fanning Island, Line Islands (J. Randall photo).

Eupomacentrus fasciolatus (about 100 mm TL), Lord Howe Island in three meters.

Eupomacentrus emeryi (46 mm SL), Pitcairn Island (J. Randall photo).

Eupomacentrus lividus (about 150 mm TL), Madang, New Guinea in three meters.

Eupomacentrus gascoynei (about 100 mm TL), One Tree Island, Great Barrier Reef in four meters.

Eupomacentrus lividus (Bloch and Schneider)
Blunt-snout Gregory

Illus. p. 141

Chaetodon lividus Bloch and Schneider, 1801: 235 (Pacific Ocean).

Diagnosis.—Dorsal rays XII, 15 to 16; anal rays II, 12 to 14; pectoral rays 18. Tubed lateral-line scales 18. Gill rakers on first arch 26 to 28. Body depth 2.0 to 2.2 in SL. Color in alcohol generally dark brown; juveniles lighter with large dark blotch at base of hindmost dorsal rays; fins dark brown except pectorals pale to dusky. Maximum size to about 110 mm SL.

Ecology.—Inhabits lagoons and coastal reefs in one to five meters. Frequently seen together with *E. nigricans* or in areas of dead staghorn coral which support a coat of filamentous algae, which these fishes apparently eat.

Distribution.—Widespread in the tropical Indo-West Pacific as far east as the Society and Line Islands.

Eupomacentrus nigricans (Lacépède)
Dusky Gregory

Illus. p. 144

Holocentrus nigricans Lacépède, 1803: 332 (no locality given).

Diagnosis.—Dorsal rays XII, 16 to 17; anal rays II, 13 to 14; pectoral rays 18 to 19. Tubed lateral-line scales 18 to 19. Gill rakers on first arch 22 to 25. Body depth 1.9 to 2.0 in SL. Color in alcohol generally tan to dark brown, usually with blackish spot about size of eye at base of hindmost soft dorsal rays; fins tan to dark brown except pectorals may be dusky with black spot on upper portion of fin base. Maximum size to about 110 mm SL.

Ecology.—Inhabits lagoons and coastal reefs in one to 12 meters. Frequently found among the branches of staghorn *(Acropora)* coral. The stomachs of several specimens collected at Palau contained algae mixed with sand grains, gastropod fragments, sponge spicules, and copepods.

Distribution.—Widespread in the tropical Indo-West Pacific as far east as the Tuamotu, Marquesas and Line Islands.

Chapter XVII
GLYPHIDODONTOPS

The genus *Glyphidodontops* includes approximately 25 species which are confined to the Indo-West Pacific; 19 are known from the "South Seas." The members of the genus are generally small, usually under 60–70 mm SL; several are sexually mature below 40 mm. The group includes some of the most brilliantly colored pomacentrids. About half of the species in the West Pacific are either bright blue or yellow, or a combination of these two colors. The genus is further distinguished by a relatively elongate body shape, the depth of which usually exceeds 2.0 in the standard length and frequently is greater than 2.3. In addition, with only a few exceptions, the members of the genus possess biserial teeth at the front of the jaws.

These fishes are found in a variety of habitats. Several species, which are primarily herbivorous, are restricted to shallow wave swept areas; these include *G. glaucus*, *G. leucopomus*, *G. niger*, and *G. unimaculatus*. Others such as *G. caeruleolineatus* and *G. starcki* are restricted to the outer reef, usually below 25 meters depth. The outer reef forms also eat algae, but a significant portion of the diet is comprised of zooplankton.

The nests of *G. biocellatus* and *G. glaucus* are often encountered in the field. The large batch of eggs, usually numbering well over 1,000, is attached to the underside of a rock or sometimes inside the valves of a dead *Tridacna* clam. The male picks away the algal growth from the substratum prior to spawning and in some cases may excavate a hollow under rocks situated in sandy locations. Courtship displays which consist of rapid chasing and stationary shaking movements with the fins erected precede the actual spawning. The male repeatedly escorts the female to the nest site for egg laying over a period of about one to two hours and then aggressively guards the nest during incubation, which lasts about four to five days. The fry are pelagic for an undetermined period after hatching.

GENUS *GLYPHIDODONTOPS* BLEEKER

Glyphidodontops Bleeker, 1877b: 128 (type species, *Glyphisodon azureus* Cuvier=*G. cyaneus* Quoy and Gaimard).

Diagnostic features.—Margin of preopercle and suborbital entire; notch between preorbital and suborbital absent; dorsal spines XIII or XIV; pectoral rays usually 14 to 19; gill rakers usually 16 to 33; tubed lateral-line scales usually 12 to 19; suborbital scaled or naked; teeth usually biserial (several species with uniserial teeth), at least anteriorly; snout scaled either to about front of orbits or about level of nostrils; greatest body depth 1.9 to 3.0 (usually 2.1 to 2.7) in SL.

Eupomacentrus.nigricans (about 125 mm TL), Great Barrier Reef, off Cairns, Queensland in five meters.

Glyphidodontops azurepunctatus (about 75 mm TL), Malakal Island, Palau Islands in five meters.

Glyphidodontops azurepunctatus (about 35 mm TL), Madang, New Guinea in two meters.

Glyphidodontops azurepunctatus (about 70 mm TL), Madang, New Guinea in three meters.

KEY TO THE SPECIES OF *GLYPHIDODONTOPS* FROM THE SOUTH SEAS

1a. Dorsal rays XIV; teeth uniserial (New Guinea; Solomon Islands).........*G. caeruleolineatus*

1b. Dorsal rays XIII; teeth uniserial or biserial...2

2a. Color of body pale, each scale with about two to four dark dots (blue in life); gillrakers 30 to 34 (East Indies; Philippines; Palau Islands; New Guinea)........... *G. azurepunctatus*

2b. Color not as in 2a; gill rakers 17 to 26......................................3

3a. Color of head and body pale with three encircling bars (New Caledonia; Fiji Islands; Samoa Islands)...*G. tricinctus*

3b. Color not as in 3a...4

4a. Dorsal fin with prominent black spot (not an ocellus), about size of eye, at base of hindmost dorsal spines; anus black; dorsal rays 10 to 12; pectoral rays 15 to 16; tubed lateral-line scales 14 to 16...5

4b. Dorsal fin without prominent black spot at base of hindmost dorsal spines, although ocellus sometimes present; anus black or same color as surrounding area; dorsal rays 11 to 16; pectoral rays 15 to 19; tubed lateral-line scales 12 to 19.............................6

5a. Head and pelvic fins pale, caudal peduncle and portion of body below soft dorsal fin brown (East Indies; Melanesia; Great Barrier Reef)...............................*G. talboti*

5b. Head and pelvic fins brown, caudal peduncle and portion of body below soft dorsal fin yellowish (Marshall and Caroline Islands)...............................*G. traceyi*

6a. Anus black, sharply contrasting with surrounding area...............................7

Anus about same color as surrounding area.......................................8

7a. Dorsal rays 10 to 11; pectoral rays 15; tubed lateral-line scales 12 to 14; color of body mostly pale (whitish in life) with dusky area encompassing last eight dorsal spines and extending to upper corner of opercle (Melanesia, except Fiji Islands; Great Barrier Reef)........*G. rollandi*

7b. Dorsal rays 12 to 13; pectoral rays 18; tubed lateral-line scales 17 to 19; color of body light brown to grey, whitish ventrally (Indo-W. Pacific)...............................*G. glaucus*

8a. Body mostly pale (whitish to yellow in life)......................................9

8b. Body mostly brown to blackish or dark only on dorsal or posterior half................11

9a. Color of body generally pale with blue to brown stripe extending from eye to base of middle soft dorsal rays, large black oblong spot frequently present at base of soft dorsal; black spot or saddle on dorsal edge of caudal peduncle; suborbital naked (W. Pacific)........*G. leucopomus*

9b. Color of body not as in 9a; black spot on dorsal edge of caudal peduncle usually absent; suborbital scaly...10

10a. Color generally brown on anterodorsal portion of head and body, remainder tan to yellowish; small dark spot at origin of lateral-line; teeth biserial anteriorly; gill rakers 17 to 19 (Ryukyu Islands; East Indies; Philippines; Palau Islands; Melanesia, except Fiji Islands; Great Barrier Reef)...*G. rex*

10b. Color uniformly pale with narrow black margin on dorsal and anal fins; small dark spot at origin of lateral-line absent; teeth uniserial; gill rakers 21 to 23 (Cook Islands; Austral Islands; Rapa; Gambier Islands; Pitcairn Group)...............................*G. galbus*

11a. Dorsal rays 10 to 11; anal rays 11 to 12; pectoral rays 14 to 15; tubed lateral-line scales 12 to 14 (Ryukyu Islands; East Indies; Philippines; N.W. Melanesia)..............*G. hemicyaneus*

11b. Dorsal rays 12 to 15; anal rays 12 to 16; pectoral rays 16 to 19; tubed lateral-line scales 15 to 19...12

12a. Pelvic and anal fins pale...13

12b. Pelvic and anal fins dark..14

13a. Dorsal rays 12 to 13; gill rakers usually 17 to 19; all fins not usually pale (except Fiji Islands and Coral Sea specimens); predorsal region dark; black spot frequently present at base of hindmost dorsal rays (W. Micronesia; Ryukyu Islands; East Indies; Philippines; Melanesia; Great Barrier Reef; Samoa Islands)..*G. cyaneus*

13b. Dorsal rays 14 to 15; gill rakers usually 20 to 22; all fins pale; predorsal region pale; black spot at base of hindmost dorsal rays absent (S.E. New Guinea; Solomon Islands; eastern Australia)..*G. flavipinnis*

14a. Color of predorsal region, dorsal fin, and caudal fin pale (yellow in life); teeth uniserial (Taiwan; Coral Sea)..*G. starcki*

14b. Color not as in 14a; teeth uniserial or biserial anteriorly.............................15

15a. Body depth 2.0 to 2.1 in SL; prominent black spot covering entire pectoral base (S.E. New Guinea; D'Entrecasteaux Islands)...*G. niger*

15b. Body depth 2.2 to 3.0 in SL; prominent black spot covering entire pectoral base absent.......16

16a. Caudal fin pale to slightly dusky; head with two dark lines from snout tip to front of orbit; gill rakers usually 17 to 19; dorsal rays 12 to 13.............................*G. cyaneus*

16b. Caudal fin dusky or entirely dark brown; head without dark lines on snout; gill rakers 19 to 25; dorsal rays 12 to 15..17

17a. Suborbital naked; body or fins usually with distinctive marking (pale bar, dark spot or ocellus); lobes of dorsal, anal, and caudal fins rounded.......................................18

17b. Suborbital scaly; body and fins without distinctive marking; lobes of dorsal, anal, and caudal fins pointed or filamentous..20

18a. Opercle with a pale bar or spot; soft dorsal fin and upper edge of caudal peduncle without dark spot or ocellus; area behind pectorals pale; pale bar frequently present at middle of sides and on caudal peduncle (W. Pacific)........................*G. leucopomus ("amabilis* variety")

18b. Opercle plain brownish; soft dorsal fin and/or upper edge of caudal peduncle frequently with dark spot or ocellus; pale bar on sides present or absent, caudal peduncle plain brownish.........19

19a. Body generally dark, frequently with pale bar on sides below middle of spinous dorsal; back with large black ocellus (in most specimens except large adults) at base of hindmost dorsal spines; small black spot on dorsal edge of caudal peduncle immediately behind dorsal fin; specimens below 40 mm frequently with narrow pale blue line from snout, across top of eye, along dorsal base to ocellus; pectoral rays usually 18; tubed lateral-line scales usually 16 to 17 (Indo-W. Pacific)..*G. biocellatus*

19b. Body generally dark or head and anterior portion of body light brown to tan and posterior half dark brown, usually without pale bar on sides; back without large ocellus at base of hindmost dorsal spines; small black spot present at base of hindmost dorsal rays, not on caudal peduncle; pectoral rays usually 19; tubed lateral-line scales usually 18 (East Indies; Philippines; Melanesia; Great Barrier Reef).......................................*G. unimaculatus*

20a. Teeth at front of jaws uniserial (New South Wales; Lord Howe Island; New Caledonia)......
....*G. notialis*

20b. Teeth at front of jaws biserial (Easter Island)................................*G. rapanui*

Glyphidodontops biocellatus (about 75 mm TL), One Tree Island, Great Barrier Reef in two meters.

Glyphidodontops caeruleolineatus (about 60 mm TL), Madang, New Guinea in 35 meters.

Glyphidodontops cyaneus (female, about 75 mm TL), Uvea, Loyalty Islands in three meters.

Glyphidodontops cyaneus (female, about 75 mm TL), Suva, Fiji Islands in three meters.

Glyphidodontops azurepunctatus (Fowler and Bean)
Blue-spot Demoiselle

Illus. pp. 144, 145

Abudefduf azurepunctatus Fowler and Bean, 1928: 149 (Philippines).
Chrysiptera melanomaculata Aoyagi, 1941: 180 (Palau Islands).

Diagnosis.—Dorsal rays XIII, 11 to 12; anal rays II, 12 to 13; pectoral rays 15. Tubed lateral-line scales 14 to 15. Gill rakers on first arch 30 to 34. Body depth 1.9 to 2.0 in SL. Color in alcohol generally pale greenish-brown to yellowish with two to four brown or reddish spots (blue in life) on each scale; breast and abdomen yellowish; anus black; fins pale. Maximum size to about 65 mm SL.

Ecology.—Inhabits sheltered lagoon and inshore reef environments among live coral in one to 16 meters. Abundant among the rock-islands of the southern Palau Group and at Kranket Lagoon, near Madang, New Guinea. Occurs in small to large groups. Feeds on plankton up to about one meter above the substratum.

Distribution.—Danawan and Si Anil Islands (off Borneo), Philippines, Palau Islands, and New Guinea.

Glyphidodontops biocellatus (Quoy and Gaimard)
Two-spot Demoiselle

Illus. p. 148

Glyphisodon biocellatus Quoy and Gaimard, 1824: 389 (Guam).
Glyphisodon zonatus Cuvier, 1830: 483 (New Guinea and Vanicolo).

Diagnosis.—Dorsal rays XIII, 12 to 14; anal rays II, 13 to 14; pectoral rays 17 to 19. Tubed lateral-line scales 17. Gill rakers on first arch 23 to 25. Body depth 2.2 to 2.5 in SL. Color in alcohol generally dark brown with whitish bar on sides; frequently with small black spot on upper caudal peduncle, immediately behind soft dorsal; fins dark brown to dusky; see remarks section below for additional comments on coloration. Maximum size to about 75–80 mm SL.

Ecology.—Inhabits lagoons, usually adjacent to shore among rubble or around rocky outcrops situated in sandy areas at depths between 0.5 and five meters. Occurs solitarily or in small groups. Feeds chiefly on benthic algae.

Distribution.—Widespread in the tropical Indo-W. Pacific to the Samoa, Marshall, and Gilbert Islands.

Remarks.—This species is very similar to *G. unimaculatus*. Both are generally drab brown or greyish in life and frequently exhibit a pale bar on the sides, although it is often lacking in *G. unimaculatus*. A detailed comparison of these species was made at One Tree Island, Great Barrier Reef in order to properly assess their taxonic status. Significant differences with regards to pectoral ray and tubed lateral-line scale counts were detected. Of 15 *G. biocellatus* examined, 13 possessed 18 pectoral rays and two had 19. A similar number of *G. unimaculatus* yielded 11 with 19 rays and four with 18. The following counts were recorded·for the lateral-line: *G. biocellatus*—17 tubed scales (11), 16 (3) and 18 (1); *G. unimaculatus*—18 tubed scales (10), 16 (3), and 17 (2). In addition, significant differences in habitat and coloration were observed. *G. unimaculatus* was usually seen on the outer reef on the leeward side of One Tree Reef, in the vicinity of the algal ridge or on the adjacent reef flat. The bottom consisted of coarse rubble or sand with beach-rock outcrops. *G. biocellatus* was observed only in the lagoon, generally near shore. *G. unimaculatus* was more or less uniformly grey-brown with a very faint bar on the sides, not nearly as strongly contrasted as the relatively wide (four to six scales) pale bar of *G. biocellatus*. There was usually a small black spot at the base of the last soft dorsal rays which extended onto the basal portion of the fin rays, followed by a pearly iridescent spot of about equal size. It was not situated on the peduncle as in *G. biocellatus*. The juveniles of these species were even more clearly separable. Specimens of *G. biocellatus* between about 25 and 40 mm SL possess a strongly contrasted white bar and an ocellus at the base of the hindmost dorsal spines. By contrast, *G. unimaculatus* of similar size were uniformly brown with a prominent black spot (not a pale-rimmed ocellus) at the base of the hindmost soft dorsal rays.

Glyphidodontops caeruleolineatus (Allen)
Blue-line Demoiselle

Illus. p. 148

Abudefduf caeruleolineatus Allen, 1973a: 35 (Madang, New Guinea).

Diagnosis.—Dorsal rays XIV, 11 to 13; anal rays II, 13 to 14; pectoral rays 15 to 16. Tubed lateral-line scales 12 to 15. Gill rakers on first arch 20 to 23. Body depth 2.3 to 2.7 in SL. Color in alcohol generally pale yellow with black edged bluish stripe extending from tip of snout to base of anteriormost soft dorsal rays; fins pale; pectorals with small black spot on upper portion of fin base. Maximum size to about 40 mm SL.

Ecology.—Inhabits outer reef slopes among rubble or small rocky outcrops which are usually situated in sand channels at depths between 30 and 62 meters. Occurs solitarily or in small groups. Feeds primarily on copepods.

Distribution.—New Guinea, D'Entrecasteaux Group, Osprey Reef, Solomon, Fiji and Samoa Islands.

Glyphidodontops cyaneus (Quoy and Gaimard)
Blue Devil

Illus. pp. 149, 152

Glyphisodon cyaneus Quoy and Gaimard, 1825: 392 (no locality given).
Glyphisodon uniocellatus Quoy and Gaimard, 1825: 393 (Coupang; Marianas Islands).
Glyphisodon azureus Cuvier, 1830: 479 (Timor and Friendly Islands).
Glyphidodon assimilis Günther, 1862: 52 (Borneo, Philippines, Indian Seas).
Abudefduf taupou Jordan and Seale, 1905: 288 (Samoa Islands).
Abudefduf turchesius Jordan and Seale, 1907: 28 (Philippines).
Abudefduf sapphirus Jordan and Richardson, 1908: 264 (Philippines).
Glyphisodon hedleyi Whitley, 1927: 20 (Great Barrier Reef).
Abudefduf elizabethae Fowler, 1959: 601 (Fiji Islands).

Diagnosis.—Dorsal rays XIII, 12 to 13; anal rays II, 13 to 14; pectoral rays 16 to 17. Tubed lateral-line scales 16 to 17. Gill rakers on first arch 17 to 19. Body depth 2.2 to 2.4 in SL. Color in alcohol either entirely brown (paler ventrally) with pale to dusky fins or dark brown on dorsal 1/2 to 2/3 of body and ventral region yellowish with fins and caudal peduncle pale (dorsal fin frequently dusky on these individuals); small black spot at base of hindmost dorsal rays frequently present on females. Maximum size to about 60 mm SL.

Ecology.—Inhabits lagoons and sheltered reef flats in 0.3 to ten meters. Occurs solitarily or in small groups. Feeds on algae, pelagic tunicates, and planktonic crustacea.

Distribution.—Mariana and Caroline Islands, Ryukyu Islands, Philippines, East Indies, New Guinea, Great Barrier Reef, New Britain, Solomon Islands, New Hebrides, Loyalty Islands, New Caledonia, Fiji and Samoa Islands.

Remarks.—The color pattern, which is variable according to sex and geographic locality, has created a good deal of confusion regarding the proper identity of this species, resulting in a long list of synonyms. *G. cyaneus* is one of the few pomacentrids which exhibits a marked sexual dichromatism. Mature males are characterized by bright orange tails and more yellow-orange color on the ventral portion of the body than is exhibited by the females. In addition, they generally lack the black spot at the base of the hindmost dorsal rays which is usually present on the females. The caudal fin of the female is translucent or slightly dusky.

Glyphidodontops flavipinnis (Allen and Robertson)
Yellow-fin Demoiselle

Illus. pp. 152, 153

Abudefduf flavipinnis Allen and Robertson, 1974: 157 (Great Barrier Reef).

Diagnosis.—Dorsal rays XIII, 14 to 15; anal rays II, 13 to 14; pectoral rays 17 to 18. Tubed lateral-line scales 15 to 18. Gill rakers on first arch 20 to 22. Body depth 2.2 to 2.6 in SL. Color in alcohol generally brownish except pale yellowish ventrally and on caudal peduncle; dorsal fin and adjacent portion of back pale yellow (yellow region extending to about rear of orbits); remainder of fins pale; small black spot on upper portion of pectoral base and axil. Maximum size to about 60 mm SL.

Glyphidodontops cyaneus (male, about 85 mm TL), Malakal Island, Palau Islands in one meter.

Glyphidodontops flavipinnis (about 40 mm TL), One Tree Island, Great Barrier Reef in two meters.

Glyphidodontops galbus (55 mm SL), Rapa (J. Randall photo).

Glyphidodontops flavipinnis (about 40 mm TL), One Tree Island, Great Barrier Reef in two meters.

Ecology.—Inhabits lagoons, passages, and outer reef slopes in three to 38 meters, usually among rubble or around dead coral outcrops which are frequently situated in sandy areas. Occurs solitarily or in small groups.

Distribution.—Samarai Island (off S.E. tip of New Guinea), Osprey Reef (Coral Sea), eastern Australia as far south as the Sydney area, and the Solomon Islands.

Glyphidodontops galbus Allen and Randall
Canary Demoiselle

Illus. p. 153

Glyphidodontops galbus Allen and Randall, 1974: 40 (Rapa).

Diagnosis.—Dorsal rays XIII, 13 to 15; anal rays II, 14 to 16; pectoral rays 17 to 18. Tubed lateral-line scales 17 to 18. Gill rakers on first arch 21 to 23. Body depth 2.4 to 3.0 in SL. Color in alcohol generally tan to pale yellow, dusky on dorsal surface of head; fins pale, dorsal and anal with narrow black margin. Maximum size to about 70 mm SL.

Ecology.—Inhabits outer reef slopes and passage areas in one to 30 meters. Forms large aggregations which feed on plankton.

Distribution.—Cook and Austral Islands, Rapa, Gambier, and Pitcairn Group.

Glyphidodontops glaucus (Cuvier)
Grey Demoiselle

Illus. p. 156

Glyphisodon glaucus Cuvier, 1830: 475 (Guam).
Glyphidodon pallidus De Vis, 1883: 452 (Bank's Group).
Chrysiptera hollisi Fowler, 1946: 155 (Ryukyu Islands).

Diagnosis.—Dorsal rays XIII, 12 to 13; anal rays II, 12 to 13; pectoral rays 18. Tubed lateral-line scales 17 to 19. Gill rakers on first arch 21 to 24. Body depth 2.2 to 2.3 in SL. Color in alcohol generally light brown to grey, whitish ventrally; anus black; fins pale to dusky; juveniles under about 25–30 mm SL with ocellus on dorsal fin. Maximum size to about 75–80 mm SL.

Ecology.—Inhabits reef flat areas exposed to mild or moderate surge in 0.5 to two meters. Occurs solitarily or in small groups. Feeds mainly on benthic algae.

Distribution.—Widespread in the tropical Indo-West Pacific to the Pitcairn Group and Line Islands.

Remarks.—I have examined the type of *Chrysiptera hollisi*, which represents the juvenile stage of *G. glaucus*.

Glyphidodontops hemicyaneus (Weber)
Azure Demoiselle

Illus. p. 157

Abudefduf hemicyaneus Weber, 1913: 351 (Tual, Kei, Indonesia).
Abudefduf parasema Fowler, 1918: 56 (Philippines).

Diagnosis.—Dorsal rays XIII, 10 to 12; anal rays II, 11 to 12; pectoral rays 14 to 15. Tubed lateral-line scales 12 to 14. Gill rakers on first arch 21 to 24. Body depth 1.9 to 2.2 in SL. Color in alcohol variable, specimens from Madang, New Guinea generally dark brown to blackish except caudal fin and peduncle, pelvic fins, and posterior portion of soft dorsal and anal fins pale (yellowish); pectoral fins translucent; specimens from the eastern tip of New Guinea mainly brown to dark brown (paler ventrally) with caudal and posterior portion of dorsal and anal fins pale to dusky.

Ecology.—Inhabits lagoons and near shore reefs in one to 16 meters, usually in the vicinity of branching corals. Occurs solitarily or in small groups. Feeds on plankton about 0.3 to 0.5 meters above the substratum.

Distribution.—Ryukyu Islands, East Indies, Philippines, New Guinea, and Solomon Islands.

Remarks.—Live individuals from the eastern tip of New Guinea and D'Entrecasteaux Islands are entirely blue with the caudal and posterior portions of the soft dorsal and anal fins translucent. They lack the bright yellow coloration found in Madang specimens (see illustration). Live individuals from the Solomon Islands are similar to the eastern New Guinea form except there is a yellowish suffusion on the pelvic, anal, and caudal fins. Individuals from the Philippines are mostly blue with a bright yellow caudal fin and peduncle, while examples from the Moluccas are blue above with the ventral 1/2 to 1/3 of the body, anal fin, caudal fin and peduncle yellow.

Glyphidodontops leucopomus (Lesson)
Surge Demoiselle

Illus. pp. 156, 160

Glyphisodon leucopomus Lesson, 1830: 189 (Caroline Islands).
Glyphisodon albofasciatus Hombron and Jacquinot, 1853: 49 (off Borneo).
Glyphidodon amabilis De Vis, 1884: 452 (South Seas).

Diagnosis.—Dorsal rays XIII, 12 to 13; anal rays II, 12 to 13; pectoral rays 18 to 19. Tubed lateral-line scales 18 to 19. Gill rakers on first arch 19 to 21. Body depth 2.3 to 2.5 in SL. Color in alcohol variable: *leucopomus* phase—generally pale with blue to brown stripes dorsally from eye to base of middle soft dorsal rays; blackish saddle on upper caudal peduncle frequently present; dorsal fin pale with black spot at base of hindmost spines, remainder of fins pale; *amabilis* or *albofasciatus* phase—generally dark brown with pale bars on opercle, middle of sides, and caudal peduncle (specimens from certain areas without two hindmost bars); fins brown. Maximum size to about 55–60 mm SL.

Ecology.—Inhabits areas exposed to mild or moderate surge in 0.2 to two meters, frequently in the vicinity of the reef crest or algal ridge. Occurs solitarily or in small groups. Feeds mostly on algae, although some crustacea are taken.

Distribution.—Widespread in the East Indies and western Pacific to the Society, Marquesas, Marshall, and Gilbert Islands.

Remarks.—The color pattern variation in this species was recently discussed by the author (Allen, in press). The *leucopomus* variety is often found under less severe surge conditions on either side of the reef crest, whereas the *amabilis* form frequents the wave swept algal ridge. Individuals exhibiting an intermediate color pattern are occasionally encountered in the transitional zone between these two habitats.

Glyphidodontops niger Allen
Black Demoiselle

Illus. p. 161

Glyphidodontops niger Allen, 1975: 89 (Cape Nelson, New Guinea).

Diagnosis.—Dorsal rays XIII, 12 to 13; anal rays II, 13; pectoral rays 17. Tubed lateral-line scales 17. Gill rakers on first arch 20 to 21. Body depth 2.0 to 2.1 in SL. Color in alcohol generally dark brown, breast paler; median fins dark brown except posterior portion of soft dorsal and caudal fins pale; pelvics brown; pectorals pale with black spot covering base and axil. Maximum size to about 50 mm SL.

Ecology.—Inhabits areas exposed to mild surge in 0.5 to two meters. Feeds primarily on algae.
Distribution.—S.E. New Guinea and the D'Entrecasteaux Islands.

Glyphidodontops notialis Allen
Southern Demoiselle

Illus. p. 161

Glyphidodontops notialis Allen, 1975: 91 (Lord Howe Island).

Diagnosis.—Dorsal rays XIII, 14 to 15; anal rays II, 15 to 16; pectoral rays 16 to 18. Tubed lateral-line scales 16 to 18. Gill rakers on first arch 20 to 23. Body depth 2.3 to 2.5 in SL. Color in alcohol generally dark brown with slightly lighter scale centers, breast and abdomen tannish, median fins dark brown to blackish, pelvic fins dusky, pectorals pale with black wedge-shaped spot covering upper portion of fin base. Maximum size to about 65 mm SL.

Ecology.—Inhabits outer rocky reefs at Lord Howe Island and coraliferous outer reef slopes at New Caledonia in seven to 45 meters. At Lord Howe Island it is one of the most common damselfishes seen outside the lagoon. Feeds mainly on algae and zooplankton.

Glyphidodontops glaucus (about 100 mm TL), One Tree Island, Great Barrier Reef in one meter.

Glyphidodontops leucopomus (about 50 mm TL), Augulpelu Reef, Palau Islands in two meters.

Glyphidodontops hemicyaneus (about 55 mm TL), Madang, New Guinea in three meters.

Distribution.—Previously reported from Lord Howe Island and New Caledonia. In addition, specimens have recently been collected near Sydney, Australia by R. Kuiter.

Glyphidodontops rapanui (Greenfield and Hensley)
Easter Demoiselle

Illus. p. 164

Abudefduf rapanui Greenfield and Hensley, 1970: 693 (Easter Island).

Diagnosis.—Dorsal rays XIII, 13 to 15; anal rays II, 14 to 16; pectoral rays 16 to 17. Tubed lateral-line scales 17 to 19. Gill rakers on first arch 21 to 22. Body depth 2.3 to 3.0 in SL. Color in alcohol generally dark brown, frequently light brown ventrally; caudal peduncle tan to whitish; dorsal and anal fins dark brown to black except posterior portions pale; caudal and pectoral fins pale; pelvics dark brown to black. Maximum size to about 55 mm SL.

Ecology.—Ubiquitous at Easter Island. Juveniles occurring in surge pools, and both adults and juveniles in three to 38 meters in rocky areas. Occurs solitarily or in aggregations of about 10 to 30 individuals, frequently in the vicinity of *Porites* coral.

Distribution.—Endemic to Easter Island.

Glyphidodontops rex (Snyder)
King Demoiselle

Illus. p. 164

Abudefduf rex Snyder, 1909: 601 (Okinawa).
Glyphidodontops cyaneus (non Quoy and Gaimard) Bleeker, 1877c: pl. 409, fig. 2 (East Indies).
Abudefduf bleekeri Fowler and Bean, 1928: 165 (Philippines).

Diagnosis.—Dorsal rays XIII, 13 to 14; anal rays II, 13 to 14; pectoral rays 16 to 17. Tub lateral-line scales 16 to 17. Gill rakers on first arch 17 to 19. Body depth 2.4 to 2.7 in SL. Color in alcohol generally brown on anterodorsal region; tan to yellowish on ventral and posterior portions of body; dorsal fin pale to dusky, remainder of fins pale. Maximum size to about 55 mm SL.

Ecology.—Inhabits the upper edge of outer reef slopes in one to six meters, frequently in surge channels. Occurs solitarily or in small groups. Feeds mainly on algae.

Distribution.—Ryukyu Islands, Philippines, Palau Islands, East Indies, New Guinea, New Britain, Solomon Islands, New Hebrides, New Caledonia, and Great Barrier Reef.

Remarks.—Live individuals from the Palau Islands have the upper portion of the head and antero-dorsal region of the body largely bluish with the remainder of the body and fins whitish. Individuals from eastern New Guinea, Melanesia, and the Great Barrier Reef are frequently charcoal-colored antero-dorsally and pale grey posteriorly with pale orange fins.

Glyphidodontops rollandi (Whitley)
Rolland's Demoiselle

Illus. pp. 164, 165

Chromis rollandi Whitley, 1961: 60 (New Caledonia).

Diagnosis.—Dorsal rays XIII, 10 to 11; anal rays II, 12 to 13; pectoral rays 15. Tubed lateral-line scales 14 to 16. Gill rakers on first arch 21 to 22. Body depth 2.1 to 2.2 in SL. Color in alcohol generally yellowish to pale grey with large dusky area encompassing about last eight dorsal spines and extending to upper corner of opercle; small dark spot near lateral-line origin, at upper pectoral base and at anal opening; fins pale. Maximum size to about 40 mm SL.

Ecology.—Inhabits lagoons, harbors, and outer reef slopes in two to 35 meters. Occurs solitarily or in small groups. Feeds primarily on zooplankton.

Distribution.—New Guinea, New Britain, Solomon Islands, New Hebrides, New Caledonia, Loyalty Islands, and Great Barrier Reef.

Glyphidodontops starcki (Allen)
Starck's Demoiselle
Illus. p. 165

Abudefduf starcki Allen, 1973a: 32 (Osprey Reef, Coral Sea).

Diagnosis.—Dorsal rays XIII, 14; anal rays II, 14 to 15; pectoral rays 16 to 17. Tubed lateral-line scales 15 to 16. Gill rakers on first arch 21 to 22. Body depth 2.2 in SL. Color in alcohol generally dark brown grading to blackish posteriorly; pale mid-dorsal stripe from forehead to origin of soft dorsal fin and covering most of region above lateral-line; spinous dorsal fin pale; soft dorsal fin pale distally and blackish basally; caudal fin and upper and lower portions of caudal peduncle pale; pelvic and anal fins blackish, pectorals pale with blackish bar covering most of fin base. Maximum size to about 50 mm SL.

Ecology.—Inhabits outer reef slopes around rocky outcrops and crevices which are frequently situated in sand channels at depths between 25 and 52 meters. Occurs solitarily or in small groups. Feeds on zooplankton a short distance above the bottom.

Distribution.—Previously known on the basis of two specimens collected at Osprey Reef. However, the species was common on the outer reef off Noumea, New Caledonia, and off Uvea Atoll, Loyalty Islands. In addition, R. Kuiter collected a single juvenile at Sydney, Australia, and H. Axelrod recently sent a photo of the species taken at Taiwan.

Glyphidodontops talboti Allen
Talbot's Demoiselle
Illus. p. 165

Glyphidodontops talboti Allen, 1975: 93 (One Tree Island, Great Barrier Reef).

Diagnosis.—Dorsal rays XIII, 11 to 12; anal rays II, 11 to 13; pectoral rays 15 to 16. Tubed lateral-line scales 14 to 16. Gill rakers on first arch 18 to 20. Body depth 2.2 to 2.3 in SL. Color in alcohol generally reddish-brown; predorsal region, side of head and ventral surface of body suffused with yellow to tan; prominent black spot about size of eye at base of hindmost dorsal spines; anal papilla black; fins pale. Maximum size to about 45 mm SL.

Ecology.—Usually inhabits outer reef slopes in six to 35 meters. Occurs solitarily or in small groups which hover a short distance above the bottom while feeding on plankton.

Distribution.—Molucca Islands, New Guinea, New Britain, D'Entrecasteaux Islands, Great Barrier Reef, Solomon Islands, New Hebrides, and Fiji Islands.

Glyphidodontops traceyi (Woods and Schultz)
Tracey's Demoiselle
Illus. p. 168

Pomacentrus traceyi Woods and Schultz, 1960: 114 (Rongelap Atoll, Marshall Islands).

Diagnosis.—Dorsal rays XIII, 10 to 12; anal rays II, 11 to 12; pectoral rays 15 to 16. Tubed lateral-line scales 14 to 16. Gill rakers on first arch 20 to 22. Body depth 2.1 in SL. Color in alcohol generally reddish-brown, posterior portion of body and caudal peduncle yellowish; prominent black spot at base of hindmost dorsal spines; spinous dorsal and anterior portion of anal fin dusky; pectorals, soft dorsal, caudal, and most of anal fin pale; pelvics brown. Maximum size to about 40–45 mm SL.

Ecology.—Observed in the lagoon at Eniwetok Atoll and the Truk Group in five to 15 meters. Two individuals were collected on the outer reef slope at Palau Islands in 20 to 30 meters. Occurs solitarily or in small groups.

Distribution.—Marshall and Caroline Islands. Probably the Philippines (erroneously reported as *Abudefduf bonang* by Fowler and Bean, 1928).

Glyphidodontops leucopomus (about 50 mm TL), Savo Island, Solomon Islands in two meters.

Glyphidodontops leucopomus (*amabilis* phase, about 70 mm TL), One Tree Island, Great Barrier Reef in two meters.

Glyphidodontops leucopomus (intermediate phase, about 70 mm TL), Palau Islands.

Glyphidodontops niger, painting of adult and juvenile individuals (about 75 mm TL and 35 mm TL, respectively) based on specimens collected at Cape Nelson, New Guinea.

Glyphidodontops notialis (about 75 mm TL), Lord Howe Island (W. Doak photo).

Glyphidodontops tricinctus Allen and Randall
Three-band Demoiselle

Glyphidodontops tricinctus Allen and Randall, 1974: 41 (Tutuila, Samoa Islands).

Diagnosis.—Dorsal rays XIII, 11 to 13; anal rays II, 12 to 14; pectoral rays 18 to 19. Tubed lateral-line scales 15 to 17. Gill rakers on first arch 23 to 26. Body depth 2.1 to 2.4 in SL. Color in alcohol generally pale with three black encircling bars; fins pale except where interrupted by bars. Maximum size to about 45–50 mm SL.

Ecology.—Inhabits coral and rock outcrops or rubble mounds situated in sandy areas in 10 to 38 meters. Occurs solitarily or in small groups.

Distribution.—New Caledonia, Fiji, and Samoa Islands.

Glyphidodontops unimaculatus (Cuvier)
One-spot Demoiselle
Illus. p. 168

Glyphisodon unimaculatus Cuvier, 1830: 478 (Timor).
Glyphidodon hemimelas Kner, 1868: 30, 350 (Fiji Islands).

Diagnosis.—Dorsal rays XIII, 13 to 14; anal rays II, 12 to 14; pectoral rays 18 to 19. Tubed lateral-line scales 16 to 18. Gill rakers on first arch 22 to 23. Body depth 2.1 to 2.4 in SL. Color in alcohol generally brown, paler ventrally; black spot at base of hindmost soft dorsal rays; dorsal fin brown, remainder of fins pale to dusky; "*hemimelas*" variety from the Fiji Islands with head and anterior portion of body light brown to tan, posterior half dark brown; see remarks section under *G. biocellatus* for additional comments on coloration. Maximum size to about 55–60 mm SL.

Ecology.—Inhabits areas exposed to mild or moderate surge in 0.2 to two meters, usually among rubble or over barren beach-rock with occasional crevices. Occurs solitarily or in small groups. Feeds mainly on benthic algae.

Distribution.—East Indies, Philippines, New Guinea, New Britain, Solomon Islands, New Hebrides, Fiji Islands, and Great Barrier Reef.

Chapter XVIII
HEMIGLYPHIDODON

The genus *Hemiglyphidodon* contains a single species which is mainly restricted to the Indo-Australian Archipelago and immediately adjacent areas, although it was recorded from Mauritius and the Seychelles during the last century. The large size, unusually high gill raker count, broad preorbital, and arrowhead-shaped body are distinguishing features. They are solitary dwellers which prefer protected inshore areas. Algae comprise the bulk of the diet. There is no information available regarding the reproductive habits.

GENUS *HEMIGLYPHIDODON* BLEEKER

Hemiglyphidodon Bleeker, 1877b: 91 (type species, *Glyphisodon plagiometopon* Bleeker).

Diagnostic features.—Margin of preopercle and suborbital entire; notch between preorbital and suborbital absent; dorsal spines XIII; pectoral rays 16 to 17; gill rakers approximately 65 to 85; tubed lateral-line scales usually 14 to 16; preorbital and suborbital naked; teeth biserial (at least anteriorly), those of outer row flared in width distally with notched to flattened tips; snout scaled to about level of nostrils; greatest body depth 1.8 to 2.0 in SL.

Hemiglyphidodon plagiometopon (Bleeker)
Lagoon Damsel
Illus. p. 169

Glyphisodon plagiometopon Bleeker, 1852a: 67 (Singapore).

Diagnosis.—Dorsal rays XIII, 14 to 15; anal rays II, 14 to 15; pectoral rays 16 to 17. Tubed lateral-line scales 14 to 16. Gill rakers on first arch about 65 to 85. Body depth 1.8 to 2.0 in SL. Color in alcohol generally dark brown; fins and pectoral base frequently darker. Maximum size to about 150 mm SL.

Ecology.—Inhabits coastal reefs in 1.5 to 20 meters. Common among the rock-islands of the southern Palau Group.

Distribution.—China, East Indies, Philippines, Palau Islands, New Guinea, northern Australia, New Britain, and Solomon Islands. The occurrence of this species at Mauritius and the Seychelles based on records from the last century is questionable.

Remarks.—Fowler and Bean (1928) reported the dentition as being uniserial; however, there is an additional row of smaller buttress teeth anteriorly just behind the primary teeth in the spaces between them.

Glyphidodontops rapanui (50 mm SL), Easter Island (J. Randall photo).

Glyphidodontops rex (about 75 mm TL), Augulpelu Reef, Palau Islands in three meters.

Glyphidodontops rollandi (about 50 mm TL), Uvea, Loyalty Islands in 10 meters.

Glyphidodontops rollandi (about 60 mm TL), One Tree Island, Great Barrier Reef in three meters.

Glyphidodontops starcki (about 75 mm TL), Noumea, New Caledonia in 25 meters.

Glyphidodontops talboti (about 50 mm TL), Efate, New Hebrides in 10 meters.

Chapter XIX
NEOPOMACENTRUS

The genus *Neopomacentrus*, described here as new, contains approximately 11 species which are restricted to the Indo-West Pacific; six are found in the "South Seas." They are generally elongate, *Chromis*-like fishes with a forked caudal fin and filamentous rays posteriorly on the median fins. They are generally coastal inhabitants, but two of the species, *N. azysron* and *N. metallicus*, occur in large aggregations on the upper edge of outer reef slopes. *N. anabatoides*, *N. cyanomos*, and *N. violascens* are frequently encountered in the vicinity of wharf pilings, and at least one member of the genus, *N. taeniurus*, penetrates freshwater streams and brackish estuaries. These fishes generally occur in small to large midwater aggregations which feed primarily on zooplankton.

Spawning of *N. cyanomos* was observed under the main wharf at Samarai Island, off the eastern tip of New Guinea. The participants engaged in chasing activities and stationary displays in which the fins were fully extended. Males exhibited a nuptial color pattern consisting of several pale bars on the dorsal portion of the body. Periodically the male was accompanied to the nest site by a gravid female whose protruding ovipositor was clearly visible. The pair would make several slow spawning passes before leaving the nest and rejoining the aggregation. The eggs were laid in a hollowed out portion of a wharf piling about four meters below the surface.

NEOPOMACENTRUS Allen, NEW GENUS

Diagnosis.—A genus of pomacentrid fishes with the following combination of characters: body elongate, depth usually 2.3 to 2.8 in SL; scales large, about 27 to 28 in a median lateral series; edge of preopercle slightly crenulate to weakly serrate; margin of suborbital usually smooth or hidden by scales; teeth biserial (at least anteriorly), an outer row of larger incisiform teeth with notched or flattened tips and an inner row of slender, nearly inconspicuous buttress teeth; dorsal rays XIII, 10 to 12; middle rays of soft dorsal and anal fins and outer rays of caudal frequently produced into long filaments.

Description.—Dorsal rays XIII, 10 to 12; anal rays II, 10 to 12; pectoral rays 15 to 18; pelvic rays I, 5; branched caudal rays 13; gill rakers on first arch 19 to 24; tubed lateral-line scales 15 to 19; vertical scale rows from upper edge of gill opening to base of caudal fin 27 to 28; horizontal scale rows from base of dorsal fin to terminal lateral-line scale (exclusive of dorsal base sheath scales) 1 to 2, and from lateral-line to anal fin origin 8 to 9; predorsal scales about 18 to 22.

Body elongate, greatest depth 2.2 to 2.8 in SL; head length 3.1 to 3.6 in SL; snout 3.8 to 4.8, eye diameter 2.8 to 3.8, interorbital width 3.7 to 4.8, least depth of caudal peduncle 1.8 to 2.1, length of caudal peduncle 1.8 to 2.4, of pectoral fin 1.0 to 1.3, of pelvic fin 0.8 to 1.3, of longest soft dorsal rays 0.6 to 1.0, of longest soft anal ray 0.7 to 1.2, all in head length. Pectorals slightly rounded; caudal forked, the lobes frequently filamentous.

Single nasal opening on each side of snout; mouth oblique, nearly terminal; lateral-line gently arched below dorsal fin, terminating 1 to 2 scale rows below base of soft dorsal; snout tip, lips, chin, and isthmus naked; remainder of head and body scaled; scales finely ctenoid; preopercle scale rows 3–4; lower margin of suborbital smooth to weakly serrate or completely hidden by scales; margin of preopercle slightly crenulate to weakly serrate; upper margin of opercle armed with 1–2 flattened spines.

Remarks.—This genus includes members which have been placed by previous authors in both *Pomacentrus* and *Abudefduf*, depending on the presence or absence of serrae on the margin of the preopercle. Species such as *bankieri* and *azysron* have been shuffled back and forth between the two genera.

Bleeker assigned several of the species to *Parapomacentrus*, the type species of which is *Pomacentrus polynema* Bleeker. I have examined the type of *P. polynema* which was kindly sent by Dr. M. Boeseman of the Rijksmuseum van Natuurlijke Histoire, Leiden. It is identifiable as *Pomacentrus pavo*. It was first distinguished from *pavo* on the basis of having a single row of teeth instead of two. However, close examination reveals a second row of narrow buttress teeth.

In addition to the species listed in the key below, the following species, with their approximate distributions indicated in parentheses, are included in *Neopomacentrus*: *N. bankieri* (China Sea); *N. fallax* (East Africa); *N. fuliginosus* (East Africa); *N. melanocarpus* (Philippines).

A detailed review of the group is presently in progress by the author. *Glyphisodon anabatoides* Bleeker is herein designated as the type species for the genus.

KEY TO THE SPECIES OF *NEOPOMACENTRUS* FROM THE SOUTH SEAS

1a. Caudal fin pale, without dark margins...2
1b. Caudal fin pale (at least on inner portion of fork), with dark margins.......................4
2a. Edge of suborbital exposed (Japan; China; Philippines; East Indies; Melanesia; northern Australia) ....*N. violascens*
2b. Edge of suborbital hidden by scales..3
3a. Pectoral base mostly dark; pectoral rays usually 18 (Philippines; East Indies; Melanesia; northern Australia) ....*N. azysron*
3b. Pectoral base with small dark spot superiorly; pectoral rays usually 16 to 17 (Philippines; East Indies; Palau Islands; Melanesia; northern Australia)......................*N.* species
4a. Edge of suborbital exposed; tubed lateral-line scales usually 15 to 16......................5
4b. Edge of suborbital hidden by scales; tubed lateral-line scales usually 17 to 18..............6
5a. Dorsal rays usually 11 (occasionally 12); pectoral base with dark bar or large wedge-shaped mark superiorly; spot at origin of lateral-line usually greater than ½ eye diameter, the outline irregular with pigment scattered on several scales; inhabits fresh and brackish water (Philippines; East Indies; Palau Islands; Melanesia)..*N. taeniurus*
5b. Dorsal rays usually 10 (occasionally 11); pectoral base with small dark spot or wedge-shaped mark superiorly; spot at origin of lateral-line if present less than ½ eye diameter, the outline round with most of pigment concentrated on a single scale; inhabits coastal reefs (Philippines; East Indies; Melanesia) ....*N. anabatoides*

Glyphidodontops traceyi (43 mm SL), Majuro, Marshall Islands (J. Randall photo).

Glyphidodontops tricinctus (35 mm SL), Tutuila, Samoa Islands (J.Randall photo).

Glyphidodontops unimaculatus (about 75 mm TL), One Tree Island, Great Barrier Reef in one meter.

Hemiglyphidodon plagiometopon (about 150 mm TL), Madang, New Guinea in four meters.

Hemiglyphidodon plagiometopon (about 40 mm TL), Madang, New Guinea in two meters.

6a. Hindmost portion of dorsal fin abruptly yellowish, frequently with whitish spot at base of last few rays; pectoral base dark, not contrasting with surrounding area or with small dark spot or wedge-shaped mark superiorly; dorsal and anal rays usually 11 (last ray branched near base); pectoral rays usually 17 (W. Indian Ocean; Ceylon; East Indies; Philippines; Melanesia; northern Australia)..*N. cyanomos*

6b. Hindmost portion of dorsal fin paler, but not abruptly yellowish, without large whitish spot at base of last few rays; pectoral base covered with large dark spot; dorsal and anal rays usually 10 (last ray branched near base); pectoral rays usually 18 (Fiji Islands; Samoa Islands)..........
.... *N. metallicus*

Neopomacentrus anabatoides (Bleeker)
Brown Demoiselle

Glyphisodon anabatoides Bleeker, 1847: 28 (Java).

Diagnosis.—Dorsal rays XIII, 10 to 11; anal rays II, 11 to 12; pectoral rays 16 to 17. Tubed lateral-line scales 15. Gill rakers on first arch 20 to 23. Body depth 2.2 to 2.6 in SL. Color in alcohol generally dark brown except hindmost portion of dorsal and anal fins pale; blackish spot at origin of lateral-line and on upper portion of pectoral fin base and axil; caudal fin pale to dusky with dark upper and lower margins. Maximum size to about 60 mm SL.

Ecology.—Inhabits lagoons, harbors, and coastal reefs in five to 12 meters.

Distribution.—East Indies, Philippines, New Guinea, New Britain, Solomon Islands, and New Caledonia.

Neopomacentrus azysron (Bleeker)
Yellow-tail Demoiselle
Illus. p. 172

Pomacentrus azysron Bleeker, 1877b: 50 (Amboina).

Diagnosis.—Dorsal rays XIII, 11 to 12; anal rays II, 11 to 12; pectoral rays 18. Tubed lateral-line scales 17 to 19. Gill rakers on first arch 20 to 23. Body depth 2.5 to 2.8 in SL. Color in alcohol generally dark brown, paler on breast; black spot at origin of lateral-line; dorsal fin dark brown to blackish except posterior half of soft dorsal pale; anal fin dusky; caudal fin and upper portion of peduncle yellowish; pectorals pale with base and axil dark brown. Maximum size to about 60 mm SL.

Ecology.—Usually inhabits outer reef slopes in one to 12 meters, frequently in the deeper surge channels.

Distribution.—Philippines, Molucca Islands, New Guinea, New Britain, Solomon Islands, New Hebrides, and northern Australia.

Neopomacentrus cyanomos (Bleeker)
Regal Demoiselle
Illus. p. 173

Pomacentrus cyanomos Bleeker, 1856b: 89 (Batavia).

Diagnosis.—Dorsal rays XIII, 11 to 12; anal rays II, 11 to 12; pectoral rays 17. Tubed lateral-line scales 17 to 18. Gill rakers on first arch 22 to 24. Body depth 2.2 to 2.6 in SL. Color in alcohol generally dark brown, paler ventrally; dark spot at lateral-line origin; dorsal, anal, and pelvic fins dark except hindmost dorsal rays pale with large whitish spot at posterior axil of fin; caudal fin pale with black upper and lower margins; pectorals pale with small black spot on upper portion of fin base. Maximum size to about 70 mm SL.

Ecology.—Inhabits lagoons, harbors, and protected outer reef slopes in five to 16 meters.

Distribution.—East Africa, Seychelles, Ceylon, East Indies, Philippines, New Guinea, New Britain, Solomon Islands, and northern Australia.

Remarks.—Smith (1960) reported this species from the western Indian Ocean as *Pomacentrus taeniurus*.

Neopomacentrus metallicus (Jordan and Seale)
Metallic Demoiselle

Illus. p. 176

Abudefduf metallicus Jordan and Seale, 1906: 289 (Samoa).

Diagnosis.—Dorsal rays XIII, 10 to 11; anal rays II, 10 to 11; pectoral rays 18. Tubed lateral-line scales 17. Gill rakers on first arch 19 to 21. Body depth 2.4 to 2.6 in SL. Color in alcohol generally dark brown, lower sides paler, sometimes with metallic sheen; fins brown to dusky; caudal fin with dark upper and lower margins. Maximum size to about 60 mm SL.

Ecology.—Inhabits outer reef slopes in two to 10 meters. Large aggregations common on the outer reef near Suva, Fiji Islands.

Distribution.—Fiji and Samoa Islands.

Neopomacentrus taeniurus (Bleeker)
Fresh-water Demoiselle

Illus. p. 176

Pomacentrus taeniurus Bleeker, 1856a: 51 (Amboina).

Diagnosis.—Dorsal rays XIII, 11 to 12; anal rays II, 11 to 12; pectoral rays 16 to 17. Tubed lateral-line scales 15 to 16. Gill rakers on first arch 21 to 23. Body depth 2.3 to 2.5 in SL. Color in alcohol generally purplish-brown to grey-brown, darker dorsally; large dark spot at lateral-line origin; spinous dorsal, pelvic, and anal fins dark brown except hindmost portion of dorsal and anal fins pale; pectorals pale with black bar at base and dark spot on upper portion of axil; caudal fin pale with dark upper and lower margins. Maximum size to about 60 mm SL.

Ecology.—Apparently restricted to brackish estuaries and freshwater streams.

Distribution.—The distribution of this species is nebulous because the name *taeniurus* has been erroneously used for other closely related species. Known for certain to occur at the Palau Islands, Molucca Islands, Philippines, New Guinea, Solomon Islands, and New Hebrides.

Neopomacentrus violascens (Bleeker)
Violet Demoiselle

Illus. p. 176

Pristotis violascens Bleeker, 1848: 637 (Sumbawa).

Diagnosis.—Dorsal rays XIII, 11 to 12; anal rays II, 10 to 11; pectoral rays 17 to 18. Tubed lateral-line scales 16 to 17. Gill rakers on first arch 20 to 22. Body depth 2.4 to 2.6 in SL. Color in alcohol generally dark brown, paler ventrally; dorsal and anal fins brown to dusky except hindmost portion of soft dorsal pale; caudal fin and peduncle yellowish; pelvics brown; pectorals pale with dark spot on fin base. Maximum size to about 50 mm SL.

Ecology.—Inhabits lagoons, harbors, and coastal reefs in five to 25 meters. Sometimes forms mixed aggregations with *Neopomacentrus* sp. Seems to prefer sandy habitats where it occurs in the vicinity of dead coral outcrops or wreckage.

Distribution.—Japan, China, Philippines, East Indies, New Guinea, New Britain, Solomon Islands, New Hebrides, and northern Australia.

Neopomacentrus sp.
Coral Demoiselle

Illus. p. 177

Parapomacentrus bankieri (non Richardson) Bleeker, 1877c: pl. 408, fig. 8 (East Indies).

Diagnosis.—Dorsal rays XIII, 11 to 12; anal rays II, 11 to 12; pectoral rays 16 to 17. Tubed lateral-line scales 16 to 17. Gill rakers on first arch 21 to 22. Body depth 2.4 to 2.5 in SL. Color in alcohol generally dark brown, yellowish ventrally; black spot about size of pupil at lateral-line origin; dorsal fin dark brown except hindmost rays of soft dorsal pale with faint spots; anal fin pale with faint spots; caudal, pelvic, and pectoral fins pale to greyish with small dark spot on upper portion of pectoral base. Maximum size to about 55 mm SL.

Neopomacentrus anabatoides (about 75 mm TL), Port Moresby, New Guinea in six meters.

Neopomacentrus anabatoides (about 55 mm TL), Rabaul, New Britain in five meters.

Neopomacentrus azysron (about 75 mm TL), Savo, Solomon Islands in three meters.

Neopomacentrus cyanomos (about 85 mm TL), Guadalcanal, Solomon Islands in 15 meters.

Neopomacentrus cyanomos (about 85 mm TL), Guadalcanal, Solomon Islands in 15 meters.

Ecology.—Inhabits lagoons, harbors, and coastal reefs in one to 10 meters, frequently in areas where silting is relatively heavy.

Distribution.—East Indies, Philippines, Palau Islands, New Guinea, New Britain, Solomon Islands, New Hebrides, and northern Australia.

Remarks.—This species has been referred to as *bankieri* by nearly all previous authors. However, the type of *bankieri* from Hong Kong, which is deposited at the British Museum (Natural History), differs significantly with regard to the condition of the suborbital series. The suborbital is scaleless and the lower margin is clearly visible. By contrast, the species treated here has a scaled suborbital and the margin is hidden. This species is probably undescribed and will be treated in a forthcoming revision of *Neopomacentrus* by the author.

Chapter XX
PARAGLYPHIDODON

The genus *Paraglyphidodon* contains 11 species which are found only in the Indo-West Pacific region; seven inhabit the "South Seas." These are medium sized pomacentrids which are relatively deep-bodied and possess biserial teeth at the front of the jaws. They appear to be related to *Glyphidodontops*. Most of the species dwell in less than 20 meters, but *P. thoracotaeniatus* is frequently encountered below this depth. They are solitary fishes or occur in small groups and are omnivorous with regard to diet. There is no information available concerning the reproductive behavior.

GENUS *PARAGLYPHIDODON* BLEEKER

Paraglyphidodon Bleeker, 1877b: 116 (type species, *Paraglyphidodon oxycephalus* Bleeker).

Diagnostic features.—Margin of preopercle and suborbital entire; notch between preorbital and suborbital absent; dorsal spines XIII or XIV; pectoral rays usually 17 to 19; gill rakers usually 20 to 26; tubed lateral-line scales usually 16 to 19; suborbital usually scaled (except naked in *P. polyacanthus*); teeth biserial, at least anteriorly; snout usually scaled to about level of nostrils or beyond; greatest body depth usually 1.7 to 2.0 in SL.

Note : The following key is for specimens in excess of about 40 mm SL. It will not work for the juveniles of *P. behni* or *P. thoracotaeniatus.* The young of the former species differs markedly from the adults and is illustrated in the figure. *P. thoracotaeniatus* juveniles are similar to the adults but possess on ocellus on the spinous dorsal fin and in this respect are similar to *P. bonang*. *P. polyacanthus* also exhibits a unique juvenile pattern, but the dorsal spine count of XIV is diagnostic.

KEY TO THE SPECIES OF *PARAGLYPHIDODON* FROM THE SOUTH SEAS

1a. Dorsal spines XIV; suborbital naked (Queensland; Lord Howe and Norfolk Islands; New Caledonia) ....*P. polyacanthus*

1b. Dorsal spines XIII; suborbital scaly..2

2a. Color entirely blackish...3

2b. Color not entirely blackish..4

3a. Body depth 1.9 to 2.1 in SL; caudal fin deeply emarginate, the lobes filamentous; middle rays of soft dorsal and anal fins prolonged, much greater than head length (Fiji Islands)........ .... *P. carlsoni*, n.sp.

3b. Body depth 1.7 to 1.8 in SL; caudal fin slightly emarginate, the lobes rounded; middle rays of soft dorsal and anal fins relatively short, about equal to or less than head length (Indian Ocean; East Indies; Ryukyu Islands; Taiwan; Philippines; Palau Islands; Melanesia; northern Australia) ....*P. melas*

4a. Ocellus at base of 9th to 11th dorsal spines present (Japan; East Indies; Solomon Islands).... .... *P. bonang*

4b. Ocellus at base of 9th to 11th dorsal spines absent......................................5

5a. Body mostly pale; anterior edge of anal fin black; pectoral rays usually 18 to 19 (Indian Ocean; East Indies; Ryukyu Islands; Philippines; Palau Islands; Melanesia; Queensland). .*P. melanopus*

Neopomacentrus metallicus (about 75 mm TL), Suva, Fiji Islands in six meters.

Neopomacentrus taeniurus (about 75 mm TL), freshwater stream on Espiritu Santo, New Hebrides.

Neopomacentrus violascens (about 75 mm TL), Espiritu Santo, New Hebrides in 20 meters.

Neopomacentrus sp. (about 70 mm TL), Malakal Island, Palau Islands in five meters.

Paraglyphidodon behni (about 125 mm TL), Augulpelu Reef, Palau Islands in 16 meters.

5b. Body mostly dark; anterior edge of anal fin pale to brown (same color as remainder of fin); pectoral rays usually 17...6
6a. Head with blackish bar behind hind border of preopercle; pelvics dark; caudal fin and posterior portion of body frequently yellowish; gill rakers 24 to 26 (Ryukyu Islands; Taiwan; East Indies; Philippines; Palau Islands; Melanesia; northern Australia)..........................*P. behni*
6b. Head and breast with two to three dark bars with whitish areas between; pelvics pale; caudal fin and posterior portion of body brownish; gill rakers 22 to 23 (Philippines; New Guinea; Solomon Islands)..*P. thoracotaeniatus*

Paraglyphidodon behni (Bleeker)
Behn's Damsel

Illus. pp. 177, 180

Glyphisodon behnii Bleeker, 1847: 25 (Batavia, Java).
Glyphisodon xanthurus Bleeker, 1853b: 345 (Amboina).
Abudefduf filifer Weber, 1913: 348 (Kei Islands, Indonesia).
Chromis bitaeniatus Fowler and Bean, 1928: 56 (Philippines).

Diagnosis.—Dorsal rays XIII, 14 to 16; anal rays II, 13 to 15; pectoral rays 17. Tubed lateral-line scales 17. Gill rakers on first arch 24 to 26. Body depth 1.8 in SL. Color in alcohol generally brown grading to yellowish at level of soft dorsal and anal fins; pelvics dark, pectorals pale with dark spot on upper portion of base; occasional specimens entirely dark brown; juveniles under about 40 mm SL pale with two dark longitudinal stripes on sides. Maximum size to about 100 mm SL.

Ecology.—Usually inhabits passages and outer reef slopes in two to 23 meters. The stomachs of New Guinea specimens contained algae, pelagic tunicates, salps, and unidentified crustacean fragments.

Distribution.—Ryukyu Islands, Taiwan, East Indies, Philippines, Palau Islands, New Guinea, Solomon Islands, New Hebrides, and northern Australia.

Remarks.—The juvenile stage, previously recorded as *Chromis bitaeniatus*, was discussed by Allen (1973c). Some doubt still remains regarding the proper specific name. It is possible that P. *behni* and P. *xanthurus*, synonymized here, are both valid. I recently acquired a 38 mm SL specimen collected at Ambon by V. Springer which agrees with the figure of *P. behni* in Bleeker's (1877c) Atlas. It is entirely dark brown and is less deep-bodied than specimens of similar size which exhibit the typical "*xanthurus*" pattern (see accompanying illustration of adult). More specimens of larger size showing the dark *behni* pattern are needed in order to solve this problem. The species as treated here would be referable to *P. xanthurus* if *P. behni* is ultimately shown to be valid.

Paraglyphidodon bonang (Bleeker)
Ocellated Damsel

Illus. p. 180

Glyphisodon bonang Bleeker, 1853: 522 (Sumatra).

Diagnosis.—Dorsal rays XIII, 15 to 16; anal rays II, 13 to 15; pectoral rays 18 to 20. Tubed lateral-line scales 20. Body depth 1.6 to 1.8 in SL. Color in alcohol generally brown, many scales with a lighter spot; bluish stripe connecting nostrils over snout; large pale-edged, dark brown ocellus between 9th to 11th dorsal spines; fins brown. Maximum size to about 110 mm SL.

Ecology.—One juvenile observed on the outer reef slope off northern Guadalcanal in 15 meters.

Distribution.—Japan, East Indies, Solomon Islands. The species reported as A. *bonang* from the Philippines by Fowler and Bean was probably *Glyphidodontops traceyi*.

Remarks.—This species is included here on the basis of a single juvenile observed at Guadalcanal, Solomon Islands. The above diagnosis was taken from De Beaufort (1940) as no specimens were collected.

Paraglyphidodon carlsoni Allen, new species
Carlson's Damsel
Illus. p. 181

Holotype.—Australian Museum, Sydney I.17689–001, 90.3 mm SL, collected with spear on lee-ward side of Yaukuve Levu Island, Great Astrolabe Lagoon, Fiji Islands, in 1–3 meters by B. Carlson on 21–22 March, 1974.

Paratypes.—AMS I.17689–002, 4 specimens, 65.7–93.0 mm SL, same collecting data as holotype; AMS I.17690–001, 72.2 mm SL, collected with spear in lagoon outside of Vaqa Bay, Beqa Island, Fiji Islands in 1–6 meters by B. Carlson and B. Goldman on 17 January, 1974; AMS I.17691–001, 57.0 mm SL, same data as holotype except collected in 1½–3 meters on 31 January, 1974.

Description.—The range of counts and proportional measurements for the paratypes are indicated in parentheses if different from the holotype. Proportional measurements for the holotype and three paratypes are expressed as percentage of the standard length in Table 5.

Dorsal rays XIII, 14 (XIII, 13½ [1], XIII, 14½[3], XIII, 15[2]) anal rays II, 13½ (one paratype with 12); pectoral rays 18 (one paratype with 19); pelvic rays I, 5; branched caudal rays 13; gill rakers on the first arch 22 (21 [2], 22 [2], 23 [2]); tubed lateral-line scales 18 (two paratypes with 17); vertical scale rows from upper edge of gill opening to base of caudal fin 27; horizontal scale rows from base of dorsal fin to terminal lateral-line scale (exclusive of dorsal base sheath scales) 1½, and from lateral-line to anal fin origin 9; predorsal scales about 24, extending to level slightly in front of nostrils; teeth biserial, close-set with rounded tips, about 48 in outer row of each jaw, an inner row of smaller, narrow buttress teeth in the spaces between the outer row teeth.

Body ovate, laterally compressed, the greatest depth 2.0 (1.9 to 2.1) in the standard length. Head profile conical, the head length contained 3.5 (3.3 to 3.5) times in the standard length; snout 3.2 (2.9 to 4.2), eye diameter 3.2 (2.8 to 3.4), interorbital width 2.8 (2.7 to 3.2), least depth of caudal peduncle 1.8 (1.7 to 1.9), length of caudal peduncle 2.9 (2.7 to 3.2), of pectoral fin 0.9 (0.8 to 1.0), of pelvic fin 0.6 (0.6 to 0.7), of longest caudal rays 0.8 (0.5 to 0.8), all in the head length.

Single nasal opening on each side of snout; mouth oblique, terminally located; lateral-line gently arched beneath dorsal fin, terminating 1½ scale rows below base of 2nd soft dorsal ray; preorbital and suborbital scaly, isthmus with row of scales except on mid-portion; snout tip, lips, and chin naked; remainder of head and body scaled; scales finely ctenoid except a few cycloid scales near tip of snout; preopercle scale rows 2, with additional row of scales on inferior limb; small sheath scales covering basal ½ to ⅔ of membranous portions of dorsal, anal, and caudal fins; margin of pre-orbital, suborbital, preopercle and opercle entire.

Origin of dorsal fin at level of 4th tubed lateral-line scale; spines of dorsal fin gradually increasing in length posteriorly; length of first dorsal spine 3.7 (3.8 to 4.3), of seventh dorsal spine 2.1 (1.8 to 2.2), of last dorsal spine 1.4 (1.5 to 1.6), of longest soft dorsal ray 0.8 (0.7 to 0.9), of first anal spine 3.4 (3.3 to 5.2), of second anal spine 1.7 (1.6 to 1.8), of longest soft anal ray 1.0 (0.6 to 1.0), all in the head length; caudal fin emarginate; pectoral fins pointed.

Color in alcohol.—Head, body, and fins entirely dark brown, nearly black except breast slightly lighter and membranous portion of pectoral fin translucent.

Color in life.—Adult specimens in excess of about 70 mm SL charcoal black, occasionally with neon blue spot on upper edge of caudal peduncle. Individuals under about 60–70 mm SL charcoal black with brilliant neon blue stripe between lateral-line and dorsal fin, extending from temporal region of head to below middle of soft dorsal fin. There is also a neon blue spot on the upper edge of the caudal peduncle and a narrow blue margin on the anterior edge of the pelvic fin.

Ecology.—According to Mr. Bruce Carlson, a resident biologist at Suva, Fiji Islands, this species appears to be very restricted with regards to habitat. Mr. Carlson has done extensive collecting and diving around the main islands of the Fiji Group, but has only encountered the species at Yaukuve Levu (type locality), Beqa Island, and on the lee side of Nanuya Levu Island in the Yasawa Group, northwest of Vitu Levu. The only place where the species was reported as being relatively common was in the Great Astrolabe Lagoon at Yaukuve Levu. All the specimens from this locality were taken

Juvenile specimen of *Paraglyphidodon behni*, approximately 30 mm Sl.
Photo by K.H. Choo.

Paraglyphidodon bonang (about 35 mm TL),
Guadalcanal, Solomon Islands in 10 meters.

Paraglyphidodon behni (about 100 mm TL), Port Moresby, New Guinea in eight meters.

Paraglyphidodon carlsoni (about 100 mm SL), Fiji Islands.

Paraglyphidodon melanopus (about 75 mm TL), One Tree Island, Great Barrier Reef in two meters.

TABLE 5

MORPHOMETRIC PROPORTIONS (IN THOUSANDTHS OF THE STANDARD LENGTH) FOR SELECTED TYPES OF *PARAGLYPHIDODON CARLSONI*

Character	Holotype AMS I.17689–001	AMS I.17689–002	Paratypes AMS I.17690–001	AMS I.17691–001
Standard length (mm)	90.3	90.0	72.2	57.0
Greatest depth of body	507	482	524	514
Greatest width of body	221	200	194	193
Head length	285	282	287	293
Snout length	89	86	79	70
Eye diameter	90	82	90	104
Interorbital width	102	104	91	95
Least depth of caudal peduncle	161	156	169	163
Length of caudal peduncle	95	89	107	111
Snout to origin of dorsal fin	390	374	409	418
Snout to origin of anal fin	664	656	693	668
Snout to origin of pelvic fin	382	399	392	386
Length of base of dorsal fin	620	597	589	614
Length of base of anal fin	244	244	245	246
Length of pectoral fin	327	322	360	365
Length of pelvic fin	454	469	464	491
Length of pelvic spine	172	178	191	181
Length of first dorsal spine	78	73	66	72
Length of seventh dorsal spine	138	131	155	158
Length of last dorsal spine	197	184	194	193
Length of longest dorsal ray	338	344	360	425
Length of first anal spine	83	87	64	56
Length of second anal spine	162	176	177	167
Length of longest anal ray	277	306	316	496
Length of caudal fin	346*	400*	374*	579

on the edge of the fringing reef on the leeward side of the island. The reef front at this location drops off vertically to an average depth of 2–3 meters and is dissected by many small channels, about 0.5–1.5 meters in width. Many of these are "roofed" over with coral rock, coralline algae, and living coral, thus forming small caves and overhangs. Virtually every cave at the type locality had one or two individuals swimming around the entrance, usually in the shadows where they were difficult to see. When pursued by a diver the fish either retreated deeper into the cave or into holes in the walls. However, they were not entirely restricted to a cave dwelling existence. Often Mr. Carlson encountered individuals swimming on the reef top, but always near the edge of the reef and never far from the home cave.

Remarks.—This species is superficially similar to *P. melas* Bleeker and is probably the species recorded under that name for the Fiji Islands by Fowler (1958). Both species are entirely black, but

*damaged

182

there are important differences in proportions and coloration of juveniles and subadults. *P. carlsoni* is more elongate (depth 1.9 to 2.1 in SL compared with 1.7 to 1.8 for *melas*). In addition, the middle rays of the soft dorsal and anal fins, and outer rays of the caudal fin in *P. carlsoni* are very elongate and produced into filaments (although the tips are easily broken and may be missing in preserved specimens). In contrast *P. melas* has relatively short fin rays (longest soft dorsal and anal rays 1.0 to 1.3 in head compared with 0.6 to 0.9, occasionally 1.0 in *carlsoni*; outer caudal rays 1.0 to 1.1 vs 0.5 to 0.8; pelvic fin length 0.8 to 1.0 vs. 0.6 to 0.7). Juveniles and subadults of *P. melas* are solid black and lack the characteristic blue markings seen on *P. carlsoni* of similar size.

P. carlsoni also bears a resemblance to *Glyphisodon cochinensis* as illustrated by Day (1877). The smallest paratype in particular resembles the fish in Day's illustration. However, the description of *cochinensis* indicates that it is a member of the genus *Neopomacentrus*. Particularly diagnostic is Day's mention of notched teeth. The teeth were described as being uniserial, which does not agree with the characteristic biserial condition found in *Neopomacentrus*. However, the row of buttress teeth in that genus is very inconspicuous, more so than in *Paraglyphidodon*. In addition, the pectoral ray count of 15 for *cochinensis* is too low for *Paraglyphidodon* and more closely approaches the minimum value of 16 recorded for *Neopomacentrus* during the present study.

Named *carlsoni* in honor of Bruce Carlson who collected the types and provided detailed habitat notes. He has contributed many new pomacentrid records for the Fiji Islands.

Paraglyphidodon melanopus (Bleeker)
Royal Damsel

Illus. p. 181

Glyphisodon melanopus Bleeker, 1856b: 82 (Java).

Diagnosis.—Dorsal rays XIII, 14 to 15; anal rays II, 13 to 15; pectoral rays 18 to 19. Tubed lateral-line scales 17. Gill rakers on first arch 20 to 22. Body depth 1.8 to 2.0 in SL. Color in alcohol generally pale grey with dorsal fin and area above lateral-line yellowish to tan; anal spines and first few rays black; remainder of fin pale; pelvics black; pectoral and caudal fins pale. Maximum size to about 75 mm SL.

Ecology.—Inhabits lagoons in one to three meters. Frequently associated with soft corals.

Distribution.—Widespread from East Africa to the East Indies, Philippines, Ryukyu Islands, Palau Islands, New Guinea, Solomon Islands, and Great Barrier Reef.

Paraglyphidodon melas (Cuvier)
Black Damsel

Illus. p. 184

Glyphisodon melas Cuvier, 1830: 472 (Java).

Diagnosis.—Dorsal rays XIII, 14 to 15; anal rays II, 13 to 14; pectoral rays 18 to 19. Tubed lateral-line scales 17. Gill rakers on first arch 20 to 21. Body depth 1.7 to 1.8 in SL. Color in alcohol generally dark brown to black including fins. Maximum size to about 125 mm SL.

Ecology.—Inhabits lagoons and outer reef slopes in one to 12 meters, usually around rocky outcrops or soft coral formations. Occurs solitarily or in small groups.

Distribution.—Widespread from East Africa to the East Indies, Philippines, Taiwan, Ryukyu Islands, Palau Islands, New Guinea, Solomon Islands, New Hebrides, and Great Barrier Reef.

Paraglyphidodon polyacanthus (Ogilby)
Multi-spined Damsel

Illus. pp. 184, 185

Glyphidodon polyacanthus Ogilby, 1889: 65 (Lord Howe Island).

Diagnosis.—Dorsal rays XIV, 13 to 14; anal rays II, 14; pectoral rays 18. Tubed lateral-line scales 18 to 19. Gill rakers on first arch 22 to 23. Body depth 1.9 to 2.1 in SL. Color in alcohol variable: adult specimens from Lord Howe Island generally dark brown without distinguishing marks; pectoral pale; pelvics pale to dusky; remainder of fins dark brown; juveniles pale and marked as shown in

Paraglyphidodon melas (about 125 mm TL), Malakal Island, Palau Islands in three meters.

Paraglyphidodon polyacanthus (about 125 mm TL), One Tree Island, Great Barrier Reef in six meters.

Paraglyphidodon polyacanthus (about 40 mm TL), Lord Howe Island in seven meters.

Paraglyphidodon thoracotaeniatus (about 100 mm TL), Guadalcanal, Solomon Islands in 10 meters.

accompanying illustration; specimens from the Capricorn Group, Great Barrier Reef dark brown on dorsal half of body, pale (yellowish) on ventral half; large black ocellus present at base of hindmost dorsal spines; dorsal fin brown to dusky; caudal pale to dusky; remainder of fins pale; pectorals with dark spot on upper portion of fin base. Maximum size to about 120 mm SL.

Ecology.—Occurs outside the lagoon usually in deeper surge channels on the leeward side of reefs in the Capricorn Group, Queensland. Ubiquitous at Lord Howe Island in two to 30 meters.

Distribution.—Previously known only from Lord Howe and Norfolk Islands, but the author recently collected specimens at the Capricorn Group and at Noumea, New Caledonia.

Paraglyphidodon thoracotaeniatus (Fowler and Bean)
Bar-head Damsel

Abudefduf thoracotaeniatus Fowler and Bean, 1928: 158 (Philippines).

Diagnosis.—Dorsal rays XIII, 12 to 14; anal rays II, 13 to 14; pectoral rays 17. Tubed lateral-line scales 16. Gill rakers on first arch 22 to 23. Body depth 1.7 to 1.9 in SL. Color in alcohol generally brownish above, grading to tan or yellowish ventrally; two to three broad dark bars on head and thorax with pale spaces between; dorsal fin brown; remainder of fins pale except caudal dusky, pectoral base and upper portion of axil dark; juveniles generally lighter and with large ocellus covering hindmost portion of spinous dorsal fin. Maximum size to about 85 mm SL.

Ecology.—Inhabits outer reef slopes in 15 to 45 meters.

Distribution.—Philippines, New Guinea and Solomon Islands.

<del>186</del>

Chapter XXI
PARMA

The genus *Parma* contains eight species which are restricted to the Australia-New Zealand region and New Caledonia. These fishes are primarily inhabitants of cooler temperate seas, but three of the species, *P. oligolepis, P. polylepis,* and an undescribed form, have distributions which overlap southern coral reefs. The members of the genus are among the largest pomacentrids and most exhibit dramatic color changes with growth. They occur solitarily or in small groups and are primarily herbivorous. The genus is morphologically similar to *Hypsypops* of southern California and Mexico.

GENUS *PARMA* GUNTHER

Parma Günther, 1862: 57 (type species, *Parma microlepis* Günther).

Diagnostic features.—Margin of preopercle and suborbital entire or crenulate; notch between preorbital and suborbital absent or poorly developed; dorsal spines XIII, vertical scale rows 30 to 46; horizontal scale rows below lateral-line to origin of anal fin usually 14 to 19; suborbital scaled; teeth uniserial, close-set and numerous; predorsal scales extending to about level of orbits; greatest body depth usually 1.6 to 1.9 in SL.

KEY TO THE SPECIES OF *PARMA* FROM THE SOUTH SEAS

1a. Vertical scale rows from upper edge of opercle to caudal base about 30 to 34; tubed lateral-line scales 22 to 24; forehead of large adults without bony tubercles (Queensland and northern New South Wales)..*P. oligolepis*

1b. Vertical scale rows from upper edge of opercle to caudal base about 36 to 44; tubed lateral-line scales usually 26 to 33; forehead of large adults with or without bony tubercles..............2

2a. Pectoral rays usually 21 (occasionally 20 or 22); vertical scale rows from upper edge of opercle to caudal base 40 to 44; forehead of adults with bony tubercles; color of adults dark brown, head sometimes lighter; two to three pale bars on sides of specimens under about 120 mm SL; ocellus at base of hindmost dorsal spines present on specimens less than about 80–90 mm SL (southern Queensland; New South Wales; Lord Howe and Norfolk Islands; New Caledonia).. .... *P. polylepis*

2b. Pectoral rays usually 22 (occasionally 21); vertical scale rows from upper edge of opercle to caudal base usually 36 to 40; forehead of adults without bony tubercles; color of adults uniformly dark brown to blackish; specimens under about 80–90 mm SL tan to brown with bluish spots on sides and blue lines extending from snout to dorsal fin, and ocellus present at base of hindmost dorsal spines (Lord Howe Island; North Island, New Zealand).........................*P.* species

Parma oligolepis Whitley
Big-scale Parma   Illus. p. 188

Parma oligolepis Whitley, 1929: 230 (Queensland).

Diagnosis.—Dorsal rays XIII, 17 to 20; anal rays II, 13 to 15; pectoral rays 20 to 22. Tubed lateral-line scales 22 to 24. Gill rakers on first arch 21 to 24. Color in alcohol generally dark brown except lighter on breast and underside of head; fins dark brown to blackish except more or less translucent on hindmost portion of soft dorsal, anal, and caudal fins; pectorals dusky with dark wedge-shaped mark on upper portion of fin base; juveniles under about 50 mm SL with pair of bluish lines extending from anterior part of head to dorsal fin, and prominent ocellus at soft dorsal junction. Maximum size to about 170 mm SL.

Parma oligolepis (about 45 mm TL), Sydney, Australia (R. Kuiter photo).

Parma polylepis (70 mm SL), Lord Howe Island (J. Randall photo).

Parma polylepis (about 125 mm TL), One Tree Island, Great Barrier Reef in three meters.

Parma sp. (about 75 mm TL), Poor Knights Islands, New Zealand (W. Doak photo).

Parma sp. (about 210 mm TL), Lord Howe Island in six meters.

Ecology.—This species was not observed during the present study. However, museum specimens indicate that it is probably most abundant in non-coral reef coastal waters, although one specimen at the Australian Museum was taken at Green Island on the Great Barrier Reef.

Distribution.—Queensland and northern New South Wales.

Parma polylepis Günther
Banded Parma

Illus. p. 188

Parma polylepis Günther, 1862: 59 (Norfolk Island).

Diagnosis.—Dorsal rays XIII, 17 to 19; anal rays II, 13 to 14; pectoral rays 20 to 22. Tubed lateral-line scales 26 to 33. Gill rakers on first arch 17 to 23. Body depth 1.6 to 1.7 in SL. Color in alcohol generally dark brown, slightly lighter on breast; fins dark brown except pectorals dusky; specimens under about 120 mm SL dark brown with pale bar on posterior part of head and two pale bars on sides; ocellus present at base of hindmost dorsal spines on specimens less than about 80–90 mm SL. Maximum size to about 180 mm SL.

Ecology.—Inhabits lagoons and outer rocky reefs in one to 30 meters. Confined to outer reef surge channels at the Capricorn Group, Great Barrier Reef, but ubiquitous at Lord Howe Island.

Distribution.—Capricorn Group (Great Barrier Reef), New South Wales, Lord Howe Island, Norfolk Island, and New Caledonia.

Remarks.—Live adults at Lord Howe Island are characterized by yellowish heads.

Parma sp.
Black Parma

Illus. p. 189

Diagnosis.—Dorsal rays XIII, 18 to 20; anal rays II, 14 to 15; pectoral rays 21 to 22. Tubed lateral-line scales 25 to 31. Gill rakers on first arch 18 to 22. Body depth 1.6 to 1.7 in SL. Color in alcohol generally dark brown; fins dark brown; juveniles mostly pale with small bluish spots on sides and ocellus on dorsal fin. Maximum size to about 220 mm SL.

Ecology.—Inhabits rocky reefs in six to 15 meters.

Distribution.—Lord Howe Island and northern New Zealand.

Remarks.—This species will be described by D. Hoese and the author in a forthcoming revision of *Parma*. Live adults frequently exhibit a white spot on the suprascapular region which can be "turned" on or off according to behavioral moods.

Chapter XXII

PLECTROGLYPHIDODON

The genus *Plectroglyphidodon* contains about 10 species, including at least two undescribed forms, which inhabit the Indo-West Pacific; eight are found in the "South Seas." These fishes occur solitarily or in small groups and are primarily herbivorous, but at least one species, *P. johnstonianus*, probably also feeds on coral polyps. *P. imparipennis*, *P. leucozona*, *P. phoenixensis*, and *P. sindonis* prefer areas exposed to mild or moderate surge. *P. dickii*, *P. flaviventris*, *P. johnstonianus*, and *P. lacrymatus* frequent coral reef areas to a depth of about 12 meters. There is no information regarding the reproductive habits of these fishes.

GENUS *PLECTROGLYPHIDODON* FOWLER AND BALL

Plectroglyphidodon Fowler and Ball, 1924: 271 (type species, *Plectroglyphidodon johnstonianus* Fowler and Ball).

Diagnostic features.—Margin of preopercle and suborbital entire; notch between preorbital and suborbital absent; dorsal spines XII; pectoral rays usually 19 to 21; gill rakers usually 10 to 17 (except 21 to 23 in *lacrymatus*); suborbital scaled; teeth uniserial, relatively elongate; snout scaled to level of nostrils or slightly beyond; greatest body depth usually 1.7 to 2.0 in SL (except *imparipennis* with 2.1 to 2.4).

Remarks.—Bleeker (1877b) included *P. dickii*, *P. lacrymatus*, and *P. leucozona* in the subgenus *Stegastes* Jenyns. The type of *Stegastes* is *S. imbricatus* Jenyns (=*Glyphisodon luridus*, see Günther, 1862, p. 56) from the Atlantic. The fact that this species has 13 dorsal spines and other morphological differences would tend to exclude it from the group for which Bleeker used *Stegastes*. Whitley (1929), recognizing this error, introduced the name *Negostegastes* with *P. leucozona* as the type species. However, *Plectroglyphidodon* was introduced earlier by Fowler and Ball and is therefore the valid generic designation.

Under their description of *Abudefduf johnstonianus*, Woods and Schultz (1960) stated:

"Fowler and Ball have made this species the type of a separate genus, *Plectroglyphidodon*, distinguished from *Abudefduf* by the plaited lips. It is true that the lips are thick, ridged, and fringed, but in other respects, e.g., scalation of orbital and opercular bones, number of dorsal fin spines, spiny dorsal outline, large number of dorsal and anal fin rays, low number of gill rakers (especially on upper branch), shape of body, and form of teeth of jaws, this species resembles the other members of the genus *Negostegastes*. '*Plectroglyphidodon*' is intermediate in lip form between *Negostegastes* and *Cheiloprion* Weber. *Cheiloprion labiatus* Day is thus related to the *Negostegastes* group, but in that species the lips are very much thickened, curled back, and fringed, in this species the jaw teeth are finer than those in species of *Negostegastes*."

They continue their discussion by stating:

"Although both *Cheiloprion labiatus* and '*Plectroglyphidodon*' *johnstonianus* may be distinguished on the basis of their thickened lips, nearly all the rest of their external characters are similar to *Abudefduf* (*Negostegastes*) *leucozona* Bleeker, the type species of this subgenus. If we recognize the genera *Cheiloprion* and *Plectroglyphidodon* we lose sight of the close relationship to *Negostegastes* and if we do not recognize them we perhaps do not sufficiently emphasize their specialization."

Plectroglyphidodon dickii (about 75 mm TL), Augulpelu Reef, Palau Islands in 10 meters.

Plectroglyphidodon flaviventris (50 mm SL), Rangiroa, Tuamotu Islands (J. Randall photo).

Plectroglyphidodon imparipennis (about 60 mm TL), Noumea, New Caledonia in three meters.

Plectroglyphidodon johnstonianus (about 100 mm TL), Osprey Reef, Coral Sea in 10 meters.

The assertion of Woods and Schultz that *johnstonianus* belongs to the "*Negostegastes*" group is correct. However, I would not include *Cheiloprion* in this genus, in spite of its resemblance to *johnstonianus* in the form of thickened lips and a reduced number of gill rakers on the upper arch. The contrary characters which exclude *Cheiloprion* from *Plectroglyphidodon* are a weakly denticulate suborbital and preopercle, thirteen dorsal spines, 17 pectoral rays, a naked preorbital and suborbital, and biserial teeth. *Cheiloprion* seems more closely allied to *Pomacentrus*. The evolution of thickened lips and reduced gill rakers in *C. labiatus* and *P. johnstonianus* may represent an example of convergence. Both species appear to be closely associated with living coral and obtain at least a portion of their nourishment from the polyps. Perhaps the thickened lips represent a form of insulation which would protect them from the stinging nematocysts.

P. imparipennis, which is smaller and more elongate than the other members of the genus, is the sole representative of a separate subgenus, *Oliglyphisodon* Fowler (1941). It is further distinguished by a low gill raker count.

The genus will be treated in detail by J. Randall and the author in a forthcoming revision.

KEY TO THE SPECIES OF *PLECTROGLYPHIDODON* FROM THE SOUTH SEAS

1a. Body depth 2.1 to 2.4 in SL; dorsal rays 14 to 15; anal rays usually 11; gill rakers 10 to 12; color usually pale without distinguishing marks (Indo-West Pacific)..............*P. imparipennis*

1b. Body depth usually 1.7 to 1.9 in SL; dorsal rays 15 to 20; anal rays 12 to 18; gill rakers 12 to 23; color not as in 1a...2

2a. Gill rakers 21 to 23; tubed lateral-line scales 18 to 19; dorsal rays usually 16 to 17; anal rays 13 to 14; color dark brown with small bluish spots (often obscure in preservative) scattered on head and back; caudal fin and posterior portion of caudal peduncle yellowish (Indo-West Pacific)......
....*P. lacrymatus*

2b. Gill rakers 12 to 17; tubed lateral-line scales 20 to 22; dorsal rays 15 to 20; anal rays 12 to 18; color usually not as in 2a..3

3a. Color entirely brown (usually dark brown) or with one to four pale bars on sides; pectoral rays 20 to 21..4

3b. Color mostly pale to brown, without pale bars on sides; pectoral rays 18 to 19..............6

4a. Dorsal rays 19 to 20; anal rays 15 to 16; color of adults entirely dark brown, juveniles and subadults with one to two pale bars on sides and large ocellus below soft dorsal junction (Hawaiian Islands)..*P. sindonis*

4b. Dorsal rays 15 to 17; anal rays 12 to 14; color of adults entirely dark brown or with one to four pale bars on sides, juveniles and subadults with ocellus on soft dorsal fin....................5

5a. Caudal peduncle with broad black bar bordered anteriorly with narrow white bar; color dark brown with three to four pale bars on sides; dorsal rays usually 16 to 17; anal rays usually 14 (occasionally 13) (West Pacific)...*P. phoenixensis*

5b. Caudal peduncle without broad black bar; color entirely dark brown or with a single pale bar below base of about 4th to 6th dorsal spines; dorsal rays usually 15 (occasionally 16); anal rays usually 12 (occasionally 13) (Indo-West Pacific).....................................*P. leucozona*

6a. Anal rays usually 14; gill rakers 16 to 17; color mostly tan to brown with black crescent-shaped bar four to five scales wide, originating on anterior soft dorsal rays and extending to tips of anterior anal rays (Indo-West Pacific)..*P. dickii*

6b. Anal rays 15 to 18; gill rakers 12 to 14; color tan to brown, frequently with broad dark bar posteriorly...7

7a. Lips swollen, with many transverse ridges (West Pacific)...................*P. johnstonianus*

7b. Lips more or less normal, without ridges (Tuamotu Islands)..................*P. flaviventris*

Plectroglyphidodon dickii (Liénard)
Dick's Damsel
Illus. p. 192

Glyphisodon dickii Liénard, 1839: 35 (Mauritius).

Diagnosis.—Dorsal rays XII, 17 to 18; anal rays II, 14 to 16; pectoral rays 19. Tubed lateral-line scales 21 to 22. Gill rakers on first arch 16 to 17. Body depth 1.8 to 1.9 in SL. Color in alcohol generally pale brown to tan with bold black bar posteriorly extending from origin of soft dorsal fin to anal fin; dorsal and anal fins mostly brownish; pelvics dusky to blackish; pectoral and caudal fins pale. Maximum size to about 85 mm SL.

Ecology.—Inhabits lagoons, passages, and the upper edge of outer reef slopes in one to 12 meters. Feeds on benthic algae. Frequently associated with *Acropora* coral heads.

Distribution.—Widespread in the Indo-West Pacific as far east as the Tuamotu and Line Isands.

Plectroglyphidodon flaviventris Allen and Randall
Yellow-belly Damsel
Illus. p. 192

Plectroglyphidodon flaviventris Allen and Randall, 1974: 44 (Tuamotu Islands).

Diagnosis.—Dorsal rays XII, 18 to 19; anal rays II, 15 to 16; pectoral rays 18 to 19. Tubed lateral-line scales 21. Gill rakers on first arch 12 to 13. Body depth 1.7 in SL. Color in alcohol generally brown, darker posteriorly from level of soft dorsal fin; lower part of head, breast, and abdomen pale brown to tan; dorsal and anal fins brown; caudal dusky; pectorals and pelvics pale. Maximum size to about 70 mm SL.

Ecology.—Inhabits outer reef slopes and passages in five to 12 meters. Usually associated with *Pocillopora* coral, generally with three to five individuals per coral head.

Distribution.—Tuamotu Islands.

Plectroglyphidodon imparipennis (Vaillant and Sauvage)
Bright Eye
Illus. p. 193

Glyphisodon imparipennis Vaillant and Sauvage, 1875: 279 (Honolulu).

Diagnosis.—Dorsal rays XII, 14 to 15; anal rays II, 11 to 12; pectoral rays 20. Tubed lateral-line scales 19. Gill rakers on first arch 10 to 12. Body depth 2.1 to 2.4 in SL. Color in alcohol generally pale, including fins, darker dorsally. Maximum size to about 45 mm SL.

Ecology.—Inhabits areas exposed to mild or moderate surge in 0.5 to three meters. The stomachs of two specimens collected at the Palau Islands contained algae mixed with sand, small shrimps, polychaetes, and gastropod fragments.

Distribution.—Widespread in the Indo-West Pacific as far east as the Pitcairn Group, Hawaiian Islands, and Line Islands.

Remarks.—An unusual color variant occurs in the Marquesas Islands. The body is generally brown or dusky with two to three poorly defined whitish bars on the sides and a prominent blackish bar on the upper half of the caudal peduncle.

Plectroglyphidodon johnstonianus Fowler and Ball
Johnston Damsel
Illus. pp. 193, 200

Plectroglyphidodon johnstonianus Fowler and Ball, 1924: 271 (Johnston Island).

Diagnosis.—Dorsal rays XII, 18 to 19; anal rays II, 16 to 18; pectoral rays 19. Tubed lateral-line scales 21 to 22; Gill rakers on first arch 12 to 14. Body depth 1.7 to 1.9 in SL. Color in alcohol brownish to tan, frequently with broad dark band just anterior to caudal peduncle; dorsal, anal, and caudal fins pale to dusky; pectorals and pelvics pale. Maximum size to about 70 mm SL.

Ecology.—Usually inhabits outer reefs and passages in two to 12 meters. Frequently associated with *Acropora* or *Pocillopora* coral heads. Feeds on algae and probably coral polyps.

Plectroglyphidodon lacrymatus (about 100 mm TL), Efate, New Hebrides in 10 meters.

Plectroglyphidodon lacrymatus (about 75 mm TL), Augulpelu Reef, Palau Islands in 10 meters.

Plectroglyphidodon leucozona (86 mm SL), from Pitcairn Island. (J. Randall photo.)

Plectroglyphidodon leucozona (about 60 mm TL), Egum Atoll, Solomon Sea in one meter.

Distribution.—Apparently widespread throughout Oceania, including the Great Barrier Reef, as far east as the Pitcairn Group and the Hawaiian Islands.

Remarks.—Specimens from the North Pacific frequently lack the pronounced dark bar on the posterior portion of the body. *P. nitidus* Smith from the western Indian Ocean may be synonymous.

Plectroglyphidodon lacrymatus (Quoy and Gaimard)
Jewel Damsel
Illus. p. 196

Glyphisodon lacrymatus Quoy and Gaimard, 1825: 388 (Guam).

Diagnosis.—Dorsal rays XII, 16 to 18; anal rays II, 13 to 14; pectoral rays 19 to 20. Tubed lateral-line scales 18 to 19. Gill rakers on first arch 21 to 23. Body depth 1.7 to 1.9 in SL. Color in alcohol generally dark brown, sometimes with small blue spots scattered on upper half of body and dorsal fin (spots more apparent on juveniles, which also have an ocellus in the middle of the dorsal fin); fins dark brown except caudal yellowish and pectorals pale with dark base. Maximum size to about 65 mm SL.

Ecology.—Inhabits lagoons, passages, and the upper edge of outer reef slopes in two to 12 meters. Feeds primarily on benthic algae.

Distribution.—Widespread in the tropical Indo-West Pacific as far east as the Society, Marshall, and Gilbert Islands.

Plectroglyphidodon leucozona (Bleeker)
White-band Damsel
Illus. p. 197

Glyphisodon leucozona Bleeker, 1859: 339 (Java).
Abudefduf corneyi Jordan and Dickerson, 1908: 613 (Fiji Islands).
Abudefduf behnii (non Bleeker) Fowler, 1959: 380 (Fiji Islands).

Diagnosis.—Dorsal rays XII, 15 to 16; anal rays II, 12 to 13; pectoral rays 20 to 21. Tubed lateral-line scales 20. Gill rakers on first arch 15 to 17. Body depth 1.9 to 2.0 in SL. Color in alcohol generally dark brown, paler on chin, breast, and abdomen; some specimens showing diffuse pale bar on middle of sides about equal to eye diameter in width; juveniles with prominent white bar on middle of sides and large ocellus at middle of dorsal fin; fins dusky to dark brown except pectorals pale with black spot on upper portion of fin base and axil. Maximum size to about 90 mm SL.

Ecology.—Inhabits shallow areas with mild to moderate surge in 0.3 to two meters. Usually found just below the zone of heavy surge, where coral growth begins. Feeds on benthic algae.

Distribution.—Widespread in the tropical Indo-West Pacific from East Africa to the Pitcairn Group in the South Pacific and the Marshall Islands in the North Pacific.

Remarks.—Known from the Indian Ocean and Red Sea as *Abudefduf cingulum* (Klunzinger).

Plectroglyphidodon phoenixensis (Schultz)
Phoenix Damsel
Illus. p. 200

Abudefduf phoenixensis Schultz, 1943: 190 (Enderbury Island, Phoenix Islands).
Abudefduf albofasciatus (non Hombron and Jacquinot) Fowler, 1928: 324 (Wake Island and Johnston Island).

Diagnosis.—Dorsal rays XII, 16 to 17; anal rays II, 13 to 14; pectoral rays 20 to 21. Tubed lateral-line scales 21 to 22. Gill rakers on first arch 14 to 16. Body depth 1.9 to 2.1 in SL. Color in alcohol generally dark brown with three to four narrow pale bars on body and broad black bar on caudal peduncle; caudal and pectorals pale; specimens under about 40 mm SL with ocellus on soft dorsal fin. Maximum size to about 70 mm SL.

Ecology.—Inhabits reefs which are exposed to mild or moderate surge in 0.1 to eight meters.

Distribution.—Johnston Island, Wake Island, Marcus Island, and the Marshall, Gilbert, Fiji, Samoa, Phoenix, Society, Tuamotu, and Marquesas Islands. Also recently collected by D. Robertson at Kenn Reef, Coral Sea. In addition, J. Randall recently collected and photographed a species at Mauritius, West Indian Ocean which is very similar and may in fact represent a color variant of *phoenixensis*.

Plectroglyphidodon sindonis (Jordan and Evermann)
Hawaiian Rock Damsel

Illus. p. 200

Glyphisodon sindonis Jordan and Evermann, 1903: 188 (Hawaii).

Diagnosis.—Dorsal rays XII, 19 to 20; anal rays II, 15 to 16; pectoral rays 21. Tubed lateral-line scales 21 to 22. Gill rakers on first arch 14 to 16. Body depth 1.6 to 1.7 in SL. Color in alcohol generally brown to dark brown with darker scale margins; juveniles and subadults with two pale bars on sides, a pale caudal, and large ocellus below soft dorsal junction; all specimens with large triangular dark spot on upper pectoral base. Maximum size to about 100 mm SL.

Ecology.—Inhabits areas exposed to mild or moderate surge, adjacent to rocky shores in 0.5 to three meters.

Distribution.—Endemic to the Hawaiian Islands.

Plectroglyphidodon johnstonianus (about 75 mm TL), Great Barrier Reef, off Cairns, Queensland in eight meters.

Plectroglyphidodon phoenixensis (70 mm SL), Eniwetok, Marshall Islands (J. Randall photo).

Plectroglyphidodon sindonis (about 110 mm TL), Hawaii, Hawaiian Islands in two meters.

Pomacentrus albimaculus (about 75 mm TL), Madang, New Guinea in 12 meters.

Pomacentrus alexanderae (about 75 mm TL), Malakal Island, Palau Islands in 10 meters.

Chapter XXIII
POMACENTRUS

The genus *Pomacentrus* is the second largest in the family; only *Chromis* contains more species. It includes approximately 35 members which are found in the Indo-West Pacific; 25 are inhabitants of the "South Seas." A serrate preopercle and biserial teeth at the front of the jaws are characteristic features of these fishes. Although a majority of the members are moderately deep-bodied, a few of the species, such as *P. australis*, *P. coelestis*, and *P. pavo*, are elongate. These latter forms tend to be bright blue in color and spend most of the time feeding in midwater on zooplankton. The other members are omnivorous feeders. Generally speaking, the drab colored species, such as *P. burroughi* and *P. wardi*, are primarily herbivorous, while more colorful species such as *P. alexanderae* and *P. popei* consume a significant amount of zooplankton. However, there are exceptions. The various species are adapted to a wide range of environmental conditions. *P. tripunctatus* is restricted to coastal reefs at depths less than about three meters. Others, such as *P. alexanderae* and *P. reidi*, are largely restricted to outer reef slopes in about 20 to 46 meters depth. *P. amboinensis* and *P. flavicauda* shelter in outcrops adjacent to sandy bottoms, while other species such as *P. lepidogenys* and *P. popei* prefer areas of rich coral growth. In short, the group is extremely successful, having invaded a wide variety of habitats.

P. wardi, a common inhabitant of the reefs surrounding One Tree Island on the Great Barrier Reef, exhibits a spawning pattern which is typical of several of the species observed during the study. Courtship activities are initiated by the more aggressive male who continually chases his mate with a "jerky" swimming motion. During courtship, spawning, and nest guarding the male frequently assumes a pattern consisting of three to four whitish bars on the upper back which are contrasted against the dark ground color. These bars vanish and re-appear periodically. Up to several thousand eggs are attached to a solid substratum, usually under a stone or on the walls or ceiling of a rocky hollow. They are guarded and cared for by the male for several days prior to hatching. The fry leave the nest immediately upon hatching and are assumed to be pelagic for at least several weeks.

GENUS *POMACENTRUS* LACEPEDE

Pomacentrus Lacépède, 1802: 505 (type species, *Chaetodon pavo* Bloch).

Diagnostic features.—Margin of suborbital usually serrate (except entire in *P. coelestis*, *P. lepidogenys*, and *P. smithi*); margin of preopercle usually with distinct serrae (weak in *P. lepidogenys* and *P. smithi*); usually a prominent notch between preorbital and suborbital, but much reduced in a few species; dorsal spines XIII to XIV (usually XIII); preorbital usually naked, but scaled in *P. lepidogenys* and with small patch of scales in *P. littoralis*; suborbital usually naked (except scaled posteriorly in *P. philippinus*); teeth biserial anteriorly; snout scaled to about level of nostrils or beyond; greatest body depth 1.7 to 2.6 in SL.

KEY TO THE SPECIES OF *POMACENTRUS* FROM THE SOUTH SEAS

1a. Dorsal spines XIV. 2

1b. Dorsal spines XIII. 4

2a. Body depth 2.2 to 2.6 in SL; pectoral base entirely dusky (eastern Australia). . . . . . .*P. australis*

2b. Body depth 1.8 to 2.0 in SL; pectoral base with dark spot superiorly. .3

3a. Gill rakers 19 to 21; pectoral rays usually 18; small dark spot on upper pectoral base (East Indies; Philippines; Palau Islands; Melanesia; Great Barrier Reef). . . . .*P. reidi*

3b. Gill rakers 26 to 29; pectoral rays usually 17; prominent wedge-shaped dark mark on upper pectoral base (Philippines; New Guinea). . . . .*P. opisthostigma*

4a. Body depth 2.4 or greater in SL. 5

4b. Body depth 2.3 or less (usually 1.8 to 2.1) in SL. 6

5a. Preorbital with one or two posteriorly directed spines; suborbital serrate; gill rakers usually 23 to 24 (Indo-West Pacific). . . . .*P. pavo*

5b. Preorbital and suborbital entire; gill rakers usually 20 to 22 (West Pacific). . . . .*P. coelestis*

6a. Pectoral base mostly covered with prominent rounded black spot. .7

6b. Pectoral base not mostly covered with prominent rounded black spot. 11

7a. Tubed lateral-line scales 13 to 15; posterior edge of dorsal and caudal fins with prominent dark margin (Moluccas; Melanesia; Great Barrier Reef). . . . .*P. nigromarginatus*

7b. Tubed lateral-line scales 16 to 19; posterior edge of dorsal and caudal fins usually without (except sometimes in *P. philippinus*) contrasting dark margin. 8

8a. Pectoral rays usually 16 to 17. 9

8b. Pectoral rays usually 18 to 19. 10

9a. Color of body generally brown except posterior portion, including caudal fin and peduncle, pale (yellow in life); anal fin mostly black (East Indies; Philippines; Palau Islands; Melanesia; northern Australia). . . . .*P. alexanderae*

9b. Color of body uniformly dark brown to blackish, including fins (Ryukyus; Taiwan; East Indies; Philippines; Marshall and Mariana Islands; Caroline Islands; Melanesia; Great Barrier Reef; Samoa Islands). . . . .*P. melanopterus*

10a. Suborbital with scales on posterior section; dorsal rays usually 14 (last ray branched near base); gill rakers usually 23 to 24; soft dorsal, anal and caudal fins without faint spots (Ryukyus; Taiwan; Philippines; Melanesia; Great Barrier Reef). . . . .*P. philippinus*

10b. Suborbital without scales; dorsal rays usually 15 (last ray branched near base); gill rakers usually 19 to 21; soft dorsal, anal, and caudal fins frequently with several rows of faint spots (East Indies; Palau Islands; Melanesia; Great Barrier Reef). . . . .*P. species*

11a. Suborbital scaly (Philippines; Melanesia; Great Barrier Reef). . . . .*P. lepidogenys*

11b. Suborbital naked. 12

12a. Caudal fin abruptly pale, strongly contrasted with adjacent caudal peduncle. 13

12b. Caudal fin not abruptly pale, either dark or pale, but not strongly contrasted with adjacent caudal peduncle 14

13a. Forehead with several narrow lines (bluish in life); each scale of body with bluish dot; ocellus generally present on soft dorsal fin of individuals of all sizes; anal fin with pale submarginal lines (Japan; Ryukyus; Taiwan; East Indies; Philippines; Palau Islands; Melanesia; Great Barrier Reef) . . . .*P. bankanensis*

13b. Forehead without narrow lines; each scale of body without bluish dot; ocellus present only on soft dorsal fin of juveniles (under about 30–40 mm SL); anal fin usually without pale submarginal lines (Ryukyus; Palau Islands; Melanesia; eastern Australia). . . . .*P. flavicauda*

14a. Color of body mostly pale, at least on ventral half of body. 15

14b. Color of body generally brown. 18

Pomacentrus amboinensis (about 100 mm TL), Augulpelu Reef, Palau Islands in 10 meters.

Pomacentrus australis (about 75 mm TL), Wistari Reef, Great Barrier Reef in 15 meters.

Pomacentrus bankanensis (about 75 mm TL), Uvea, Loyalty Islands in five meters.

Pomacentrus bankanensis (about 75 mm TL), Augulpelu Reef, Palau Islands in five meters.

15a. Dorsal rays 12 to 13; anal rays 13 (last ray branched near base); body depth 2.1 to 2.2 in SL; tubed lateral-line scales 15 to 16 (Philippines; Melanesia)....................*P. smithi*

15b. Dorsal rays 14 to 16; anal rays 14 to 16; body depth 1.8 to 2.1 in SL; tubed lateral-line scales 16 to 18 16

16a. Anterodorsal portion of body usually dark, more or less sharply contrasted with remainder of body; ocellus present at soft dorsal junction on juveniles under about 40–50 mm SL (Ryukyus; Taiwan; East Indies; Philippines; Palau Islands; Melanesia)..................*P. moluccensis*

16b. Anterodorsal portion of body generally same color or only slightly darker than remainder of body...17

17a. Prominent dark spot about ⅓ to ½ pupil diameter, on upper pectoral base; body depth 2.0 to 2.1 in SL; side of head frequently with whitish blotches; soft dorsal fin with ocellus on most individuals under about 50 mm SL; dorsal and anal fins without narrow black margin (East Indies; Philippines; Palau Islands; Melanesia; eastern Australia)..............*P. amboinensis*

17b. Small dark spot, much less than ⅓ pupil diameter, on upper pectoral base; body depth 1.8 to 1.9 in SL; side of head without whitish blotches; soft dorsal fin without ocellus on individuals of all sizes; dorsal and anal fins with narrow black margin (Philippines; Palau Islands; Moluccas; Melanesia; Great Barrier Reef)........................*P. popei*

18a. Forehead with several narrow lines (bluish in life); each scale of body with bluish dots; ocellus or black spot usually present on soft dorsal fin of individuals of all sizes; forehead and upper portion of back usually pale (orange in life) (West Pacific).......................*P. vaiuli*

18b. Forehead without several narrow lines (except in small juveniles); each scale of body without bluish dots; ocellus on soft dorsal fin present or absent; forehead and upper portion of back usually same color as body (brown)...19

19a. Gill rakers 26 to 30; color mostly brown with pale spots on side of head; bluish spot on dorsal edge of caudal peduncle when alive (Philippines; Palau Islands; New Guinea; Solomon Islands) ....*P. grammorhynchus*

19b. Gill rakers 20 to 24; color not as in 19a.................................20

20a. Pectoral rays usually 18 to 19.....................................21

20b. Pectoral rays usually 16 to 17.....................................23

21a. Dorsal edge of caudal peduncle with black spot or saddle (Melanesia; Queensland)..........
....*P. tripunctatus*

21b. Dorsal edge of caudal peduncle without black spot................................22

22a. Dorsal and anal rays 13 to 14; gill rakers 23 to 24; body depth 1.9 to 2.0 in SL; caudal whitish (Palau Islands; New Guinea)............................*P. emarginatus*

22b. Dorsal and anal rays 15 to 16; gill rakers 20 to 22; body depth 1.9 to 2.0 in SL (eastern Australia)...*P. wardi*

23a. Tubed lateral-line scales 14 to 16; gill rakers 24 to 25; color generally dark brown, frequently with one to two pale blotches at base of soft dorsal fin (Philippines; Palau Islands; New Guinea; Solomon Islands)...*P. burroughi*

23b. Tubed lateral-line scales 16 to 17; gill rakers 20 to 22; color generally brown, sometimes with ocellus on soft dorsal fin.....................................24

24a. Body light brown to brown with darker scale margins, whitish to tan saddle on dorsal edge of caudal peduncle; tubed lateral-line scales usually 15 to 16 (New Guinea)........*P. albimaculus*

24b. Body uniformly brown without pale area on dorsal edge of caudal peduncle; tubed lateral-line scales usually 17 (East Indies; Palau Islands; Melanesia; Great Barrier Reef)..*P. taeniometopon*

Pomacentrus albimaculus Allen
White-spot Damsel

Illus. p. 201

Pomacentrus albimaculus Allen, 1975: 96 (Madang, New Guinea).

Diagnosis.—Dorsal rays XIII, 14 to 15; anal rays II, 15 to 16; pectoral rays 17. Tubed lateral-line scales 16 to 17. Gill rakers on first arch 20 to 21. Body depth 1.9 to 2.0 in SL. Color in alcohol generally brown, scale margins and top of head darker; upper portion of caudal peduncle tan; dorsal, anal, and caudal fins brown, pectorals and pelvics pale with diffuse dark spot on upper pectoral base; ocellus present on soft dorsal fin of specimens under about 40 mm SL. Maximum size to about 70 mm SL.

Ecology.—Observed only at Madang, New Guinea where it is found in the harbor, around wharf pilings and rocky outcrops in 10 to 20 meters. Occasional individuals are encountered outside the harbor, but inside the outer reef. Occurs solitarily or in small groups. Feeds mainly on algae.

Distribution.—Presently known only from Madang, New Guinea, but certainly more widespread.

Pomacentrus alexanderae Evermann and Seale
Alexander's Damsel
Illus. p. 201

Pomacentrus alexanderae Evermann and Seale, 1907: 91 (Philippines).
Pomacentrus nigromanus Weber, 1913: 338 (Amboina).

Diagnosis.—Dorsal rays XIII, 13 to 14; anal rays II, 14 to 15; pectoral rays 17. Tubed lateral-line scales 16 to 17. Gill rakers on first arch 20 to 22. Body depth 2.0 to 2.1 in SL. Color in alcohol brown grading to yellowish posteriorly; anterior half of spinous dorsal fin brown, remainder of fins and soft dorsal yellowish; anal fin black except hindmost portion abruptly pale; caudal yellowish; pelvic spine and first ray black, remainder of fin pale yellow; pectorals pale with prominent black spot covering fin base and axil. Maximum size to about 70 mm SL.

Ecology.—Inhabits lagoons, passages, and outer reef slopes in six to 60 meters. Occurs solitarily or in small groups. The stomach of a specimen from Palau contained algae, barnacle nauplii, copepods, fish eggs, and a small gastropod.

Distribution.—East Indies, Philippines, Palau Islands, New Guinea, northern Australia (except Great Barrier Reef), New Britain, Solomon Islands, and New Hebrides.

Pomacentrus amboinensis Bleeker
Ambon Damsel
Illus. p. 204

Pomacentrus amboinensis Bleeker, 1868: 334 (Amboina).

Diagnosis.—Dorsal rays XIII, 14 to 16; anal rays II, 14 to 16; pectoral rays 17. Tubed lateral-line scales 16 to 17. Gill rakers on first arch 22 to 24. Body depth 2.0 to 2.1 in SL. Color in alcohol generally tan to yellowish, darker dorsally; small dark spot near lateral-line origin; fins pale, prominent black spot on upper portion of pectoral fin base; juveniles under about 40–50 mm SL with ocellus on soft dorsal fin. Maximum size to about 80 mm SL.

Ecology.—A ubiquitous species inhabiting lagoons, coastal reefs, passages, and outer reef slopes in two to 40 meters. Occurs in sandy areas around coral heads, rocky outcrops or other protective shelter. Food consists chiefly of algae, but zooplankton is also taken.

Distribution.—East Indies, Philippines, Palau Islands, New Guinea, New Britain, Solomon Islands, New Hebrides, Loyalty Islands, New Caledonia, and tropical eastern Australia.

Remarks.—Live individuals are variable in color, ranging from drab pale-purplish to bright yellow.

Pomacentrus australis Allen and Robertson
Australian Damsel
Illus. p. 204

Pomacentrus australis Allen and Robertson, 1973: 158 (Great Barrier Reef).

Diagnosis.—Dorsal rays XIV, 13 to 14; anal rays II, 14 to 15; pectoral rays 17 to 19. Tubed lateral-line scales 17 to 19. Gill rakers on first arch 19 to 21. Body depth 2.2 to 2.6 in SL. Color in alcohol generally bluish to brown, paler ventrally and on caudal peduncle; dorsal and anal fins grey or dusky; remainder of fins pale to dusky; pectoral base dusky. Maximum size to about 65mm SL.

Ecology.—At One Tree Island, Great Barrier Reef this species inhabits lagoon and outer reef environments in 12 to 35 meters. The habitat consists of open sandy areas or rubble areas with

Pomacentrus burroughi (about 100 mm TL), Madang, New Guinea in five meters.

Pomacentrus burroughi (about 40 mm TL), Madang, New Guinea in two meters.

Pomacentrus coelestis (about 60-70 mm TL), Malakal Pass, Palau Islands in three meters.

Pomacentrus coelestis (about 75 mm TL), Malakal Pass, Palau Islands in two meters.

occasional coral outcrops. Occurs solitarily or in small groups which typically feed on zooplankton a short distance above the bottom.

Distribution.—Apparently confined to the southern half of the Great Barrier Reef and New South Wales as far south as the Sydney area.

Pomacentrus bankanensis Bleeker
Speckled Damsel

Illus. p. 205

Pomacentrus bankanensis Bleeker, 1853d: 513 (Banka, Indonesia).
Pomacentrus dorsalis Gill, 1859: 147 (Japan).
Pomacentrus delurus Jordan and Seale, 1905: 738 (Philippines).

Diagnosis.—Dorsal rays XIII, 15 to 16; anal rays II, 15 to 16; pectoral rays 18. Tubed lateral-line scales 17 to 19. Gill rakers on first arch 20 to 22. Body depth 2.0 to 2.1 in SL. Color in alcohol generally brown with caudal fin and peduncle abruptly whitish; small dark spot near lateral-line origin and on upper portion of pectoral fin base; fins brown except pectorals pale; ocellus present on hindmost dorsal rays; specimens from certain localities sometimes entirely brown or with only slightly lighter caudal fin and peduncle; see remarks section for comments on juvenile coloration. Maximum size to about 70 mm SL.

Ecology.—Inhabits lagoons, reef flats, passages, and outer reef slopes in one to 12 meters. Occurs solitarily or in small groups. Feeds mainly on algae, but copepods, isopods, and pelagic tunicates also taken.

Distribution.—Japan, Ryukyu Islands, Taiwan, East Indies, Philippines, Palau Islands, New Guinea, Great Barrier Reef, New Britain, Solomon Islands, New Hebrides, New Caledonia, and Fiji Islands.

Remarks.—The juveniles of *P. bankanensis*, *P. flavicauda*, and *P. vaiuli* are similar, but easily distinguished on the basis of live coloration. Unlike *P. bankanensis* and *P. flavicauda*, which exhibit an abrupt boundary between the dark body color and the whitish caudal fin and peduncle, *P. vaiuli* shows a gradual transition of color in this area. *P. flavicauda* differs from the other two species by lacking bluish stripes on the forehead, which is generally brown. The forehead region of *P. bankanensis* and *P. vaiuli* is orange (actually more reddish in *P. bankanensis*) with several bluish stripes extending from the snout and interorbital region to the dorsal fin base. *P. vaiuli*, however, differs from *P. bankanensis* by lacking a bluish stripe on the exact mid-dorsal line of the snout, interorbital, and forehead.

Pomacentrus burroughi Fowler
Burrough's Damsel

Illus. p. 208

Pomacentrus burroughi Fowler, 1918: 46 (Philippines).
Pomacentrus cranei Herre, 1935: 409 (Solomon Islands).

Diagnosis.—Dorsal rays XIII, 15 to 16; anal rays II, 15 to 16; pectoral rays 16 to 17. Tubed lateral-line scales 14 to 16. Gill rakers on first arch 24 to 25. Body depth 1.8 to 2.0 in SL. Color in alcohol generally dark brown, frequently with one or two pale blotches at base of soft dorsal fin; fins dark brown except pectorals pale with small black spot on upper portion of fin base. Maximum size to about 65 mm SL.

Ecology.—Inhabits lagoons and coastal reefs in two to 16 meters. Occurs solitarily or in small groups. Feeds mainly on benthic algae.

Distribution.—Presently known from the Philippines, Palau Islands, New Guinea, and the Solomon Islands.

Remarks.—Fowler's description of *P. burroughi* does not mention the characteristic pale spot(s) at the base of the soft dorsal fin. However, these markings are frequently absent in preserved material. The low lateral-line count (usually 14 to 15) given by Fowler in combination with the dark coloration is distinctive.

Pomacentrus coelestis Jordan and Starks
Neon Damsel

Illus. p. 209

Pomacentrus coelestis Jordan and Starks, 1901: 383 (Japan).

Diagnosis.—Dorsal rays XIII, 13 to 15; anal rays II, 14 to 15; pectoral rays 17 to 18. Tubed lateral-line scales 17 to 18. Gill rakers on first arch 20 to 22. Body depth 2.5 to 2.6 in SL. Color in alcohol generally dark brown, pale (yellowish) on chin, breast, and abdomen; dorsal fin brown except hindmost rays pale; anal fin usually pale, occasionally brown or dusky; caudal fin and sometimes peduncle yellowish; pelvics and pectorals pale with darkish base and axil on latter fin. Maximum size to about 70 mm SL.

Ecology.—Inhabits outer reef slopes in one to 12 meters, frequently among dead coral rubble. Occurs in small to large aggregations comprised of hundreds of individuals. Feeds in midwater on zooplankton, but some algae taken from the substratum.

Distribution.—Japan, Ryukyu Islands, Philippines, Molucca Islands, Melanesia, eastern Australia as far south as Sydney, and Oceania in general as far east as the Tuamotu and Line Islands.

Pomacentrus emarginatus Cuvier
Outer-reef Damsel

Illus. p. 212

Pomacentrus emarginatus Cuvier, 1830: 422 (Waigiu).

Diagnosis.—Dorsal rays XIII, 14; anal rays II, 13 to 14; pectoral rays 18. Tubed lateral-line scales 17 to 18. Gill rakers on first arch 23 to 24. Body depth 2.0 to 2.1 in SL. Color in alcohol generally brown; fins slightly dusky to brown, except caudal and pectorals pale; base of pectoral fin darker than adjacent part of body. Maximum size to about 75 mm SL.

Ecology.—Inhabits the upper edge of outer reef slopes in four to 12 meters. Occurs solitarily or in small groups. Feeds on benthic algae and zooplankton.

Distribution.—Known from the Palau Islands and Waigeo Island, off Western New Guinea.

Remarks.—I tentatively identify the species treated here as *P. emarginatus*. It differs from the type of this species (kindly sent from Paris by Dr. M. L. Bauchot), however, with regards to gill raker count (19 to 20 in the type) and suborbital serration (well-developed in the type, but poorly developed in Palau specimens). In addition, the type is slightly more elongate (depth 2.2 in SL vs. 2.0 to 2.1). It is possible that my Palau specimens represent an undescribed species.

Pomacentrus flavicauda Whitley
White-tail Damsel

Illus. p. 212

?*Pomacentrus chrysurus* Cuvier, 1830: 432 (Southern Sea).
Pomacentrus flavicauda Whitley, 1928b: 298 (Northwest Islet, Queensland).

Diagnosis.—Dorsal rays XIII, 14 to 16; anal rays II, 15 to 16; pectoral rays 18. Tubed lateral-line scales 18 to 19. Gill rakers on first arch 18 to 19. Body depth 1.9 to 2.2 in SL. Color in alcohol generally dark brown with caudal fin abruptly pale; remainder of fins dark brown except pectorals pale; juveniles with ocellus on hind portion of dorsal fin. Maximum size to about 65–70 mm SL.

Ecology.—Inhabits lagoons and reef flats in 0.5 to three meters, usually around rocky outcrops surrounded by sand. Occurs solitarily or in small groups. Feeds primarily on algae.

Distribution.—Ryukyu Islands, Palau Islands, New Guinea, Great Barrier Reef, Solomon Islands, Loyalty Islands, and New Caledonia. Probably more widespread, but included in the synonymy of other species by previous authors.

Remarks.—I have examined the type of *P. chrysurus* which is deposited at Paris (MNHN). The lack of distinguishing color features and absence of information regarding the type locality make a positive determination of the status difficult.

Pomacentrus flavicauda (about 75 mm TL), One Tree Island, Great Barrier Reef in two meters.

Pomacentrus emarginatus (about 100 mm TL), Augulpelu Reef, Palau Islands in 10 meters.

Pomacentrus lepidogenys (about 75 mm TL), One Tree Island, Great Barrier Reef in 15 meters.

Pomacentrus lepidogenys (about 75 mm TL), Great Barrier Reef, off Cairns, Queensland in seven meters.

Pomacentrus grammorhynchus Fowler
Blue-spot Damsel

Illus. p. 216

Pomacentrus grammorhynchus Fowler, 1918: 44 (Philippines).

Diagnosis.—Dorsal rays XIII, 14 to 15; anal rays II, 14 to 15; pectoral rays 17 to 18. Tubed lateral-line scales 16 to 17. Gill rakers on first arch 26 to 30. Body depth 1.8 to 2.0 in SL. Color in alcohol generally brown; caudal peduncle frequently with darkened area on dorsal surface; dorsal and anal fins mostly brown; caudal dusky; pectorals and pelvics pale; base of pectoral fin dark; see additional comments on coloration under remarks section. Maximum size to about 80–90 mm SL.

Ecology.—Inhabits lagoons and passages in two to 12 meters, usually among branching corals. Occurs solitarily or in small groups. Feeds mainly on benthic algae.

Distribution.—Philippines, Palau Islands, New Guinea, Solomon Islands and Great Barrier Reef. Probably more widespread.

Remarks.—The bright blue spot on the dorsal surface of the caudal peduncle and yellowish pectoral fins are characteristic features of live individuals. The ground color of the body ranges from brown to tan. Juveniles are very similar to *P. moluccensis* but have a blue dot on the upper part of the caudal peduncle.

Pomacentrus lepidogenys Fowler and Bean
Scaly Damsel

Illus. p. 213

Pomacentrus lepidogenys Fowler and Bean, 1928: 98 (Philippines).

Diagnosis.—Dorsal rays XIII, 14 to 15; anal rays II, 14 to 15; pectoral rays 18. Tubed lateral-line scales 17 to 18. Gill rakers on first arch 20 to 22. Body depth 2.0 to 2.3 in SL. Color in alcohol generally brown to greyish, darker dorsally; fins light brown to translucent; small dark spot on upper portion of pectoral base. Maximum size to about 70 mm SL.

Ecology.—Inhabits lagoons, passages, and outer reef slopes in one to 12 meters. Occurs solitarily or in small groups. Feeds on zooplankton a short distance above the substratum.

Distribution.—Philippines, Molucca Islands, New Guinea, New Britain, Solomon Islands, New Hebrides, Loyalty Islands, New Caledonia, Fiji Islands, and Great Barrier Reef.

Pomacentrus species
Speckled-fin Damsel

Illus. p. 216

Diagnosis.—Dorsal rays XIII, 15 to 16; anal rays II, 15 to 16; pectoral rays 18 to 19. Tubed lateral-line scales 17 to 19. Gill rakers on first arch 19 to 21. Body depth 1.9 to 2.0 in SL. Color in alcohol generally dark brown (scale centers may be pale brown); spinous dorsal fin dark brown; remainder of fins brown to pale, frequently with several rows of pale spots on soft dorsal, anal, and caudal fins; specimens from the Great Barrier Reef with more or less abrupt transition from dark color of body to pale caudal fin; juveniles with ocellus on dorsal fin, occasionally persisting in adults. Maximum size to about 80 mm SL.

Ecology.—Inhabits lagoons, harbors, passages, and outer reef slopes in three to 35 meters, usually in sandy areas. Occurs solitarily or in small groups. Feeds primarily on zooplankton up to about two meters above the substratum, although some benthic algae is taken.

Distribution.—East Indies, Palau Islands, New Guinea, Great Barrier Reef, New Britain, Solomon Islands, New Hebrides, Loyalty Islands, and New Caledonia.

Pomacentrus melanopterus Bleeker
Charcoal Damsel

Illus. p. 217

Pomacentrus melanopterus Bleeker, 1852b: 562 (Amboina).
Pseudopomacentrus rainfordi Whitley, 1935: 236 (Hayman Island, Queensland).

Diagnosis.—Dorsal rays XIII, 13 to 15; anal rays II, 14 to 15; pectoral rays 16 to 17. Tubed lateral-line scales 16 to 17. Gill rakers on first arch 19 to 21. Body depth 1.8 to 2.0 in SL. Color in alcohol generally dark brown to blackish; fins dark brown to blackish except pectorals pale with intense black spot covering fin base and axil. Maximum size to about 80 mm SL.

Ecology.—Inhabits passages and outer reef slopes in six to 40 meters. Occurs solitarily or in small to large groups. Feeds on zooplankton and benthic algae.

Distribution.—Ryukyu Islands, Taiwan, East Indies, Philippines, Marshall Islands, Mariana Islands, Caroline Islands, New Guinea, Great Barrier Reef, New Britain, Solomon Islands, New Hebrides, Loyalty Islands, New Caledonia, Fiji Islands, and Samoa Islands.

Pomacentrus moluccensis Bleeker
Molucca Damsel
Illus. pp. 217, 220

Pomacentrus moluccensis Bleeker, 1853c: 118 (Amboina).
Pomacentrus tropicus Seale, 1909: 517 (Philippines).

Diagnosis.—Dorsal rays XIII, 14 to 16; anal rays II, 14 to 15; pectoral rays 17. Tubed lateral-line scales 16 to 17. Gill rakers on first arch 21 to 23. Body depth 2.0 to 2.1 in SL. Color in alcohol generally tan to yellowish, except dorsal part of head and portion of body above lateral-line dark brown; spinous dorsal fin brown, remainder of fins pale; pectorals with small black spot on upper portion of fin base; juvenile pattern as illustrated. Maximum size to about 70 mm SL.

Ecology.—Inhabits silty lagoons, coastal reefs, and harbors in 0.3 to 10 meters. Occurs solitarily or in small groups. Feeds mainly on benthic algae.

Distribution.—Ryukyu Islands, Taiwan, East Indies, Philippines, Palau Islands, New Guinea, New Britain, Solomon Islands, and New Hebrides.

Pomacentrus nigromarginatus Allen
Black-margined Damsel
Illus. p. 220

Pomacentrus nigromarginatus Allen, 1973a: 41 (Madang, New Guinea).

Diagnosis.—Dorsal rays XIII, 14 to 15; anal rays II, 14 to 15; pectoral rays 16 to 17. Tubed lateral-line scales 13 to 15. Gill rakers on first arch 20 to 21. Body depth 2.1 in SL. Color in alcohol generally grey to brown with darker scale margins giving reticulated appearance; fins mostly pale to dusky except dorsal and caudal fins with prominent black margin on their posterior edge; intense black spot covering pectoral base. Maximum size to about 65 mm SL.

Ecology.—Inhabits outer reef slopes in 20 to 46 meters, frequently around rocky outcrops situated in sandy areas. Feeds on algae and zooplankton.

Distribution.—New Guinea, New Britain, Solomon Islands, Osprey Reef (Coral Sea), and northern Great Barrier Reef. Additionally, I have recently examined specimens from the Molucca Islands collected by V. Springer and M. Gomon.

Pomacentrus opisthostigma Fowler
Brown Damsel
Illus. p. 220

Pomacentrus opisthostigma Fowler, 1918: 51 (Philippines).

Diagnosis.—Dorsal rays XIV, 13 to 14; anal rays II, 15 to 16; pectoral rays 17. Tubed lateral-line scales 15 to 16. Gill rakers on first arch 26 to 29. Body depth 1.9 to 2.0 in SL. Color in alcohol generally brown, paler on breast and abdomen; dorsal and anal fins brown; pelvics and pectorals pale, caudal dusky, prominent wedge-shaped dark mark on upper portion of pectoral base. Maximum size to about 65 mm SL.

Ecology.—Collected only at Goodenough and Fergusson Islands, D'Entrecasteaux Group from near shore reefs in six to 16 meters.

Distribution.—Philippines and New Guinea.

Pomacentrus grammorhynchus (about 100 mm TL), Alite Reef, Solomon Islands in 10 meters.

Pomacentrus species (about 80 mm TL), One Tree Island, Great Barrier Reef in six meters.

Pomacentrus melanopterus (about 80 mm TL), Efate, New Hebrides in 10 meters.

Pomacentrus moluccensis (about 75 mm TL), Guadalcanal, Solomon Islands in three meters.

Pomacentrus pavo (Bloch)
Blue Damsel

Illus. p. 221

Chaetodon pavo Bloch, 1787: 60 (East Indies).

Diagnosis.—Dorsal rays XIII, 13 to 14; anal rays II, 12 to 14; pectoral rays 17. Tubed lateral-line scales 16 to 17. Gill rakers on first arch 23 to 24. Body depth 2.4 to 2.6 in SL. Color in alcohol generally brown, lighter ventrally, with blue to grey streak on each scale; dark spot about size of pupil near lateral-line origin; spinous dorsal fin brown; remainder of fins pale to dusky. Maximum size to about 85 mm SL.

Ecology.—Inhabits lagoons and coastal reefs, usually in sandy areas around coral outcrops or alcyonarian growths, in one to 16 meters. Feeds on plankton and also filamentous algae. Occurs in small to large groups.

Distribution.—Widespread in the tropical Indo-West Pacific as far east as the Tuamotu, Marshall, and Gilbert Islands.

Pomacentrus philippinus Evermann and Seale
Philippine Damsel

Illus. pp. 221, 225

Pomacentrus philippinus Evermann and Seale, 1907: 91 (Philippines).
Pseudopomacentrus imitator Whitley, 1964: 175 (Lihou Atoll, Coral Sea).

Diagnosis.—Dorsal rays XIII, 14 to 15; anal rays II, 14 to 16; pectoral rays 18 to 19. Tubed lateral-line scales 17 to 18. Gill rakers on first arch 23 to 24. Body depth 1.9 to 2.0 in SL. Color in alcohol generally dark brown; scale centers lighter; dorsal and anal fins brown to blackish except hindmost portion pale; caudal pale; pectorals pale with black spot covering base; pelvics black; specimens from the Great Barrier Reef entirely blackish with pale streak on each scale. Maximum size to about 70–80 mm SL.

Ecology.—Inhabits passages and outer reef slopes in 1.5 to 12 meters, usually around coral outcrops or in the shadows of overhanging cliffs and ledges. Occurs solitarily or in small groups.

Distribution.—Ryukyu Islands, Taiwan, Philippines, New Guinea, Great Barrier Reef, Solomon Islands, New Hebrides, New Caledonia and Fiji Islands.

Pomacentrus popei Jordan and Seale
Lemon Damsel

Illus. p. 224

Pomacentrus popei Jordan and Seale, 1907: 90 (Philippines).
Pomacentrus sufflavus Whitley, 1927: 18 (Michaelmas Cay, Queensland).

Diagnosis.—Dorsal rays XIII, 14 to 15; anal rays II, 14 to 15; pectoral rays 17. Tubed lateral-line scales 17 to 18. Gill rakers on first arch 23 to 24. Body depth 1.8 to 1.9 in SL. Color in alcohol generally yellowish to light brown; small dark spot near origin of lateral-line and another on upper portion of pectoral fin base; fins pale. Maximum size to about 55–60 mm SL.

Ecology.—Inhabits lagoons, passages, and outer reef slopes in one to 14 meters, usually in the vicinity of live coral. Occurs solitarily or in small to large aggregations. Feeds chiefly on algae and planktonic crustacea.

Distribution.—Philippines, Palau Islands, Molucca Islands, New Guinea, Great Barrier Reef, New Britain, Solomon Islands, New Hebrides, Loyalty Islands, New Caledonia, and Fiji Islands.

Remarks.—W. Taylor of USNM has kindly compared the types of *P. popei* with specimens of *P. sufflavus* from the Great Barrier Reef. He reported that they are identical.

A unique variety, which is characterized by a purplish-brown coloration, exists in the Fiji Islands. However, the young are similar to specimens from other areas.

Pomacentrus reidi Fowler and Bean
Reid's Damsel

Illus. p. 225

Pomacentrus reidi Fowler and Bean, 1928: 99 (Philippines).

Diagnosis.—Dorsal rays XIV, 13 to 15; anal rays II, 15 to 16; pectoral rays 17 to 18. Tubed lateral-line scales 16 to 17. Gill rakers on first arch 19 to 21. Body depth 1.8 to 2.0 in SL. Color in alcohol generally greyish, slightly yellowish ventrally; dorsal and anal fins grey; remainder of fins pale; small dark spot on upper portion of pectoral base. Maximum size to about 90 mm SL.

Ecology.—Inhabits outer reef slopes in 12 to 70 meters. At Palau this was one of the most common pomacentrids between 20 and 40 meters.

Distribution.—Celebes, Molucca Islands, Philippines, Palau Islands, New Guinea, Solomon Islands, New Hebrides, and Great Barrier Reef.

Pomacentrus smithi Fowler and Bean
Smith's Damsel

Illus. p. 228

Pomacentrus smithi Fowler and Bean, 1928: 75 (Philippines).

Diagnosis.—Dorsal rays XIII, 12 to 13; anal rays II, 13 to 14; pectoral rays 16 to 17. Tubed lateral-line scales 15 to 16. Gill rakers on first arch 21 to 22. Body depth 2.1 to 2.2 in SL. Color in alcohol generally tan to brown, scale margins frequently darker giving appearance of oblique lines on sides and five to six horizontal lines on caudal peduncle; ventral portion of head and body whitish to silvery; spinous dorsal fin brown; remainder of fins pale; pectorals with small dark spot on upper portion of fin base. Maximum size to about 50–55 mm SL.

Ecology.—Inhabits lagoons, harbors, and coastal reefs in two to 14 meters, frequently where silting is relatively heavy. Occurs in small to large groups which feed in midwater above live coral heads.

Distribution.—Philippines, New Guinea, Solomon Islands, and New Hebrides.

Pomacentrus taeniometopon Bleeker
Dusky Damsel

Illus. p. 229

Pomacentrus taeniometopon Bleeker, 1852c: 283 (Ceram).

Diagnosis.—Dorsal rays XIII, 15 to 16; anal rays II, 14 to 15; pectoral rays 17. Tubed lateral-line scales 17. Gill rakers on first arch 21 to 22. Body depth 1.9 to 2.0 in SL. Color in alcohol generally brown; small dark spot near lateral-line origin and on upper portion of pectoral fin base frequently present; dorsal, anal, and pelvic fins dark brown with ocellus frequently present on posterior portion of dorsal; caudal pale (at least distally) to dark brown. Maximum size to about 60 mm SL.

Ecology.—Inhabits lagoons, harbors, coastal reefs and outer reef slopes in two to eight meters, frequently among branching corals and alcyonarians. Occurs solitarily or in small groups. Feeds mainly on benthic algae.

Distribution.—East Indies, Palau Islands, New Guinea, Great Barrier Reef, New Britain, Solomon Islands, New Hebrides, and New Caledonia. Probably more widespread but included as a synonym of *P. tripunctatus* by most authors.

Pomacentrus tripunctatus Cuvier
Three-spot Damsel

Illus. pp. 228, 229

Pomacentrus tripunctatus Cuvier, 1830: 421 (Vanicolo, Santa Cruz Islands).
Pomacentrus vanicolensis Cuvier, 1830: 421 (Vanicolo, Santa Cruz Islands).
Pomacentrus obscurus Alleyne and Macleay, 1877: 343 (Torres Strait).
Pomacentrus macleayi Whitley, 1928a: 221 (Torres Strait).
Pseudopomacentrus wardi macleayi Whitley, 1932a: 291 (Torres Strait).

Diagnosis.—Dorsal rays XIII, 14 to 15; anal rays II, 14 to 15; pectoral rays 18. Tubed lateral-line scales 17 to 18. Gill rakers on first arch 20 to 22. Body depth 1.8 to 2.0 in SL. Color in alcohol

Pomacentrus moluccensis (about 35 mm TL), Malakal Island, Palau Islands in three meters.

Pomacentrus nigromarginatus (about 100 mm TL), Malaita, Solomon Islands in 20 meters (W. Starck photo).

Pomacentrus opisthostigma, painting of 80 mm TL specimen collected at Goodenough Island, D'Entrecasteaux Group.

Pomacentrus philippinus (about 100 mm TL), Michaelmas Cay, Great Barrier Reef in five meters.

Pomacentrus pavo
(about 100 mm TL),
One Tree Island,
Great Barrier Reef in
six meters.

Pomacentrus pavo (about 75 mm TL), Guadalcanal, Solomon Islands in three meters.

generally brown; small dark spot at lateral-line origin (often lacking in preserved specimens) and blackish saddle on dorsal edge of caudal peduncle; fins slightly dusky to brown; juveniles with ocellus on soft dorsal fin. Maximum size to about 75 mm SL.

Ecology.—Inhabits harbors and coastal reefs in 0.2 to three meters. Occurs solitarily or in small groups. Feeds chiefly on benthic algae.

Distribution.—Known to occur for certain at New Guinea, N.E. Queensland, New Britain, Solomon Islands, Santa Cruz Islands, and New Hebrides. Probably occurs throughout the Indo-Malayan region, but distribution records are obscured because many species have been misidentified as *P. tripunctatus* by previous authors.

Remarks.—The name *tripunctatus* has been indiscriminately attached to a variety of non-descript *Pomacentrus* by many authors. Bleeker (1877c) illustrated five color varieties of "*tripunctatus*," only one of which actually represents this species. More recent workers have placed numerous species in the synonymy of *tripunctatus*. For example, Fowler and Bean (1928) and De Beaufort (1940) each list 22 nominal synonyms. Many of these represent valid species and the task of "unscrambling" this confused synonymy is a formidable one. The true *tripunctatus* is easily distinguished by the black spot on the upper caudal peduncle. I have examined the types (MNHN 8245, 4 specimens, 30.3–33.4 mm) which were kindly sent by Dr. M. L. Bauchot. They represent the juvenile stage. In addition, the types of *P. vanicolensis*, *P. obscurus*, and *P. macleayi* were examined.

Pomacentrus vaiuli Jordan and Seale
Princess Damsel

Illus. pp. 232, 233

Pomacentrus vaiuli Jordan and Seale, 1906: 280 (Samoa Islands).

Diagnosis.—Dorsal rays XIII, 15 to 16; anal rays II, 15 to 16; pectoral rays 17 to 18. Tubed lateral-line scales 17 to 18. Gill rakers on first arch 20 to 21. Body depth 1.9 to 2.1 in SL. Color in alcohol generally brown, paler ventrally; most scales on body with two to three dark spots; dorsal and anal fins brown with black spot on basal portion of hindmost dorsal rays; caudal fin pale to dusky; pelvic and pectoral fins pale; pelvic fins and pectoral base usually darker in specimens from the Great Barrier Reef; see remarks section under *P. bankanensis* for comments on the live colors of juveniles.

Ecology.—Inhabits lagoons, passages, and outer reef slopes in three to 40 meters. Usually confined to the latter habitat in Melanesia and the Great Barrier Reef. Occurs solitarily or in small groups.

Distribution.—Molucca Islands, Melanesia, Great Barrier Reef, and western Oceania in general as far east as the Samoa, Marshall, and Gilbert Islands.

Pomacentrus wardi Whitley
Ward's Damsel

Illus. p. 233

Pomacentrus wardi Whitley, 1927: 301 (Heron Island, Queensland).

Diagnosis.—Dorsal rays XIII, 15 to 16; anal rays II, 15 to 16; pectoral rays 18 to 19. Tubed lateral-line scales 18 to 19. Gill rakers on first arch 20 to 21. Body depth 1.9 to 2.0 in SL. Color in alcohol generally dark to light brown, paler ventrally; scale centers usually lighter than ground color, small dark spot near origin of lateral-line; dorsal, anal, and pelvic fins dark brown to blackish; pectorals pale, frequently with black wedge-shaped mark on upper portion of fin base; caudal fin dusky. Maximum size to about 80 mm SL.

Ecology.—Inhabits lagoons and outer reef slopes in one to 20 meters. Abundant at the Capricorn Group, Great Barrier Reef. Occurs solitarily or in small groups. Feeds chiefly on benthic algae.

Distribution.—Apparently confined to eastern Australia as far south as Sydney, and possibly the Gulf of Carpentaria.

Remarks.—The color pattern of live juveniles is similar to that of *P. moluccensis*. At One Tree Island in the Capricorn Group, the adults exhibit three distinct color varieties. Individuals which live in the shallow lagoon where the reef is dead and covered with algae tend to be a bleached grey-brown; those which live on the outer reef are bluish dorsally and frequently retain the dorsal ocellus as adults. Specimens from a wide area of the lagoon are brown without an ocellus except in juveniles.

Chapter XXIV
POMACHROMIS

The genus *Pomachromis* is comprised of four species which inhabit the Indo-West Pacific; all are found in the "South Seas." These are elongate *Chromis*-like fishes which frequently form small to large midwater feeding aggregations. Although occasionally seen in lagoons, the outer reef slope appears to be the primary habitat. The reproductive habits are unknown.

GENUS *POMACHROMIS* ALLEN AND RANDALL

Pomachromis Allen and Randall, 1974: 45 (type species, *Abudefduf richardsoni* Snyder).

Diagnostic features.—Scales relatively large, about 28 in a median lateral series; body depth 2.7 to 2.9 in SL; dorsal spines XIV; margin of opercle, subopercle, and interopercle smooth, except small spine on upper edge of opercle; margin of suborbital and preopercle smooth, crenulate, or weakly denticulate; teeth incisiform, basically uniserial (irregularly biserial at front of jaws in some specimens).

KEY TO THE SPECIES OF *POMACHROMIS* FROM THE SOUTH SEAS

1a. Caudal fin and peduncle entirely pale (Mariana Islands)..........................*P.* species
1b. Caudal fin with dark upper and lower margins or large black spot on upper caudal peduncle....2
2a. Upper and lower margins of caudal fin dark brown; dark color of upper caudal peduncle not forming large isolated blotch extending onto basal portion of caudal fin....................3
2b. Upper and lower margins of caudal fin pale; dark color of upper caudal peduncle forming large isolated blotch extending onto basal portion of caudal fin (Marshall and Caroline Islands)....
....*P. exilis*
3a. Brown coloration of sides confined to area above tubed lateral-line and upper edge of caudal peduncle; color abruptly pale below lateral-line (Society Islands; Pitcairn Group)..........
....*P. fuscidorsalis*
3b. Brown coloration of sides not confined to area above tubed lateral-line and upper edge of caudal peduncle; color generally brown above and below lateral-line, gradually fading to tan on central portion of body (Samoa Islands; Fiji Islands, Loyalty Islands, Great Barrier Reef, Ryukyu Islands, Mauritius)..*P. richardsoni*

Pomachromis exilis (Allen and Emery)
Slender Reef-Damsel   Illus. p. 233

Pomacentrus exilis Allen and Emery, 1972: 565 (Truk Islands).

Diagnosis.—Dorsal rays XIV, 12 to 13; anal rays II, 12 to 13; pectoral rays 19. Tubed lateral-line scales 17 to 18. Gill rakers on first arch 22 to 24. Body depth 2.7 to 2.9 in SL. Color in alcohol generally tan, paler on ventral surface; large dark brown blotch covering upper half of caudal peduncle and extending onto basal portion of caudal fin; fins pale tan; dark spot on upper half of pectoral fin base and axil. Maximum size to about 60 mm SL.

Pomacentrus popei (about 60 mm TL), Suva, Fiji Islands in 10 meters.

Pomacentrus popei (about 75 mm TL), Malakal Pass, Palau Islands in 10 meters.

Pomacentrus reidi
(about 125 mm TL),
Guadalcanal,
Solomon Islands in
20 meters.

Pomacentrus reidi (about 40 mm TL), Madang, New Guinea in 30 meters.

Pomacentrus philippinus (*imitator* variety, about 75 mm TL), Suva, Fiji Islands in 10 meters.

Ecology.—Inhabits lagoons and outer reef slopes in eight to 12 meters. Frequently occurs in small groups composed of about two to ten individuals which characteristically hover about one meter above the bottom while feeding on zooplankton

Distribution.—Known from Eniwetok Atoll, Marshall Islands, and the Truk Group, Caroline Islands.

Pomachromis fuscidorsalis Allen and Randall
Tahitian Reef-damsel

Illus. p. 236

Pomachromis fuscidorsalis Allen and Randall, 1974: 46 (Tahiti).
Abudefduf sp. one Harry, 1953: 103 (Raroia Atoll, Tuamotu Islands).

Diagnosis.—Dorsal rays XIV, 13; anal rays II, 13; pectoral rays 19 to 20. Tubed lateral-line scales 17 to 18. Gill rakers on first arch 24 to 27. Body depth 2.7 to 2.9 in SL. Color in alcohol generally pale except dark brown on upper portion of head and above lateral-line; spinous dorsal fin dusky; remainder of fins pale except caudal with dark upper and lower margins; small brown spot on upper portion of pectoral base. Maximum size to about 60 mm SL.

Ecology.—Inhabits passages, outer reef slopes, and surge channels, in one to 18 meters.

Distribution.—Society Islands and Pitcairn Group.

Pomachromis richardsoni (Snyder)
Richardson's Reef-damsel

Illus. p. 236

Abudefduf richardsoni Snyder, 1909: 600 (Okinawa).

Diagnosis.—Dorsal rays XIV, 13 to 14; anal rays II, 13; pectoral rays 19. Tubed lateral-line scales 18 to 19. Gill rakers on first arch 24 to 25. Body depth 2.5 to 2.7 in SL. Color in alcohol generally dark brown on dorsal half of body grading to whitish or tan below, scale edges darker; dorsal fin mostly dark brown except posterior portion of soft dorsal pale; anal fin pale basally and blackish distally; pelvics and pectorals pale; black spot on upper portion of pectoral base; caudal pale with prominent black margins on upper and lower edge. Maximum size to about 60 mm SL.

Ecology.—Inhabits outer reef slopes in 10 to 20 meters.

Distribution.—Previously known from the Ryukyu Islands, but collected recently by J. Randall and the author at Mauritius, the northern Great Barrier Reef, Loyalty Islands, and Samoa Islands. In addition, specimens were recently received from B. Carlson collected at the Fiji Islands.

Pomachromis sp.*
Guam Reef-damsel

Illus. p. 236

Diagnosis.—Dorsal rays XIV, 13; anal rays II, 13; pectoral rays 18. Tubed lateral-line scales 17. Gill rakers on first arch 22. Color in alcohol generally brown dorsally grading to tan ventrally and on caudal peduncle, scale edges darker; whitish blotches on head; fins pale; small dark spot on upper edge of pectoral base. Maximum size to about 60 mm SL.

Ecology.—Inhabits outer reef slopes in five to 15 meters.

Distribution.—Known only on the basis of three specimens collected off Targuisson Point, Guam, Mariana Islands. According to H. Larson (personal communication) the species was relatively common where these were taken.

Remarks.—The above diagnosis is based on only one individual. The other known specimens were unobtainable at the time this was written. The species will be described by H. Larson and the author in a forthcoming publication.

---

* This species has recently been described as *P. guamensis* (Allen and Larson, 1975, Micronesia 11 (1): 123-126).

Chapter XXV
PRISTOTIS

The genus *Pristotis* contains three species which inhabit the Indo-West Pacific; only one, *P. jerdoni*, resides in the "South Seas." They generally inhabit sandy areas, and the diet consists chiefly of zooplankton.

GENUS *PRISTOTIS* RÜPPELL

Pristotis Rüppell, 1838: 128 (type species, *Pristotis cyanostigma* Rüppell).

Diagnostic features.—Margin of preopercle and subopercle serrate; notch between preorbital and suborbital absent; dorsal spines XIII; teeth uniserial; predorsal scales extending to about mid-interorbital; greatest depth about 2.5 to 2.9 in SL.

Remarks.—I have united *Pristotis* and *Daya* Bleeker (1877b) as I find no significant differences between them. Tyler (1966) mentioned that *Daya* differed from *Pristotis* by having the first anal spine almost as long as the second, four to five rows of scales on the preoperculum, the caudal more deeply forked and the lobes of equal length, and 17 pectoral fin rays. After examining many specimens of *P. jerdoni* (type species of *Daya*) I find they differ from other *Pristotis* only with regard to the number of preopercle scale rows (usually two to three in the other two members of the genus, *P. cyanostigma* Rüppell from the Red Sea and *P. judithae* Tyler from the Seychelles). This difference is not sufficient to merit generic distinction.

Pristotis jerdoni (Day)
Gulf Damsel

Illus. p. 237

Pomacentrus jerdoni Day, 1873: 237 (Madras, India).

Diagnosis.—Dorsal rays XIII, 12 to 13; anal rays II, 12 to 14; pectoral rays 17 to 18. Tubed lateral-line scales 19 to 20. Gill rakers on first arch 26 to 28. Body depth 2.5 to 2.8 in SL. Color in alcohol generally pale with dark spot on upper portion of pectoral fin base. Maximum size to about 110 mm SL.

Ecology.—Inhabits flat sandy bottoms, usually in 15 to 40 meters, but one individual sighted in five meters at One Tree Island, Great Barrier Reef. The stomach of a specimen taken at Egum Atoll, Solomon Sea contained mostly harpactacoid copepods.

Distribution.—Persian Gulf, India, Indonesia, Gulf of Carpentaria, Egum Atoll (Solomon Sea), Western Australia, eastern Australia as far south as the Sydney area, and Taiwan.

Pomacentrus smithi (about 75 mm TL), Efate, New Hebrides in three meters.

Pomacentrus tripunctatus (about 100 mm TL), Guadalcanal, Solomon Islands in three meters.

Pomacentrus taeniometopon (about 100 mm TL), Malakal Pass, Palau Islands in three meters.

Pomacentrus tripunctatus (about 40 mm TL), Guadalcanal, Solomon Islands in three meters.

APPENDIX TABLE I

POMACENTRIDS OF THE SOUTH SEAS
(except Hawaiian Islands and S.E. Oceania, see Appendix Table II)

Abbreviations:
LI = Line Islands
MI = Marshall Islands
PI = Palau Islands
NG = New Guinea
GBR = Great Barrier Reef
LH = Lord Howe Island
SI = Solomon Islands
NH = New Hebrides
NC = New Caledonia-Loyalty Islands
FI = Fiji Islands

*denotes new locality record

Taxon	LI	MI	PI	NG	GBR	LH	SI	NH	NC	FI
Abudefduf										
bengalensis					X					
sp.		X	X				X			
coelestinus		X	X	X	X	X	X	X	X	X
notatus			X*							
saxatilis		X	X*	X	X		X	X	X*	X
septemfasciatus	X	X	X*	X	X		X	X		X
sordidus	X	X	X*	X	X	X*	X*	X	X	
whitleyi					X				X*	
Acanthochromis										
polyacanthus				X	X		X	X		
Amblyglyphidodon										
aureus		X	X*	X*			X*	X*	X*	X*
curacao		X	X	X			X	X*		X
leucogaster		X*	X*	X*	X		X	X*	X	X*
ternatensis		X*	X				X*			
Amblypomacentrus										
breviceps				X			X*			
Amphiprion										
akindynos					X			X		
chrysopterus		X	X	X			X*	X*		X
clarkii		X	X				X	X*	X	
latezonatus						X				
mccullochi						X				
melanopus		X	X	X	X		X	X*	X	
leucokranos				X			X*			
percula				X	X		X	X		
rubrocinctus										X
perideraion		X	X	X	X*		X*	X*	X	X*
polymnus				X			X			
sandaracinos				X			X			
tricinctus		X								
Cheiloprion										
labiatus			X	X	X		X			
Chromis										
acares	X	X		X			X			
agilis		X				X*	X	X*	X	
amboinensis		X*	X	X	X*		X*	X*	X*	X*
analis			X	X			X*	X*	X*	X*
atripectoralis	X*	X	X*	X*	X*	X*	X	X*	X*	X*
atripes			X*	X*	X*		X*	X*	X*	
caerulea	X*	X	X	X	X		X*	X	X*	X
chrysura					X*			X*	X	X*
elerae		X*	X*				X*			X*
hypsilepis						X				
iomelas			X*	X*				X*	X*	X*
kennensis						X*		X*		
lepidolepis	X*	X	X*	X*	X*		X*	X*	X*	X*
lineata			X	X*				X*		
margaritifer	X	X	X*	X	X*		X*	X*	X	X*
nitida						X	X*			
weberi	X*	X*	X*	X*	X*		X*	X*	X*	X*
retrofasciata			X*	X*	X*		X*	X*	X*	X*
ternatensis		X	X	X	X*		X	X	X*	X*
vanderbilti	X					X*	X	X*	X*	X*
xanthochir			X*	X*			X*			
xanthura		X*	X*	X*	X*		X*	X*	X*	X*
sp. #A			X*	X*			X*	X*	X*	
sp. #C			X*				X*			
sp. #D			X*	X*			X*	X*		X*

Taxon	LI	MI	PI	NG	GBR	LH	SI	NH	NC	FI
Dascyllus										
aruanus	X	X	X	X	X	X*	X	X	X	X
melanurus		X*	X	X*			X		X	
reticulatus		X	X	X	X			X*	X	X
trimaculatus	X	X	X*	X	X	X*	X*	X	X*	X
Dischistodus										
chrysopoecilus			X	X				X*		
fasciatus				X						
notopthalmus		X*	X	X				X		
perspicillatus			X	X				X*	X*	
prosopotaenia			X	X				X	X*	
pseudochrysopoecilus			X	X				X*		
Eupomacentrus										
albifasciatus	X	X	X	X*	X		X	X	X*	X
apicalis		X								
aureus	X									
fasciolatus		X	X*	X*	X*	X	X*	X*	X*	X
gascoynei						X*	X*		X*	
lividus	X*	X	X	X			X	X	X	X
nigricans	X	X	X	X			X	X	X*	X
Glyphidodontops										
azurepunctatus			X	X*						
biocellatus	X	X	X	X	X		X		X	X
caeruleolineatus								X*		X*
cyaneus		X	X	X				X	X	
flavipinnis		X	X					X		
glaucus	X	X	X*		X		X*			X
hemicyaneus				X*				X*		
leucopomus	X	X	X	X	X*		X	X	X*	X
niger		X								
notialis						X			X	
rex		X*	X*	X*			X*	X*	X*	
rollandi		X*	X*					X*	X*	
starcki									X*	
talboti			X	X			X	X		X
traceyi		X	X*							
tricinctus									X	X
unimaculatus				X*	X			X*	X*	X*
Hemiglyphidodon										
plagiometopon			X*	X	X*			X		
Lepidozygus										
tapeinosoma	X*		X	X	X			X*	X*	X*
Neopomacentrus										
anabatoides				X				X*		X
azysron				X*	X*			X*	X*	
cyanomos				X	X			X*		
metallicus										X*
taeniurus		X*	X	X[1]				X	X	
violascens			X	X				X*	X	
sp.		X	X	X				X	X*	X
Paraglyphidodon										
behni			X	X				X	X*	
bonang				X						
carlsoni										X*
melanopus		X*	X*	X				X*		
melas		X	X	X				X	X	X
polyacanthus			X*	X					X	
thoracotaeniatus			X*					X*		
Parma										
oligolepis				X						
polylepis						X*	X		X*	
sp.						X*				
Plectroglyphidodon										
dickii	X	X	X*	X*	X*	X*	X	X*	X*	X*
imparipennis	X	X	X*					X*	X*	X*
johnstonianus		X	X*		X*		X*	X*	X*	X*
lacrymatus		X	X*	X	X*		X*	X*	X*	X*
leucozona		X	X	X*	X	X*	X*	X	X*	X
phoenixensis		X								X*

[1]coastal Queensland only

POMACENTRIDS OF HAWAIIAN ISLANDS AND S.E. OCEANIA

	LI	MI	PI	NG	GBR	LH	SI	NH	NC	FI
Pomacentrus										
albimaculus				X						
amboinensis			X	X	X		X	X	X	
australis				X						
bankanensis			X	X*	X		X	X	X*	X*
burroughi			X*	X*			X			
coelestis	X	X	X*	X*	X*	X*	X*	X*		X*
emarginatus			X*							
flavicauda			X*	X*	X		X*		X*	
grammorhynchus			X*	X*	X*		X*			
lepidogenys				X*	X*		X*	X*	X*	X*
sp.			X*	X	X*		X*	X*	X*	X*
melanopterus		X		X	X		X	X*	X*	
moluccensis			X*	X			X	X		
alexanderae			X	X			X*	X*		
nigromarginatus				X	X		X*	X*		X*
opisthostigma			X*							
pavo		X	X	X	X*	X*	X	X	X	X*
philippinus				X*	X*		X*	X*	X	X*
popei			X*	X	X		X	X*	X	X*
reidi			X*	X*	X*		X*	X*		
smithi			X*				X*	X*		
taeniometopon			X*	X*	X*		X*	X*	X*	
tripunctatus				X	X		X	X		
vaiuli		X	X*	X*	X*		X*	X*	X*	X*
wardi				X						
Pomachromis										
exilis		X								
richardsoni					X				X	X*
sp.[2]*										
Premnas										
biaculeatus				X	X		X	X		
Pristotis										
jerdoni				X*	X					
TOTAL SPECIES	22	43	77	103	91	26	98	78	66	60

[2]known only from Guam, Mariana Islands

Abbreviations:

HAW = Hawaiian Islands		MAR = Marquesas Islands	
TAH = Tahiti		RAP = Rapa	
TUA = Tuamotus		PIT = Pitcairn Group	
		EAS = Easter Island	

	HAW	TAH	TUA	MAR	RAP	PIT	EAS
Abudefduf							
abdominalis	X						
coelestinus		X	X		X*		
saxatilis				X			
septemfasciatus		X	X				
sordidus	X	X	X	X	X*	X	
Amphiprion							
chrysopterus		X	X				
melanopus		X					
Chromis							
acares	X	X				X	
agilis	X	X	X		X	X	
atripectoralis		X		X*			
caerulea		X	X				
hanui	X						
iomelas		X					
leucura	X	X		X			
margaritifer		X	X*				
opercularis		X	X*	X*		X*	
ovalis	X						
randalli							X
struhsakeri	X						
vanderbilti	X	X	X		X	X	
verater	X						
sp. A		X					
sp. B			X*				
sp. E					X*		
sp. F			X*				
sp. G			X*				
sp. H					X*	X*	
Dascyllus							
albisella	X						
aruanus		X	X	X*	X*		
reticulatus		X	X		X*	X*	
strasburgi			X				
trimaculatus		X	X			X*	
Eupomacentrus							
albifasciatus		X	X				
aureus		X*	X*				
emeryi		X			X		
fasciolatus	X	X			X*	X*	X
lividus		X					
nigricans		X	X	X			
Glyphidodontops							
galbus		X			X	X	
glaucus		X	X				
leucopomus		X		X			
rapanui							X
Lepidozygus							
tapeinosoma		X	X*	X*			
Plectroglyphidodon							
dickii		X	X	X*			
flaviventris		X					
imparipennis	X	X	X	X	X*	X*	
johnstonianus	X	X	X*	X*	X*	X*	
lacrymatus		X					
leucozona				X	X*	X*	
phoenixensis		X	X	X*			
sindonis	X						
Pomacentrus							
coelestis			X*				
pavo		X	X				
Pomachromis							
fuscidorsalis		X	X			X	
TOTAL SPECIES	15	30	27	19	13	16	3

Pomacentrus vaiuli (about 75 mm TL), Augulpelu Reef, Palau Islands in 10 meters.

Pomacentrus vaiuli (about 75 mm TL), Suva, Fiji Islands in 10 meters.

Pomacentrus wardi (about 100 mm TL), One Tree Island, Great Barrier Reef in three meters.

Pomachromis exilis (43 mm SL), Eniwetok Atoll, Marshall Islands (J. Randall photo).

Pomacentrus vaiuli (about 75 mm TL), Wistari Reef, Great Barrier Reef in 14 meters.

BIBLIOGRAPHY

Abe, T. 1939. A list of the fishes of the Palao Islands. Palao Tropical Biol. Sta. Studies, No. 4: 523–583.

Allen, G. R. 1972. Anemonefishes, their classification and biology. T.F.H. Publications Inc., New Jersey. 288 pp.

——. 1973a. Three new species of deep-dwelling damselfishes (Pomacentridae) from the south-west Pacific Ocean. Aust. Zool. 18(1): 31–42.

——. 1973b. *Amphiprion leucokranos*, a new species of pomacentrid fish, with notes on other anemonefishes of New Guinea. Pac. Sci. 27(4): 319–326.

——. 1973c. *Chromis bitaeniatus* Fowler and Bean, the juvenile of *Abudefduf behni* (Bleeker). Trop. Fish Hobbyist 21: 5–15.

——. 1975. Four new damselfishes from the southwestern Pacific Ocean (Pisces: Pomacentridae). Proc. Linn. Soc. N.S.W. 99(2): 87–99

—— and A. R. Emery, 1972. *Pomacentrus exilis*, a new species of damselfish from the central-west Pacific. Copeia, 3: 565–568.

—— and J. E. Randall. 1974. Five new species and a new genus of damselfishes (family Pomacentridae) from the South Pacific Ocean. Trop. Fish Hobbyist. 22: 36–49.

—— and D. R. Robertson. 1974. Descriptions of four new damselfishes (Pomacentridae) from Papua-New Guinea and eastern Australia. Rec. Austr. Mus. 29(4): 153–167.

Alleyne, H. G. and W. M. Macleay. 1877. The ichthyology of the Chevert Expedition. Proc. Linn. Soc. N.S.W. 1: 321–359.

Aoyagi, H. 1941. One new species of the Pomacentridae, Pisces, from the Palau Islands. Zool. Mag. (Tokyo), 53(3): 180–181.

Baissac, L. 1956. Poissons de L'ile Maurice. Proc. Roy. Soc. Mauritius, 1(4): 332–333.

Bennett, J. W. 1830. A selection of rare and curious fishes found upon the coast of Ceylon. London, 1828–30, 6 pts., 3 pls.

Bleeker, P. 1847. Labroideorum ctenoideorum bataviensium diagnoses et adumbratonis. Verh. Bat. Gen. 21(1): 1–33.

——. 1848. A contribution to the ichthyology of Sumbawa. Journ. Ind. Arch. 2(9): 632–639.

——. 1852a. Bijdrage tot de kennis der ichthyologische fauna van Singapore. Nat. Tijdschr. Ned. Ind. 3: 51–86.

——. 1852b. Nieuwe bijdrage tot de kennis der ichthyologische fauna van Amboina. Nat. Tijdschr. Ned. Ind. 3: 545–568.

——. 1852c. Bijdrage tot de kennis der ichthyologische fauna van de Moluksche eilanden. Visschen van Amboina en Ceram. Nat. Tijdschr. Ned. Ind. 3: 229–309.

——. 1853a. Bijdrage tot de kennis der ichthyologische fauna van Ternate. Nat. Tijdsch. Ned. Ind. 4: 131–140.

——. 1853b. Vierde bijdrage tot de kennis der ichthyologische fauna van Amboina. Nat. Tijdschr. Ned. Ind. 5: 317–352.

——. 1853c. Derde bijdrage tot de kennis der ichthyologische fauna van Amboina. Nat. Tijdschr. Ned. Ind. 4: 91–130.

——. 1853d. Nieuwe tientallen diagnostische beschrijvingen van nieuwe of weinig bekende vischsoorten van Sumatra. Nat. Tijdschr. Ned. Ind. 5: 495–534.

——. 1854a. Derde bijdrage tot de kennis der ichthyologische fauna van de Banda-eilanden. Nat. Tijdschr. Ned. Ind. 6: 89–114.

——. 1854b. Bijdrage tot de kennis der ichthyologische fauna van het eiland Flores. Nat. Tijdschr. Ned. Ind. 6: 311–338.

——. 1855. Bijdrage tot de kennis der ichthyologische fauna van het eiland, Groot-Obi. Nat. Tijdschr. Ned. Ind. 9: 431–438.

——. 1856a. Beschrijvingen van nieuwe en weinig bekende vischsoorten van Amboina, verzameld op eene reis door den Molukschen Archipel, gedaan in het gevolg van den Gouverneur-Generaal Duymaer van Twist in September en October 1855. Act. Soc. Sci. Indo-Neerl. 1: 1–76.

——. 1856b. Verslag omtrent eenige vischsoorten gevangen aan de zuidkust van Malang in Oast-Java. Nat. Tijdschr. Ned. Ind. 11: 81–92.

——. 1856c. Zevende bijdrage tot de kennis der ichthyologische fauna van Ternate. Nat. Tijdschr. Ned. Ind. 10: 357–386.

——. 1859. Over eenige vischsoorten van de zuidkustwateren van Java. Nat. Tijdschr. Ned. Ind. 19: 329–352.

——. 1868. Description de trois espèces inédites de poissons des iles d'Amboine et de Waigion. Versl. Akad. Amsterdam (2)II: 331–335.

——. 1873. Description d'une espèce inédite de Heliases d'Amboine. Ned. Tijdschr. Dierk. 4: 111–112.

——. 1877a. Description de quelques espèces inédites de Pomacentroides de l'Inde archipélagique. Versl. Akad. Amsterdam (2) 10 (1876): 384–391.

——. 1877b. Mémoire sur les Chromides marins ou Pomacentroides de l'Inde archipélagique. Nat. Verh. Holl. Maatsch. Wetensch. 3(6): 1–166.

——. 1877c. Atlas Ichthyologique des Indes Orientales Néerlandaisis, publié sous les auspices du Gouvernment Colonial Néerlandais. Amsterdam. Müller. 1862–77, 9 vols., 420 pls.

Bliss, R. 1883. Descriptions of new species of Mauritian fishes. Trans. Roy. Soc. Mauritius: 45–56.

Bloch, M. E. 1790. Naturgeschichte der ausländischen Fische. Berlin, 9 pts. in 2 + atlas (3 vols.), 324 clr. pls. 1787–95.

—— and J. E. Schneider. 1801. Systema Ichthyologiae iconibus ex illustratum. Post. obitum auctoris opus inchoatum absolvit correxit, interpolabit Jo. Gottlob. Schneider. Saxo Berolini, lx, 584 pp., 110 clr. pls.

Brock, V. E. and T. C. Chamberlain. 1968. A geological and ecological reconnaissance off western Oahu, principally by means of the research submarine "Asherah." Pac. Sci. 22(3): 373–394.

Castelnau, F. 1873. Contributions to the ichthyology of Australia. Proc. Zool. Acclim. Soc. Victoria, 2: 37–158.

——. 1875. Researches on the fishes of Australia. Intercol. Exhib. Essays, Victorian Dept., 2: 34.

Cuvier, G. L. C. F. D. 1814. Mémoire de la composition de la mâchoire supérieure des poissons, et sur le parti qu'on peut en tirer pour la distribution méthodique de ces animaux. Bull. Soc. Philom. Paris: 73–90.

——. 1817. Le règne animal distribué d'après son organisation, pour servir de base à l'histoire naturelle des animaux et d'introduction à l'anatomie comparie. Paris. Poissons, 2: 532 pp.

——. 1829. Le règne animal distribué d'après son organisation, pour servir de base à l'histoire naturelle des animaux et d'introduction à l'anatomie compaire, 2nd ed., 5 vols., Paris, 1829.

———. 1830. Histoire naturelle des Poissons. Paris, F. G. Levrault, 5: 499 pp.

Day, F. 1869. Remarks on some of the fishes in the Calcutta museum. Proc. Zool. Soc. London: 511–527.

———. 1873. On new or imperfectly known fishes of India. Proc. Zool. Soc. London: 236–240.

———. 1877. The fishes of India; being a natural history of the fishes known to inhabit the seas and freshwaters of India, Burma, and Ceylon. London. 1875–78, xx, 778 pp., 198 pls.

De Beaufort, L. F. 1940. The fishes of the Indo-Australian Archipelago. Vol. 8, Percomophi (continued), Cirrhitoidea, Labriformes, Pomacentriformes. Leiden; E. J. Brill, 508 pp., 56 text-figs.

De Vis, C. W. 1884. Fishes from South Sea islands. Proc. Linn. Soc. N.S.W., 8: 445–457.

———. 1885. New Australian fishes in the Queensland Museum. Proc. Linn. Soc. N.S.W., 9: 869–887.

Doak, W. 1972. Fishes of the New Zealand Region. Hodder and Stoughton, Auckland. 132 pp.

Ekman, S. 1953. Zoogeography of the Sea. London, Sidwick and Jackson, Ltd., 417 pp.

Evermann, B. W. and A. Seale. 1907. Fishes of the Philippine Islands. Bull. Bur. Fish. 26(1906): 49–110.

Forskål, P. 1775. Descriptiones animalium avium, amphibiorum, piscium, insectorum, vermium; quae in itinere orientali observivit. Post. morten auctoris edidit Carsten Niebuhr. Havinae, 164 pp., 43 pls.

Fowler, H. W. 1904. A collection of fishes from Sumatra. Journ. Acad. Nat. Sci. Philad. 2 ser: 495–560.

———. 1918. New and little-known fishes from the Philippine Islands. Proc. Acad. Nat. Sci. Philad.: 2–143.

———. 1927. Fishes of the tropical central Pacific. B. P. Bishop Mus. Bull. 38: 3–32.

———. 1928. The fishes of Oceania. Mem. Bernice P. Bishop Mus., 10: 540 pp.

———. 1941. The George Vanderbilt Oahu survey—the fishes. Proc. Acad. Nat. Sci. Philad. 93: 247–279.

———. 1943. Descriptions and figures of new fishes obtained in Philippine Seas and adjacent waters by the United States Bureau of Fisheries Steamer "Albatross." U.S.N.M. Bull. 100, 14(2): 53–91.

———. 1946. A collection of fishes obtained in the Riu-Kiu Islands by Captain Ernest R. Tinkham A.U.S. Proc. Acad. Nat. Sci. Philad. 98: 123–218.

———. 1959. Fishes of Fiji. Govt. of Fiji, Suva, Fiji, 670 pp., 243 figs.

——— and S. C. Ball. 1924. Descriptions of new fishes obtained by the Tanager Expedition of 1923 in the Pacific Islands west of Hawaii. Proc. Acad. Nat. Sci. Philad.: 269–274.

——— and B. A. Bean. 1928. The fishes of the families Pomacentridae, Labridae and Callyodontidae, collected by the United States Bureau of Fisheries steamer "Albatross," chiefly in Philippine seas and adjacent waters. Bull. U.S. Nat. Mus., 100, 7: 525 pp.

Gilbert, C. H. 1905. The deep-sea fishes of the Hawaiian Islands. Bull. U.S. Fish. Comm. for 1903, 23(2), sect. 2: 575–713.

Gill, T. 1859. Notes on a collection of Japanese fish, made by Dr. J. Morrow. Proc. Acad. Nat. Sci. Philad.: 144–150.

———. 1862. Catalogue of the fishes of lower California in the Smithsonian Institution, collected by Mr. Xantus. Proc. Acad. Nat. Sci. Philad., 14: 140–151.

———. 1863. Synopsis of the pomacentroids of the western coast of North and Central America. Proc. Acad. Nat. Sci. Philad., 15: 213–221.

Gosline, W. A. and V. E. Brock. 1960. Handbook of Hawaiian fishes. Univ. Hawaii Press, Honolulu, 372 pp.

Greenfield, D. W. 1968. The zoogeography of Myripristis (Pisces: Holocentridae). Systematic Zoology 17(1): 76–87.

——— and D. A. Hensley. 1970. Damselfishes (Pomacentridae) of Easter Island, with descriptions of two new species. Copeia, 4: 689–695.

Günther, A. 1862. Catalogue of the fishes of the British Museum, 8 vols., London. 1859–70, Vol. 4: 534 pp.

———. 1867. Additions to the knowledge of Australian reptiles and fishes. Ann. Mag. Nat. Hist. 3(20): 45–68.

Harry, R. R. 1953. Ichthyological field data of Raroia Atoll, Tuamotu Archipelago. Atoll Res. Bull. No. 18: 190 pp.

Helfrich, P. 1958. The early life history and reproductive behavior of the maomao, Abudefduf abdominalis (Quoy and Gaimard). Ph.D Dissertation, Univ., Hawaii, 228 pp.

Herre, A. C. 1935. New fishes obtained by the Crane Pacific Expedition. Field Mus. Nat. His. Zool. Ser. 335, 18(12): 383–438.

Hombron, H. and V. Jacquinot. 1853. Voyage au Pôle Sud et dans l'Océanie sur L'Astrolabe et La Zélée, pendant 1837–40, Zool. 3(2): 29–56.

Jenkins, O. P. 1901. Descriptions of fifteen new species of fishes from the Hawaiian islands. Bull. U.S. Fish Comm. 19: 387–404.

Jordan, D. S. 1917. The Genera of Fishes. Leland Stanford Junior Univ. Publ. 1: 161 pp.

——— and M. Dickerson. 1908. On a collection of fishes from Fiji with notes on certain Hawaiian fishes. Proc. U.S.N.M., 34: 603–617.

——— and B. W. Evermann. 1903. Descriptions of new genera and species of fishes from the Hawaiian Islands. Bull. U.S. Fish Comm., 22: 161–208.

——— and C. W. Metz. 1912. Descriptions of two new species of fishes from Honolulu, Hawaii. Proc. U.S.N.M., 42: 525–527.

——— and R. E. Richardson. 1908. Fishes from islands of the Philippine Archipelago. Bull. Bur. Fish. 27: 233–287.

——— and A. Seale. 1905. List of fishes collected by Dr. Bashford Dean on the island of Negros, Philippines. Proc. U.S.N.M. 28 (1407): 769–803.

———. and A. Seale. 1905. The fishes of Samoa, description of the species found in the archipelago, with a provisional check-list of the fishes of Oceania. Bull. Bur. Fish. (1906), 25: 175–455.

——— ———. 1907. Fishes of the islands of Luzon and Panay. Bull. Bur. Fish. 26 (1906): 1–48.

——— and E. C. Starks. 1901. Description of three new species of fishes from Japan. Proc. Cal. Acad. Sci. (3): 381–386.

Klausewitz, W. 1960. Dascyllus strasburgi, ein neuer fisch aus dem Pacific. (Pisces, Perciformes, Pomacentridae). Bull. aquat. Biol. 2: 45–49.

Kner, R. 1868. Ueber neue Fische aus dem museum der Herren J. C. Godeffroy und Sohn in Hamburg. Sitzgsber. Ak. Wiss. Wien. 58: 26–31.

Lacépède, B. G. 1803. Histoire naturelle des poissons, (Vol. 1) par le citoyen Lacépède, membre de l'Institut

Pomachromis fuscidorsalis (58 mm SL), Tahiti, Society Islands (J. Randall photo).

Pomachromis sp., painting of 60 mm TL specimen collected at Guam, Mariana Islands.

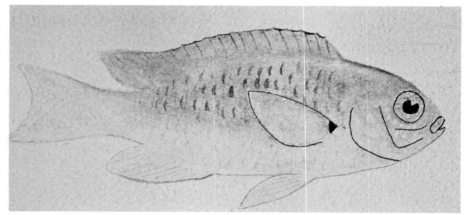

Pomachromis richardsoni (about 75 mm TL), Uvea, Loyalty Islands in 10 meters.

Pristotis jerdoni
(about 75 mm TL),
Sydney, Australia.

Pristotis jerdoni (45.6 mm SL), Taiwan (S. Shen photo).

National, et Professeur der Muséum d'Histoire Naturelle Tome premier, Paris, 1798–1803, 1st ed. (1799–1802), 14 vols., 4: 472 pp.

Lesson, R. P. 1830. *In:* Duperrey Voyage autour du monde . . . sur la corvette . . . "La Coquille" . . . Zoologie, 471 pp., atlas, A. Bertrand, Paris.

Liénard, 1839. (title of paper not available), Soc. Hist. Nat. Maurice, 10: 35.

Linnaeus, C. 1758. Systema naturae. Edition 10: 824 pp., London.

Macleay, W. J. 1878. The fishes of Port Darwin. Proc. Linn. Soc., N.S.W. 2: 344–367.

——. 1883. Contribution to a knowledge of the fishes of New Guinea. Proc. Linn. Soc. N.S.W., 8(2): 252–280.

Norman, J. R. 1966. A draft synopsis of the orders, families and genera of recent fishes and fish-like vertebrates. Trustees of the Brit. Mus.: 1–606.

Ogilby, J. D. 1889. The reptiles and fishes of Lord Howe Island. Mem. Austr. Mus. 2: 51–74.

——. 1913. On six new or rare Queensland fishes. Mem. Qld. Mus., Brisbane, 2: 81–89.

Pietschmann, V. 1934. Drei neue Fische aus den hawaiischen Küstengewassern. Anz. Akad. Wiss. Wien. 71: 99–100.

Playfair, R. L. and A. Günther. 1866. The fishes of Zanzibar, with a list of the fishes of the whole east coast of Africa. London. 156 pp.

Quoy, J. R. C. and J. P. Gaimard. 1825. Voyage autour du monde, Entrepris par Ordre du Roi, exécute sur les corvettes de "S. M. l'Uranie" et at "Physicienne," pendant les annes 1817, 1818, 1819, et 1820, par M. Louis de Freycinct: Zoologie, Poissons: 329–424.

Randall, J. E. 1956. A revision of the surgeon fish genus *Acanthurus*. Pac. Sci. 10(2): 159–235.

——. 1968. Caribbean Reef Fishes. T.F.H. Publications, Inc., New Jersey, 318 pp.

Randall, J. E. and S. N. Swerdloff. 1973. A review of the damselfish genus *Chromis* from the Hawaiian Islands, with descriptions of three new species. Pac. Sci. 27(4): 327–349.

Richardson, J. 1842. Contributions to the ichthyology of Australia. Ann. Mag. Nat. Hist., 9: 384–392.

——. 1846. Report on the ichthyology of the seas of China and Japan. Rept. Brit. Assoc. Adv. Sci., 15 meet. 1845: 187–320.

Rüppell, W. P. E. S. 1828. Atlas zu der Reise im nördichen Afrika. Zoologie, Fische des Rothen Meeres, 4 vols., Frankfurt-a-M. 1826–28, 119 pls.

——. 1835. Neue Wirbelthiere zu der Fauna von Abyssinien gehörig. 2 vols., Frankfurt-a-M., 1835–40.

Schmidt, P. J. 1930. Fishes of the Riu-Kiu Islands. Trans. Pacif. Comm., Leningr. 1: 19–156.

Schultz, L. P. 1943. Fishes of the Phoenix and Samoan Islands collected in 1939 during the expedition of the U.S.S. "Bushnell." Bull. U.S.N.M. 180: 316 pp.

—— and A. Welander. 1953. (*In:* Schultz, L. P. *et al.*). Fishes of the Marshall and Marianas Islands. Vol. 2, Bull. U.S.N.M., 202: 438 pp.

Schlegel, H. and S. Müller. 1839–44. Overzigt den iut de Sunda en Moluksche zeeen bekende visschen, van de geslachten *Amphiprion, Premnas, Pomacentrus, Glyphisodon, Dascyllus,* en *Heliases.* Verh. Natuur. Gesch. Leiden, 1839–44, 2: 17–26.

Seale, A. 1909. New species of Philippine fishes. Philipp. Journ. Sci. 4(6): 491–543.

Smith, J. L. B. 1960. Coral fishes of the family Pomacentridae from the western Indian Ocean and the Red Sea. Ichthyol. Bull. 19: 317–349. Dept. Ichthyol., Rhodes Univ., Grahamstown, S. Afr.

Snyder, J. O. 1909. Descriptions of new genera and species of fishes from Japan and the Riu Kiu islands. Proc. U.S.N.M. 36(1688): 597–610.

Steindachner, F. 1900. Fische aus dem Stillen Ocean. Ergebnisse einer Reise nach dem Pacific (Schauensland 1896–97). Denkschr. Akad. Wiss. Wien. 70: 483–521.

Swerdloff, S. N. 1970. Behavioral observations on Eniwetok damselfishes (Pomacentridae: *Chromis*) with special reference to the spawning of *Chromis caeruleus.* Copeia, 2: 371–374.

Thiolliere, V. J. 1856. Montrouzier. X. Suite de la faune de l'ile de Woodlark on Moiou. Ichthyologie. Ann. Soc. Agric. Lyon, 8: 393–504.

Tyler, J. C. 1966. A new species of damselfish (Pomacentridae) from the western Indian Ocean, *Pristotis judithae.* Notul. Nat., 393: 1–6.

Vaillant, L. and H. E. Sauvage. 1875. Note sur quelque espèces nouvelles de poissons des iles Sandwich: Rev. Mag. Zool. 3rd ser. 3: 278–287.

Waite, E. R. 1900. Additions to the fish fauna of Lord Howe Island. Rec. Austr. Mus., 3: 193–209.

Wang, K. F. 1941. The labroid fishes of Hainan. Contr. Biol. Lab. Sci. Soc. China Nanking Zool., 15: 87–119.

Weber, M. 1913. Die Fische der Siboga Expedition. Siboga Expeditie., Vol. 57: 710 pp.

Welander, A. and L. P. Schultz. 1951. *Chromis atripectoralis,* a new damselfish from the tropical Pacific, closely related to *C. caeruleus,* family Pomacentridae. Journ. Wash. Acad. Sci. 42(3); 107–110.

Whitley, G. P. 1927. The fishes of Michaelmas Cay, North Queensland. Rec. Austr. Mus. 16(1): 1–32.

——. 1928a. Studies in Ichthyology, No. 2. Rec. Austr. Mus. 16(4): 211–239.

——. 1928b. Fishes from the Great Barrier Reef collected by Mr. Melbourne Ward. Rec. Austr. Mus. 16(6): 294–304.

——. 1929. Some fishes of the order Amphiprioniformes. Mem. Queensland Mus., Brisbane, 9(3): 207–246.

——. 1932a. Fishes. Great Barr. Reef. Exped. Sci. Rept. (London) 4(9): 267–316.

——. 1932b. Marine zoogeographical regions of Australasia. Aust. Nat. 8(pt. 8): 166–167.

——. 1933. Studies in Ichthyology, No. 7. Rec. Austr. Mus. 19: 60–112.

——. 1935. Studies in Ichthyology, No. 9. Rec. Austr. Mus. 19(4): 215–250.

——. 1954. New locality records for some Australian fishes. Proc. Roy. Zool. Soc., N.S.W., 1952/53: 23–30.

——. 1961. Fishes from New Caledonia. Proc. Roy. Zool. Soc., N.S.W., 1958–59: 60–65.

——. 1964. Fishes from the Coral Sea and the Swain Reefs. Rec. Austr. Mus. 26(5): 145–195.

Woods, L. P. and L. P. Schultz. 1960. (*In:* Schultz, L. P. *et al.*). Fishes of the Marshall and Marianas Islands. Vol. 2, Bull U.S.N.M., 202: 1–438.

INDEX